TERRORISM, TICKING TIME-BOMBS, AND TORTURE

TERRORISM, TICKING TIME-BOMBS, AND TORTURE

A Philosophical Analysis

FRITZ ALLHOFF

The University of Chicago Press

Chicago and London

FRITZ ALLHOFF is associate professor of philosophy at Western Michigan University and senior research fellow at the Australian National University. He is the editor or coeditor of eighteen books and the coauthor, with Patrick Lin and Daniel Moore, of *What Is Nanotechnology and Why Does It Matter?*

The University of Chicago Press, Chicago 60637
The University of Chicago Press, Ltd., London
© 2012 by The University of Chicago
All rights reserved. Published 2012.
Printed in the United States of America

21 20 19 18 17 16 15 14 13 12   1 2 3 4 5

ISBN-13: 978-0-226-01483-8 (cloth)
ISBN-10: 0-226-01483-5 (cloth)

Library of Congress Cataloging-in-Publication Data

Allhoff, Fritz.
   Terrorism, ticking time-bombs, and torture : a philosophical
   analysis / Fritz Allhoff.
        p. cm.
   Includes bibliographical references and index.
   ISBN-13: 978-0-226-01483-8 (cloth : alkaline paper)
      ISBN-10: 0-226-01483-5 (cloth : alkaline paper) 1. Torture—
Moral and ethical aspects. 2. Terrorism—Prevention—Moral and
ethical aspects.   I. Title.
   HV8593 .A425 2012
   174'.936467—dc23

                                                2011029348

♾ This paper meets the requirements of ANSI/NISO Z39.48-1992
(Permanence of Paper).

Contents

Preface

For unrelated reasons, I started writing this book on January 21, 2009, the day after Barack Obama was inaugurated as the forty-fourth president of the United States. Obama's inauguration marked the end of President George W. Bush's unpopular presidency, a presidency whose hallmarks were 9/11 and the associated military responses in Iraq and Afghanistan. Were anything else to associate as strongly with the Bush administration and its so-called War on Terror, it would be the economic decline of the administration's closing months; this latter owes in no small part to the former. As Bush headed back to Texas, I wondered whether his legacy could possibly be repaired, whether the ensuing protection against further terrorist attacks or the liberation of future generations of Iraqis could redeem him under American or international judgment. I suspect not, that the costs borne in pursuit of these objectives will be insuperable toward resurrecting any sort of esteem for his eight years in office.

The attacks of September 11, 2001, irrevocably changed Bush's presidency as well as the lives of most Americans. That day is one of the worst we can imagine; almost three thousand lives were lost under the destructive power of four airplanes. I remember living in California and being awakened by the phone just after 6:37 A.M., minutes after American Airlines flight 77 hit the Pentagon. My parents lived about a mile away from the crash site, and phones were out for several distressing hours. They turned out to be safe, unlike the 189 people killed in the crash. Were there to be a silver lining in the attacks, it would be that Americans were brought together in a mutual support; as striking as some of the scenes of destruction was Bush hugging Senate majority leader—and Democrat—Tom Daschle before Bush's September 20 address to a joint session of Congress.

Bush's response to 9/11 was swift and unequivocal. Operation Enduring Freedom (Afghanistan) was launched in less than a month. Within two months, the USA PATRIOT Act—decried by critics as a violation of civil liberties—was passed into law. Operation Iraqi Freedom began in March 2003, only a few weeks after the creation of the Department of Homeland Security. And, from the outset of Operation Enduring Freedom, captives were taken to a detention facility in Guantánamo Bay, Cuba, a facility at which they were denied due process as well as various Geneva Convention protections. At the time of writing, Guantánamo housed 174 detainees—almost as many as were killed in the Pentagon attack—and 775 had been sent to the facility since October 2001.

Allegations of prisoner mistreatment have abounded for as long as captives have been held at Guantánamo. There have been confirmed cases of waterboarding, and so-called stress and duress tactics have been employed; these include wall standing, hooding, noise exposure, sleep deprivation, and food and drink deprivation. Behavioral science consultation teams (BSCTs) were tasked with the development of detention and interrogation strategies, generating outcry regarding the professional codes of ethics that the associated physicians and psychologists were ostensibly violating. Things got worse in April 2004 with revelations about prisoner abuse in Abu Ghraib. It was little coincidence that Major General Geoffrey Miller was sent to run this facility in 2003 after previously running Guantánamo; part of his mission—under Secretary of State Donald Rumsfeld's directive—was to increase the intelligence production of those detained in Iraq.

It is in this milieu that Obama came into office, replacing an unpopular president who perhaps overzealously responded to the 9/11 attacks. Within a mere two days of his inauguration, he signed an executive order to have Guantánamo closed within a year—which has yet to happen over a year and a half later—and reiterated the mantra that the United States does not torture. This executive order is as much symbolic as it is substantive, especially as the population at Guantánamo continues to dwindle. To wit, it is Obama's public rebuke of the Bush presidency, a rebuke meant to close an unpalatable chapter in American history and to restore the status of *American* both domestically and internationally.

But what is it, exactly, that Bush was supposed to have gotten so wrong? 9/11 was an absolutely horrible event, and, since it, there has not been another successful terrorist attack on U.S. soil. Or, depending on whether we think the Fort Hood shootings were terroristic—and I am inclined not to—such an attack took place under Obama's administration and not Bush's. In any case, the unassailable fact is that the Bush administration kept us safe from terrorism since 9/11; this is probably even more striking if we consider the ill will that his military operations surely generated.

The question, then, is not whether his strategies worked—in some relevant sense, they did—but rather whether they were necessary and/or justified. In other words, could we have otherwise been safe? Or is our safety worth the costs that have been incurred?

These questions are too complicated for me to answer and, regardless, require more empirical facility than a philosopher would be able to offer. In all this, however, there is a core philosophical question: What are we able to do to protect ourselves? Or to put it another way: How far can we go to disarm terrorist threats? In both public debate and public consciousness, this question is particularly acute when we consider the moral status of interrogational torture. If such torture is necessary for the abrogation of some terrorist threat, would that torture be justified? This book considers that question and, in short, answers in the affirmative. The central contention is that lesser harms are always preferable to greater harms and that, while bad, torture could nevertheless be the lesser harm in exceptional cases. And, furthermore, this *could* need not be that of wild philosophical fantasy since it is able to gain traction in the real world.

The philosophical debate on torture is, to my mind, severely misguided. On my desk right now, I have five books dedicated to the moral status of torture, and *every one* of them features some nefarious-looking chair, either occupied by a bound detainee or else tantalizingly inviting one.[1] With few exceptions, this iconography is emblematic of a discourse that places the significant moral locus of torture on the person being tortured. We are resounded by platitudes about how torture violates the rights of the tortured, how it compromises their dignity, and so on. Interrogational torture, however, is not primarily about the tortured: it is about the lives threatened by terrorist attacks. If there were no terrorist attacks, there would be no (good) reason to torture. Approaching the torture debate by placing a premium on the lives of innocents—rather than the putative rights of suspected terrorists—recasts it in a morally significant way. And this is true whether torture is even very likely to be effective insofar as a moderate—or even low—chance of saving a significant number of lives might well be one of which we should avail ourselves.

For these reasons, I think it is critical to approach the morality of torture within the context of terrorism. Much of the literature, however, treats the issues in precisely the vacuum that I want to avoid. To that end, the structure of this book is quite straightforward. Part I is about terrorism: what it is; why it is bad; and how the contemporary advent of terrorism challenges traditional norms. These first three chapters lay the foundation for the rest of the book insofar as they delineate the context in which the question of torture becomes most poignant.

Part II then turns to the philosophical underpinnings of torture. Chapter 4 asks what torture is and why it is (intrinsically) wrong; whatever else I go on to say about torture, it is important to acknowledge that torture constitutes a moral wrong. That said, it is still an open question whether torture could be the lesser of two wrongs, one of which is ineluctable. That question gives rise to the infamous ticking-time-bomb scenarios in which we are asked whether torture would be justifiable if it would surely save myriad lives that would otherwise be lost. Chapter 5 explores the methodological underpinnings of ticking-time-bomb thinking, arguing that some of the standard criticisms thereof are unwarranted. That chapter, however, is completely methodological; the point is merely to critically explore the way in which ticking-time-bomb cases appear in the debate. Normative questions are still left: even if ticking-time-bomb cases have some legitimate role in our moral discourse, should we torture in those cases? That is the topic of chapter 6, in which a variety of moral approaches to torture are considered.

Everything in these middle chapters is purely philosophical insofar as no engagement with the real world has yet been made. That engagement becomes the focus of part III, starting with empirical objections to torture. In particular, people have argued that torture does not work, that it requires institutions, that the (unjustified) incidence of torture would spread, that there are better alternatives to torture, or that ticking-time-bomb cases are never actually realized. Chapter 7 considers these and other criticisms against torture. If we are going to allow for torture in exceptional cases, then something should be said about how this would be legislatively or judicially authorized; this is the focus of chapter 8. Ultimately, I prefer the necessity defense to high-profile proposals involving torture warrants, but other possibilities are also discussed. Finally, chapter 9 concerns the limits of torture. In a manuscript that defends the moral permissibility of torture, it bears emphasis that this defense applies only to exceptional cases and is highly circumscribed. Lest my position ultimately be misunderstood, this last chapter provides an important close to the book.

In some sense, this book started shortly after 9/11: I remember watching an interview with Alan Dershowitz on CNN, and, shortly thereafter, I wrote my first paper on torture.[2] This paper was published while I was still in graduate school, but it was an odd direction to take insofar as my dissertation and other work had to do with metaethics and the philosophy of biology; the interest in torture really did not connect with any prior interests or training. From that first paper through the next near decade, the moral status of interrogational torture has become a core element of my research agenda. An important part of that agenda has been discussing these ideas with others; I am grateful for their discourse and for pressing me to strengthen my own views.

Various presentations have generated valuable feedback, including ones given at the City College of New York (2003), Loyola Marymount University (2003), the Australian National University (2005), the Australasian Association of Philosophy (Sydney, Australia, 2005), the American Society of Bioethics and the Humanities (Washington, DC, 2005), the University of Michigan (2005), the Association of Practical and Professional Ethics (Jacksonville, FL, 2006), Western Michigan University (2006), Western Michigan University (2008), the International Intelligence Ethics Association (Baltimore, MD, 2008), the University of São Paulo (2008), the Australian National University (2008), the Australian Association of Philosophy (Melbourne, Australia, 2008), the Association for Professional and Practical Ethics (Cincinnati, OH, 2008), the University of Utah (2009), the American Society of Bioethics and Humanities (Washington, DC, 2009), and Western Michigan University (2010). In all cases, I thank my interlocutors for their comments and challenges.

In spring 2009, I led a graduate seminar entitled "War, Terrorism, and Torture." In the seminar, we read and discussed the literature on which much of this book is based; the seminar also occurred during the months in which I started writing. It is hard to overstate what a great opportunity it was to have a few hours a week dedicated to these topics, particularly when those hours were spent with such strong students. In addition to the opportunity to engage the literature, the students also provided insightful commentary on earlier drafts of some of this book's chapters. For their participation and dialogue, I thank Christopher Boss, David Charlton, Nicolas Frank, Vishal Garg, Donald Kinnee, Joseph Lamia, Timothy Linnemann, Nicholas Sars, Joseph Spino, and Nathan Stout.

In February 2010, Vishal helped me organize a workshop at Western Michigan University wherein we had dedicated sessions for the chapters of the book; this was a tremendously valuable opportunity to get detailed feedback on the manuscript. Commentators were assigned to various chapters, and I thank Christopher, David, Michael Davis, Jeremy Wisnewski, Jessica Wolfendale, and Vishal for the criticisms they developed on their respective chapters. This workshop was funded by the Center for the Study of Ethics in Society, the Department of Philosophy, the College of Arts and Sciences, and the Office of the Vice President for Research; I thank all these units for their support and Vishal for his organization.

Sample chapters and a book proposal were vetted by three anonymous reviewers for the University of Chicago Press; I thank them for their referee reports as well as for their comments on the final manuscript. At the Press, I thank the Faculty Board for its support of the project, including the opportunity to pursue an unpopular thesis. Elizabeth Branch Dyson was my point of contact, and I appreciate her conversation and patience. Finally, I thank Anne Goldberg for editorial assistance, Joseph Brown for copyediting and manuscript preparation, Katherine Frentzel for coordinating production, and Robert Hunt for marketing and promotions.

After spending so much of my life reading books, it was humbling to realize how difficult it was to actually write my first. The whole process was such a valuable one in terms of intellectual growth and development, but those mentioned above made it so much more rewarding. I must single out Elizabeth for her eternal positivity. And I also want to acknowledge my then fiancée and now wife, Jenna Praner, for her constant emotional support. Between figuring out how to write a book and the tumult of its central thesis, Jenna was subjugated to long walks, a barrage of querulous discussions, and never-ending consternation; throughout, I appreciate her partnership and love.

Chapter 3 was published in an earlier and somewhat modified form as "The War on Terror and the Ethics of Exceptionalism," *Journal of Military Ethics* 8, no. 4 (2009): 265–88. Chapter 6 expands on arguments developed in two earlier publications: "Terrorism and Torture," *International Journal of Applied Philosophy* 17, no. 1 (2003): 105–18; and "A Defense of Torture: Separation of Cases, Ticking Time-Bombs, and Moral Justification," *International Journal of Applied Philosophy* 19, no. 2 (2005): 243–64. Chapter 8 was developed into a stand-alone paper: "Torture Warrants, Self-Defense, and Necessity," *Public Affairs Quarterly* 25, no. 3 (2011): 217–40. All relevant permissions have been obtained.

FRITZ ALLHOFF
Kalamazoo, MI
November 2010

PART I

TERRORISM

1

What Is Terrorism?

The debate over torture is deeply embedded in the context of terrorism. Ticking-time-bomb cases, for example, make this link explicit by asking us to contemplate the torture of a detained terrorist in the hope of saving innocent lives. And interrogational torture was, at least in most enlightened societies, widely decried before 9/11; it is these terrorist attacks that have rejuvenated discussions about torture, particularly as pertains to alleviating future attacks. To my mind, this connection is somewhat overextended insofar as there are other contexts wherein we might legitimately wonder about the moral permissibility of torture. Kidnapping cases, for example, are usually going to be nonterroristic and might better approximate some of the structural features of ticking-time-bomb cases than the terroristic contexts in which those cases are frequently deployed; I will return to this issue in §5.1. Regardless, however attenuated some of the epistemic links between torture and saving lives might be in many actual terrorist cases, the potential damages in those cases are unquestionably substantial and probably more substantial than any other context in which we consider torture.

Given the focus—both public and academic—of the relationship between torture and terrorism, terrorism bears privileged discussion. Again, this discussion does not preclude other contexts for torture but recognizes only its most visible. In this chapter, I will develop an account of terrorism that elucidates its conceptual underpinnings and, in the next, will consider why terrorism is wrong and whether it can ever be justified. The third chapter of the first part of the book offers a more general account of exceptionalism wherein the contemporary advent of terrorism is considered as well as how such terrorism bears on more traditional norms inveighing against various practices.

Terrorism derives from the Latin verb *terrere* (to frighten) and through the French *terrorisme*. It was originally used to characterize the tactics of the Jacobins during the French Revolution, especially their so-called Reign of Terror (La Terreur), which began fifteen months after the onset of the Revolution and lasted from September 5, 1793, through July 28, 1794.[1] During this time, the Jacobins exerted their influence under the ill-named Committee of Public Safety; this committee, under the charge of Maximilien de Robespierre, was meant to suppress counterrevolutionary activity and to recruit soldiers for the French military.[2] The suppression of this perceived counterrevolutionary activity led to the deaths of an estimated twenty to forty thousand people, many thousands of whom died under the guillotine. Once deposed, Robespierre himself was executed on the aforementioned July date.

The primary aim of the Reign of Terror was to eliminate opposition to the revolutionary government, but this aim was accomplished precisely by terrorizing the population (including would-be antirevolutionaries). The message was clear: oppose the Revolution, and be decapitated under the guillotine. Furthermore, the standards for conviction were extremely low, so low that mere suspicion of antirevolutionary sentiment would suffice for execution. Because these standards were low, almost anyone could have been executed, whether they were antirevolutionaries or not. And therein lies a central feature of terrorism: it fails to discriminate—whether adequately or at all—between those who are legitimate targets and those who are not. This is to say, not that anyone could have been justly executed by the Jacobins, but only that, *if* anyone could have been, it would have been the antirevolutionaries. As the Reign of Terror was practiced, however, everyone lived in fear, not just the antirevolutionaries. This historical example gives us two features that are, therefore, important for our characterization of terrorism: nondiscrimination and the use of violence to promote fear. More will be said about both of these as I proceed, particularly in the context of just war theory, but they bear early mention. It is also important *why* terrorism is practiced, and, in this case, the aim was political or, more broadly speaking, ideological: the suppression of antirevolutionaries.

Contemporary accounts of terrorism take a wide range of approaches and emphases. C. A. J. Coady, for example, identifies the following six elements of terrorism, all of which play different roles in different accounts: the effect of extreme fear, either as intended or as achieved; an attack on the state from within; the strategic purposes for which political violence is used; the supposedly random or indiscriminate nature of terrorist violence; the nature of the targets of political violence; and secrecy in the use of political violence.[3] On another approach, David Rodin derives a fourfold classificatory scheme for accounts of terrorism: tactical and operational; teleological; agent focused; and object focused.[4] Tactical and operational accounts focus on the type of violence used or the way in which it is deployed; teleological accounts focus on why the violence is deployed. Agent-focused accounts focus on who deploys the violence, and object-focused accounts focus on those against whom the violence is deployed.

There is no doubt that approaches to understanding terrorism vary widely, though a broad survey of these accounts is not important for present purposes. Rather, let me just offer the conception of *terrorism* that I will use and then go on to explore and defend some of its elements. For our purposes, let us understand terrorism as *the intentional use of force against noncombatants or their property to intentionally instill fear in the hopes of realizing some ideological aim*. This definition bears similarities and differences to others. For example, Coady defines terrorism as "a political act, ordinarily committed by an organized group, which involves the intentional killing or other severe harming of noncombatants or the threat of the same or intentional severe damage to the property of noncombatants or the threat of the same."[5] Or consider Igor Primoratz, who defines terrorism as "the deliberate use of violence, or threat of its use, against innocent people, with the aim of intimidating some other people into a course of action they would not otherwise take."[6] Another definition is Lionel McPherson's: "the deliberate use of force against ordinary noncombatants, which can be expected to cause wider fear among them, for political ends."[7] Rodin denies the intentional/deliberate requirement on force, characterizing terrorism as "the deliberate, negligent, or reckless use of force against noncombatants, by state or nonstate actors for ideological ends and in the absence of a substantively just legal process."[8]

I offer this range of definitions, not to be comprehensive, but rather to identify some of the features that are in all accounts of terrorism as well as to indicate those features on which people disagree. In the first category, note that the related concepts of *force*, *violence*, *killing*, and *harming* occur in every definition. Note also that *innocent* and *noncombatant* are similarly in common. While there might be principled reasons for preferring one of these locutions in each of the two shared categories—some of which will be explored below—there is, nevertheless, agreement that something of this sort belongs. Among the differences, note that Coady and Primoratz allow for the *threat* of terrorism to be terroristic, whereas

McPherson, Rodin, and I do not.[9] Coady and I allow that *property* can be the target of terrorism, whereas Primoratz, McPherson, and Rodin do not include any mention of property in their definitions.[10] Let us now consider some of these features in more detail.

1.2 THE INTENTIONAL USE OF FORCE

Note that some of these conceptions use *force* while others use *violence*; Coady's invocation of "the intentional killing or other severe harming" seems pretty clearly to concord with the invocation of *violence*.[11] I take it that there can be nonviolent force, and it seems to me that such force can still be used in terrorism. The *Oxford English Dictionary* defines *violence* as "the exercise of physical force so as to inflict injury on, or cause damage to, persons or property." So imagine that a group of terrorists went around kidnapping people and locking them in rooms for some nonthreatening period of time only thereafter to release them (e.g., for some shortish number of days with food and drink provided); the terrorists do this to spread fear and to realize some ideological aim. While there is not, per the aforementioned definition, any *violence* perpetuated against these detainees, the act nevertheless seems terroristic. Force, however, is clearly used, particularly whatever force would be necessary to effect the detention. Examples like this make me think that *force* is more appropriate than *violence* and that Coady's *killing* and *severe [physical] harm* are overstated. This is not to say that terrorism does not often (or even usually) involve violence, just that it need not as a matter of conceptual necessity.

Second, Coady and Primoratz allow for *threats* of violence to be terroristic, while I reject this; the unqualified notion of a threat has to be too weak.[12] Imagine, for example, that some terrorist threatened to destroy a populated building. At least something else would have to attain in order for this to be anything close to terrorism. Presumably, the threat would have to be credible; otherwise there would be no reason for anyone to be fearful. Even if the threat were attenuated, it seems to me that it could still be a threat, though nevertheless insufficient to substantiate a claim to terrorism. In other words, it does not lose its status of being a threat if the outcome it threatens is unlikely to occur; it just makes the threat less credible. So maybe Coady and Primoratz just mean something like that—namely, that the threat has to be a credible one and one of the sort that could actually generate fear in some population—even if they do not say so explicitly.

Regardless, there has to be a difference between *threatening* violence and actually perpetuating that violence.[13] If a terrorist threatens violence, then he has not *actually* committed terrorism but rather threatened to do something that would be tantamount to terrorism. It is true that the threat of violence could create fear, but so could many other things, like earthquakes. To put it another way, the mere creation of fear is insufficient to ground terrorism. Once we recognize that, why say that the (credible) threat to commit violence *is* to commit terrorism rather than say that such a threat *threatens* terrorism? If the threat of violence is terroristic, then it would be conceptually impossible to threaten terrorism (e.g., through the threat of violence) since the word *threat* would, therefore, be redundant. But it does not seem conceptually impossible to threaten terrorism; therefore, the threat of violence is not terroristic.[14]

Putting these two pieces together, let me comment on an account of nonviolent terrorism developed by Carl Wellman. In particular, Wellman argues that terrorism is "the use or attempted use of terror as a means to coercion . . . violence is not essential to terrorism and, in fact, most acts of terrorism are non-violent." The examples of allegedly nonviolent terrorism that Wellman gives are judges who sentence criminals to deter future crime, blackmail, and threatening students with failure for submissions past the due date.[15] The sentencing of criminals through incarceration, for example, would satisfy my requirement for force since the state would use force to restrict the liberties of the convicted; execution would obviously count as well. Therefore, it is possible for my account of terrorism to incorporate these cases, but I suspect that they will usually fail the fear requirement detailed in §1.4 below. Blackmail constitutes a threat, as does the threat against students. Depending on the details of the blackmail cases, it is plausible to think that these threats do not involve the use of force, but, per the above arguments, threats are insufficient to ground terrorism. Therefore, Wellman's three counterexamples are disarmed, and we still have no reason to think that terrorism could be effected without force. One of his points might have been that it can be effected without violence, though, of course, I agree and already argued for this above.

Finally, I take it that the use of force must be intentional. As I will discuss further below, terrorism is teleological: the terrorist deploys force *in order to* bring about fear. Without the requirement of intentionality, the terrorist would not have the requisite end, at least as pertains to the putatively terroristic act under consideration. The terrorist might, for example, intend to bring about fear as a general endeavor while unintentionally bringing about fear in some particular case: consider one who accidentally knocks off a windowsill a bomb that thereafter detonates in a crowded street. This accident does not seem terroristic even if the terrorist would have otherwise (even imminently) used it in an act of terrorism. Or imagine that the terrorist does not knock over the bomb at all; rather, a cleaning person does, failing to notice it. The cleaning person cannot have committed terrorism even though the effects could be exactly the same as if the terrorist (intentionally) did the exact same thing.

Or at least so go my intuitions. Rodin has argued explicitly against this position, allowing that the use of force in terrorism can be intentional, reckless, or negligent.[16] His position stems from, among other reasons, a dissatisfaction with the moral status of intentional action. Rodin takes particular issue with the doctrine of double effect, which, on Frances Kamm's formulation, holds:

> One may never intentionally bring about an evil, either as an end in itself, or as a means to some greater good. Nonetheless, one may use neutral or good means to achieve a greater good which one foresees will have evil consequences provided that (i) the evil consequences are not disproportionate to the intended good, (ii) the action is necessary in the sense that there is no less costly way of achieving the good.[17]

This principle dates to Saint Thomas Aquinas and has been often discussed in contemporary literature.[18]

Rodin is skeptical about why *intention*, used in this sense, is so relevant to the morality of actions. Following Judith Jarvis Thomson's example, consider a bombing pilot who asks about the permissibility of a bombing raid that will destroy a military installation and cause civilian casualties; whether this raid is permissible or not hardly depends on whether the pilot *intends* to cause the civilian casualties or whether those casualties are unforeseen or merely intended.[19] Rodin extends skepticism about this principle by considering recklessness or negligence, neither of which squares well with the doctrine of double effect. To use his example, consider a motorist who drives across a crowded playground to deliver a sick person to a hospital; the deaths of those on the playground would be foreseeable but unintended, and the case can be developed so that the requirement of proportionality was also satisfied. Nevertheless, we might think that the motorist has behaved impermissibly because "persons have rights against being harmed or used for the benefit of others, rights which can only be alienated in very specific ways, usually having to do with actions and decisions they have freely and responsibly taken."[20] Rodin therefore proposes that we think about the standard of care that is owed in the use of force and not grant a moral pass to operations that (merely) fail to satisfy the doctrine of double effect.

But reconceiving terrorism to require, not intention, but only violations of the relevant standard of care would be a major revision of the notion of *noncombatant immunity* that just war theory usually prescribes; it would give noncombatants almost absolute immunity from any use of force that could be expected to harm them and, therefore, rule out otherwise just instances of collateral damage.[21] I disagree with Rodin's skepticism about violating someone's rights for the benefit of others' (pace §6.2 below), though I nevertheless maintain that recklessness and negligence can be morally blameworthy. But the way to go here is not to jettison the notion of *intentionality* from our definitions, at least insofar as there are strong intuitions toward retaining it, as, in the case of terrorism, I think there are. Rather, we can acknowledge that, just because something fails to be terroristic, it hardly follows that it is morally permissible. In other words, we need not expand our conception of *terrorism* merely so that we can hold those morally accountable who violate whatever standards of care we think appropriate. Instead, we can still issue moral indictments against those, just not under the banner of terrorism.

And, at the end of his essay, Rodin seems to allow for this:

> I think that there are two entirely reasonable ways to settle the terminological question. The first is to restrict the definition of terrorism to the intentional . . . use of force against noncombatants and to categorize the reckless and negligent use of force as a separate class of offense. . . . The second response, reflected in my moral definition, is to hold that the crucial point about terrorism is not the direct intention of the agent but the wrongfulness of the act.[22]

I prefer the first way on the grounds that it preserves the intuitions that I have and has no costs; the second has the cost of being counterintuitive without anything else to suggest it.

1.3 AGAINST NONCOMBATANTS OR THEIR PROPERTY

If the targets of some terrorist activity were combatants rather than noncombatants, then we would call the act, not one of terrorism, but rather one of *war*. Therefore, one of the central features of terrorism is that it targets noncombatants. The combatant/noncombatant distinction is not perfect, though it roughly tracks the relevant features under consideration. The civilian/military distinction is not the right one insofar as some civilians are combatants (e.g., civilian contractors on some forward deployment) and some military personnel are noncombatants (e.g., chaplains and medics). And some definitions, such as Primoratz's, appeal to the notion of *innocence*, though I find this similarly unhelpful for various reasons. First, *innocence* is a very theoretically laden concept in moral philosophy, and importing it into definitions of terrorism brings needless complications and interpretive issues.[23] Second, innocence prejudges the moral status of terrorism insofar as there has to be something at least prima facie wrong with the use of force against innocents. By understanding terrorism as against noncombatants, the moral status of terrorism is an open and substantive issue that we can debate. Third, noncombatancy status is a central feature of just war theory, so, by understanding terrorism in relationship to noncombatants, we connect with that tradition in a way that a focus on innocence does not do as readily.

Nevertheless, the idea of noncombatancy is not without its difficulties. The easy contrast is that between an armed soldier on the battlefield and an unarmed civilian outside the theater. Consider the following anecdote from Robert Graves:

> While sniping from a knoll in the support line, where we had a concealed loop-hole, I saw a German, about seven hundred yards away, through my telescopic sights. He was taking a bath in the German third line. I disliked the idea of shooting a naked man, so I handed the rifle to the sergeant with me. "Here, take this. You're a better shot than I am." He got him; but I had not stayed to watch.[24]

Michael Walzer maintains that, "once war has begun, soldiers are subject to attack at any time (unless they are wounded or captured)."[25] And this is probably right, though I still sense a strong discomfort targeting the unarmed man. But, of course, that unarmed man could be shooting first tomorrow.[26] Cases like the bombing of Pearl Harbor and the attack on the USS *Cole* are interesting because, even though these were military targets, there was no declared war between the United States and its attackers. Civilians working in munitions factories or even the civilian population of a country that provides the tax base necessary to execute the war effort should presumably not be targeted, though one could hardly blame the enemy for wishing the latitude.[27]

At any rate, I do not plan to develop a thoroughgoing account of the combatant/noncombatant distinction, but, for my purposes, it does not much matter: whatever the right account of that distinction is, it can be readily incorporated into my account of terrorism. What matters is that terrorism is propagated against noncombatants and not, specifically, who the noncombatants are. This is not meant to pass the buck on an important theoretical question; it is only to say that the answer to that question does not figure centrally into the present project.

In addition to targeting noncombatants, I maintain that the targeting of their property can be legitimately counted as terroristic. Most commentators have failed to include attacks on property as terroristic, so this deserves some discussion. Coady is one of the few who specifically make such an endorsement,[28] though others are unconvinced. Jenny Teichman, for example, writes: "It may be grossly unfair and unjust to destroy the property of noncombatants, but unless that property is needed for life itself it isn't terroristic."[29] Primoratz agrees, imagining that it could be terroristic to destroy the crops that are the only source of livelihood for a village; we might similarly think that poisoning a water supply, burning all the housing, and so on are terroristic. These cases can be contrasted with destroying some statue in a museum, which most of us do not intuit to be terroristic. That said, there are at least two ways of analyzing the differences in these cases. First, there is the aforementioned distinction as to whether lives are put at risk through the actions. But, second, there is the distinction as to whether the actions cause fear. The destruction of a museum statue would simply not frighten the majority of the public. Maybe they would be angry, or maybe they would not even care. Maybe some art connoisseurs would fear the further destruction of the artistic corpus, but I doubt that this sentiment would be terribly widespread; if it were, then perhaps this could be full-fledged act of terrorism.

What matters, however, is, not what is targeted, but rather whether that targeting generates fear (cf. §1.4 below). Imagine some fatalistic population that simply would not worry if their crops were destroyed; insofar as they do not have a disposition toward fear, the prospects for terrorism are ruled out. But not only are risks to life—whether direct or indirect and in conjunction with other features developed thus far in the chapter—insufficient to ground terrorism; they are also not necessary. For example, consider 9/11 and the destruction of the World Trade Center in which 2,974 noncombatants were killed. Imagine, contrary to fact, that the attack took place at night, when the building was unoccupied; for the sake of this thought experiment, assume that there is not a single person inside and, furthermore, that no one is killed by the falling building. Unlike the case of crop destruction, there is no risk to life. But would this be an act of terrorism? I think that the answer is obviously yes, and it seems to me that it is no less an act of terrorism—even if a less bad one—than when the buildings were hit that Tuesday morning. Why? The answer has to do with fear.

1.4 INTENTIONALLY INSTILLING FEAR

Surprisingly, not all accounts of terrorism place a premium on the terror to which those accounts are etymologically connected; I think that this is a bad mistake. We saw above that *terrorism* derives from the Latin *terrere*, which means "to frighten." To then have an account of terrorism that gives no place to the notion of *terror* or *fear* sounds to me like an account of solar power for which the sun is superfluous. The relationship between *terror* and *fear*, however, is an interesting one: the *Oxford English Dictionary* characterizes *terror* as the state of being "*greatly* frightened" or bearing "*intense* fear" (emphasis added). These definitions preserve the intuition that fear could fall short of terror, even if the Latin did not. Regardless, I have yet to find a single discussion of terrorism that contemplates how much fear is required for terrorism, and I will not undertake that project here. Rather, I shall just use the concepts roughly interchangeably, not making a substantive distinction between *fear* and *intense fear*; should the reader object, feel free to substitute the latter for the former in all instances. Rather, the central question is whether terrorism requires fear at all, the answer to which I take to be obviously yes.

Rodin, for example, consciously omits the notion of *fear* from his account. He argues: "It does not seem to be the case that terrorism invariably has the effect of causing terror in a population. On the contrary, there have been instances in which communities have grown stronger and more resilient as a result of terrorist attacks."[30] But it cannot matter whether people grow stronger and more resilient some indeterminate time down the road from terrorist attacks. New Yorkers, for example, might have developed some solidarity since 9/11, or maybe even all Americans have. However, this does not mean that those attacks were not terrifying when they happened or in their aftermath as further attacks were feared. The important feature is not whether, ultimately, terrorism might lead to some benefits in a community; rather, it is whether fear is generated by the attacks themselves or in the near to midterms that follow thereafter.[31]

Rodin also doubts that the intention to bring about fear is necessary for terrorism; I again disagree. Consider a terrorist who mistakenly thinks that some act will bring about fear and, furthermore, intends to bring about that fear. But, once the act is effected, the consequences are not those that the would-be terrorist expected: rather, the population celebrates the consequences. So, while terror was the aim of the terrorist, he failed to execute his goals in a relevant way, and, therefore, the act itself is not one of terrorism. And consider the contrary case: someone aims at doing good but, because of mistaken beliefs, brings about terror. For example, imagine that this person has a justified but false belief that some noncombatant poses a threat to some larger group of noncombatants and kills the individual. And, furthermore, this happens regularly amid a crisis of violence in some town, thus spreading fear throughout the rest of the (noncombatant) population. Nevertheless, the assailant did not *intend* to cause terror, and this case lacks the nefarious sense that archetypal cases of terrorism portend.

Therefore, intending to cause fear without causing fear cannot ground terrorism. And neither can causing fear without intending to cause it. The obvious way to fix this is to require both: terrorism requires the intentional instilling of fear. In other words, the terrorist must *intend* to instill fear, and, furthermore, he must succeed. Failing either of these two conditions, the act fails to be one of terrorism. This, then, precludes the counterexamples and preserves the link between terrorism and terror. And, contra Rodin, it preserves the intuition that "we will look pretty silly if we do not mention terror in our account of terrorism."[32]

Coady also objects to the inclusion of *fear* in an account of *terrorism*; in response to Primoratz's definition, Coady makes a few remarks as to why he does not include it. The first is that terrorism may be perpetuated "for publicity value, for 'symbolic reasons,' or merely to strike the only blow thought to be possible."[33] An example that he uses is a group that destroys a loaded school bus in order to cause anger. Coady counts this as terrorism. I disagree and think that, if the act aims at anger rather than fear, it is not terrorism. And, even if fear results, it is still not terroristic since that fear was unintended. However, this is a potential objection to my account: imagine that the terrorists who perpetuated 9/11 did not intend the fear that the attacks inspired. For me, this would not be an instance of terrorism since they lack the relevant intentions. Suffice it to say, I am fully confident that those intentions were present, though we can imagine that they were absent. Regardless, if the attacks caused terror without trying to, I do not see how they can be terroristic. The problem with including them is that doing so weakens the notion of *terrorism* such that it might include any act that brought about fear, even if the intentions were *positive*. A response here could be to limit applications of *terrorism* somewhat more broadly than fear, perhaps including anger. But I do not see what we gain by doing this or how such a list of "allied emotions" could be anything other than ad hoc. Denying that an attack that aims at terror is terrorism has no implications for the moral status of that act; there are certainly many ways that acts can fail to be permissible beyond merely that they aim at terror. Coady wants to preserve the claims that these acts have as terroristic, whereas my approach is to reject those claims while still being able to offer other moral indictments.

There is one worry with my (substantial) reliance on fear: Who is it that is supposed to be afraid? And what is it that these people are supposed to be afraid of? On 9/11, most of us did not live in New York City or Washington, DC, so we certainly were not in immediate physical threat from the attacks. Many of us had family or friends in those locations, and certainly we feared for their safety; my own parents, for example, were living a mile from the Pentagon. But what of those of us without exposed family or friends? Were we afraid? Should we have been? Of what? I am not sure what the answers to these questions are, but a conceptual requirement of terrorism cannot be that everyone is made afraid; some people perhaps even took sadistic pleasure in the events' unfolding, yet this cannot undermine the status of those events as terroristic.[34]

And it is not even clear what *everyone* would mean as, surely, it is not the world's population. I doubt that it is even the whole population that is the victim of the attack: even all Americans were not fearful. Yet it has to be broader than just New Yorkers and Washingtonians as the effects of the attack resonated far beyond those cities. The way in which my account fixes the intentions of the terrorists matters as well: since I require that the terrorists intended to cause fear, do I further have to indicate the targets of the fear? That would be a disaster for the account since it could preclude an attack from being terroristic if the terrorists meant to instill fear nationwide and "only" succeeded in a narrower context. These issues are alluring, though part of that allure owes to Sorites-like seductions that I shall herein avoid. More substantively, the relevant condition is that terrorism requires the intentional instilling of fear in some significant subset of the attacked population, making loose provisions for what constitutes a population. If those in New York and Washington were afraid, as were their friends and family elsewhere, that certainly suffices for an act of terrorism; it makes no difference if some Americans were untouched and unmoved (were there to be such people).[35]

This allows us to return to the issue of property and whether it can be targeted in acts of terrorism. On my account, it can. The intuition that the aforementioned statues were not subject to terrorist attacks is accommodated, not through their exclusion as property, but rather by the fact that their destruction would not promote fear. On the other hand, the imaginary destruction of the unoccupied World Trade Center would be terroristic insofar as it aimed at and promoted fear. And—stipulating the former—we can quite reasonably suppose that such an act would promote fear. To wit, the targeting of such a central cultural icon, particularly in such a violent manner, would have deep implications for the sense of security that many Americans possessed. Furthermore, these implications would be radically different from those derived through the destruction of art; alternatively, if crops really were necessary for the survival of some population, then their destruction would be terrifying. To make this point more generally, there is no point in hanging on the status of property or even whether its destruction threatens people's lives. Rather, we can leave the issue of property completely open, always having recourse to the notion of *fear* at which terrorism necessarily aims and results.

1.5 FOR IDEOLOGICAL AIMS

While fear is the proximate aim of terrorism, it is hardly the ultimate: terrorists perpetuate terrorism for ideological aims. Many commentators, including Coady and McPherson, hold that the aims of terrorism are political, but this is surely too narrow. For our purposes, let us assume that the ideological is broader than the political yet includes political ideologies (among others). In other words, political aims are ideological, yet ideological aims are not necessarily political.[36] There is no doubt that much (or maybe even most) terrorism seeks political change, but this hardly seems a conceptual necessity. Al-Qaeda's attacks, for example, are often interpreted as objecting to the American presence in the Middle East; these attacks are meant to change our policies in such regards. But the target of the attacks could be plausibly interpreted as broader than any particular policy that we have and perhaps even to the very roots of our culture, a culture that is disseminated around the world. It is hard to think about how some political recourse would mitigate this cultural diffusion, so the goal of the attacks might be more broadly speaking ideological: the attacks are against the very ideas that our Western culture purportedly stands for and spreads.

In this regard, I agree with Rodin that terrorism should not be narrowly conceived toward political ends because such a conception "fails to capture the numerous species of terrorist motivation beyond the purely political."[37] Coming up with the cases can be controversial, but the aforementioned cultural one could work. Religious terrorism is another plausible (and perhaps common) example. Attacking a religious facility would not have any overt political aim; rather, it would "merely" constitute an expression of disapprobation toward the practitioners of that religion. Some of those attacks might be peripherally related to some political ends (e.g., anti-Zionism), though not necessarily so.

Ecoterrorism could be political insofar as it highlights putative injustices against the environment, but, for example, the freeing of animals from some research facility probably has more to do with those particular animals than with any broader political agenda. Or consider France's José Bové, who dismantled a McDonald's in Millau, France, in 1999. The purpose of this action was a protest against globalization and fast food, not to effect any sort of political change. I doubt that these examples portend terrorism simply because they do not elicit fear, but I think that they could be if they did elicit fear, independently of whether the actions are political. It is hard to think of a simple example of terrorism that is overtly nonpolitical in the sense that many of the putative cases risk the entanglement of political and nonpolitical features. Religious terrorism, for example, is sometimes talked about as nonpolitical (cf. Rodin), but I wonder whether, in practice, this distinction holds up, particularly in theocratic regimes. Is a Muslim suicide bomber in Israel to be construed as pursuing a political aim? This answer could go either way—perhaps depending on the specific details of the case—and I shall not pursue it here. Regardless, the point is meant to be that we need not rule out ideological yet nonpolitical instances of terrorism as a matter of conceptual necessity.

In this context, it is useful to consider an idea espoused by Primoratz, namely, that terrorism is perpetuated against some group such that some other group does something the latter would not otherwise be willing to do. This makes obvious sense in the political context but could easily be understood in the more broadly speaking ideological one as well.[38] As Primoratz writes:

> Terrorism has a certain structure. It has two targets: the primary and the secondary. The latter target is directly hit, but the objective is to get at the former, to intimidate the person or persons who are the primary target into doing things they otherwise would not do.[39]

This has intuitive resonance, though it needs to be somewhat modified. First, making the case for it, consider 9/11. The direct victims of the attack, mostly killed, cannot do anything. Rather, the government (political/ideological) or our culture (ideological) could make various capitulations, and it is those capitulations at which the terrorists ultimately aim.

The modification, however, pertains to the necessity of the targeted group being distinct from the action-leading group; surely this is saying too much. In 2001, for example, letters containing anthrax were sent to U.S. senators Tom Daschle (then majority leader) and Patrick Leahy at their Capitol offices; five people were killed, and seventeen others were infected.[40] In this case, we might expect the terrorist to just not care about what others do, such as Daschle and Leahy's congressional colleagues or even the U.S. government more broadly. Rather, assuming—perhaps contrary to fact—that there was some coherent plan behind this attack, the idea would be that Daschle and Leahy *themselves* bring about some different government or legislative ethos or at least contribute to such an effort. The waiting objection would be that this could not be part of the attack, which aimed to leave Daschle and Leahy dead. That depends on the specific details of the case, but perhaps the goal was merely to infect them. Regardless, the point is that terrorists could easily use force against *the very people* whom they wish to influence; nothing about the concept of *terrorism* need rule out this possibility. Primoratz is surely correct that terrorism is usually deployed against some such that others will do something, but this mere propensity is not made explicit in his definition. Since this dual-target notion is, therefore, not necessary for terrorism, I will not incorporate it into my definition, though I acknowledge that it is often—or even usually—appropriate.

As a final point, let us consider who is trying to realize these ideological aims. In particular, much of the discussion of terrorism privileges nonstate actors over state actors, but there is no conceptual requirement to that effect. In other words, states can promulgate terrorism just as nonstates can, even if the latter have borne more attention.[41] One of our exemplars of terrorism was the Reign of Terror, which was effected by the French revolutionary government. During World War II, the Allied forces bombed Hamburg, killing as many as fifty thousand noncombatants; the later Dresden bombings killed tens of thousands more.[42] These attacks were clearly designed to destroy the morale of the Germans and Japanese and to bring about a quick surrender to end the war. All these bombings satisfy the requirements for terrorism on the account thus far developed, and there is no reason to exclude them merely because they were led at the behest of states. This is not to say anything about the morality of the attacks or even anything about the moral status of state-sponsored terrorism more generally. Rather, the purpose of this chapter so far has been to develop an account of what terrorism is, and it is to the moral status of terrorism that I now turn.

2

The Moral Status
of Terrorism

Now armed with the account of terrorism developed in the previous chapter, I turn my inquiry to its moral status. One merit of that account is that it leaves open the question of whether terrorism could ever be morally permissible. In fact, there is really no moral language in the definition at all. The word *noncombatant* is going to do most of that work, but, so far, it has not been normatively loaded; words like *unjustified*, *immoral*, and so on do not appear anywhere in the account. As previously explained, this was one reason not to incorporate notions like *innocents* into the definition as such incorporations bring with them a substantial amount of moral baggage. Rather, I now turn to the consideration of the moral status of terrorism unencumbered by any definitional commitments in that regard. So: Is terrorism impermissible? If so, why? And, even if it is, can it ever be justified? These are the questions of concern in this chapter.

2.1 NONCOMBATANT IMMUNITY

On my account, terrorism is necessarily directed against noncombatants. And herein lies the first thing that we can say about the morality of terrorism, particularly as we can conjoin that discussion with the just war tradition. In that tradition, a distinction is commonly drawn between *jus ad bello* and *jus in bello*: the former concerns the morality of the war itself, whereas the latter concerns the morality of practices within the war. To quote Michael Walzer at length:

> War is always judged twice, first with reference to the reasons states have for fighting, secondly with reference to the means they adopt. The first kind of judgment is adjectival in character: we say that a particular war is

just or unjust. The second is adverbial: we say that the war is being fought justly or unjustly. Medieval writers made the difference a matter of prepositions, distinguishing *jus ad bellum*, the justice of war, from *jus in bello*, justice in war. . . . *Jus ad bellum* requires us to make judgments about aggression and self-defense; *jus in bello* about the observance or violation of the customary and positive rules of engagement. The two sorts of judgment are logically independent. It is perfectly possible for a just war to be fought unjustly and for an unjust war to be fought in strict accordance with the rules.[1]

This independence of *jus ad bellum* and *jus in bello* is hardly straightforward,[2] but the point now is to introduce the distinction and to acknowledge the moral requirement of fighting justly. A central tenet therein is that of noncombatant immunity: force may only be deployed against those who wield it against us. Whether this is an absolute value or merely a very important one is critical, but it is at least the latter. The reason is that there is no need to target noncombatants because they do not pose a threat to us. Immunity is lost through aggression but is otherwise retained; all people have this immunity until they forfeit it.[3] Terrorism, which necessarily targets noncombatants, is, therefore, morally problematic in the sense that it violates noncombatant immunity: it deploys force against those who have moral protection against the use of force because they have not taken up the use of force against others.[4]

This central feature of terrorism establishes a strong case against its moral permissibility. But can noncombatant immunity be justifiably infringed? Walzer, for example, thinks that some of the Allied bombings of German cities were justified given, as Coady puts it, the "enormity of the Nazi threat and the reasonable fear of its imminent triumph."[5] John Rawls expressed a similar view while, at the same time, condemning the bombings of Hiroshima and Nagasaki.[6] World War II invites us to consider a terrible evil against which victory is absolutely necessary. By bombing German cities—so-called terror bombing—we had the opportunity to affect the morale of the population, perhaps undermining support for Hitler, making it harder for the German government to stay in the war as its own civilians were killed, and so on. There is no doubt that the killing of these civilians was a tragedy, but let us suppose that the tragedy is less than the one we would have otherwise been forced to face, whether through more war or a stronger and more dominant Nazi Germany.

Such scenarios give rise to what Walzer calls "supreme emergencies," which he characterizes in terms of their seriousness and imminence.[7] If the threat is not sufficiently serious, then there is no point in countenancing the violation of noncombatant immunity; the moral harm of violating this principle could not be sufficiently countervailed by any other moral good. And, if the threat is not imminent, then there is similarly no reason to jeopardize noncombatant immunity since some other solution might present itself before the threat is actualized. The details of the cases are, of course, going to make all the difference; C. A. J. Coady, for example, is skeptical about whether the imminence condition was actually satisfied in terror bombings of German cities undertaken from February 1942, presumably including the cases that Walzer wants to defend.[8] I lack the expertise to render any commentary in this regard but rather make this acknowledgment to highlight the fact that there are few to no uncontroversial cases that everyone agrees would satisfy Walzer's desideratum. And, as we will see below, even if there were, the support for violating noncombatant immunity hardly follows.

Before returning to supreme emergencies, however, let us consider another prospect for justifiable terrorism: revolutionary terrorism. Leon Trotsky, the leader of the Bolsheviks during the Russian Revolution and the ensuing civil war, ardently defended the use of terrorism during the so-called Red Terror that led to the killing of over 200,000 and the arrest and imprisonment—with high mortality rates—of hundreds of thousands more.[9] Trotsky, then the commissar of war, published a lengthy defense of state-sponsored terrorism in his *Terror and Communism*.[10] He argues against a book of the same principal title published by his fellow Marxist Karl Kautsky, who, as Igor Primoratz puts it, rejected the "necessity of large-scale violence, and in particular of terrorism, as a means of dismantling the existing, capitalist society and replacing it by a socialist political and economic system."[11] Unlike invocations of supreme emergency, revolutionary terror does not aim to remediate an imminent and serious danger. Rather, the concern is the ongoing moral harms perpetuated by the existing state; without revolutionary terror, such harms will continue indefinitely. (Relevant harms might be to the safety of the citizenry, their fair participation in the state's economic apparatus, and so on.) Terrorism against the state is aimed at dismantling the state in favor of a more just one. Revolutionary terrorism therefore shares a central feature with supreme emergencies, namely, the justification of some moral harm in light of more extended considerations.

Or so the story goes. My primary worry here is not with this sort of moral framework but rather with whether the calculus ever comes out as the revolutionaries would hope. The Soviet Red Terror, for example, ultimately led to the deaths of *hundreds of thousands* of noncombatants, many of them poor and disenfranchised peasants. It is certainly not inconceivable that the balance sheets are going to be positive; imagine, for example, that the Red Terror was necessary such that millions more would flourish under some new government such that the losses are warranted. But, setting aside critical debates about whether the rights of some can be violated such that the rights of others are promoted,[12] extreme skepticism should be afforded to the proposition that revolutionary terrorism ever has these results.[13] The French Reign of Terror and the Soviet Red Terror have hardly been judged positively by historians and certainly have been judged more negatively than the pre-1943 terror bombings of World War II (i.e., the ones that at least some people think were justified). These consequences may have more to do with the empirical than with the structural features of the cases, but I am skeptical as to whether the large-scale violence that many political revolutions portend could discharge its associated moral burdens.

2.2 SUPREME EMERGENCIES

Let us now return to the notion of supreme emergency on the premise that, if terrorism can be morally justified, that justification will more plausibly appeal to supreme emergency than to revolutionary terror. As we saw above, this invocation appeals to seriousness and imminence, and those are important empirical challenges that must be addressed in any case of terrorism that seeks justification. Granting this possibility, and even being sympathetic to its actualization during World War II, there are, nevertheless, important theoretical challenges in addition to the empirical ones. Many of these have been lodged most powerfully by Coady, so let us consider them directly.

First, Coady complains that Walzer codifies a "pro-state bias" in the latter's defense of supreme emergencies: "A striking curiosity of Walzer's argument is that it is presented only as an argument available to states and their representatives."[14] For example, Walzer asks: "Can soldiers and statesmen override the rights of innocent people for the sake of their own political communities? I am inclined to answer the question affirmatively, though not without hesitation and worry."[15] However, despite the fact that Walzer thinks noncombatant immunity can be justifiably infringed, he nevertheless seems to think that terrorism is always morally wrong. For example, he writes: "I take the principle for granted: that every act of terrorism is a wrongful act."[16] There has to be a tension here as Walzer thought that some terror bombings could be justified yet he thinks that terrorism is never justified. Why does he allow for supreme emergencies yet nevertheless categorically condemn terrorism? Maybe the resolution is meant to be that, so long as states execute the attacks, they are not terrorists. This would, indeed, lead to a prostate bias and, as argued in §1.5 above, has the more profound drawback of making state-sponsored terror a conceptual impossibility. Walzer does think that "the survival and freedom of political communities . . . are the highest values of international society,"[17] so maybe he does take this prostate bias seriously, even if never explicitly defending it.

Regardless of what Walzer actually means, let us disentangle supreme emergency from statehood: if states can appeal to supreme emergency to justify terrorism, then nonstates should be able to as well. This is just to recognize that concepts like *imminence* and *seriousness* are just as at home in nonstate contexts as they are in state contexts, and it morally discriminates against nonstates to preclude them from defending themselves against attack or destruction. The differences between states and nonstates are more sophisticated than needs to be discussed for these purposes, but just consider some small group of people not linked by any sort of political or legislative features or else not otherwise recognized by other states. To say that mere statehood privileges these latter over the former in such a dramatic way that the former are patently ruled out from the terrorism allowed to the latter has to be going too far. This is not to say that, as suggested by Walzer, statehood is not an important moral good, only that statehood should not be able to categorically trump all other goods such that whatever values allow states to appeal to imminence and seriousness are completely off the table to nonstates. Perhaps, given the value of statehood, the moral calculus should set the bar higher for nonstates to appeal to terrorism, but that is just to allow for the introduction of statehood as one value among others rather than for it to assert complete preeminence over those values. Contra Walzer, then, we should allow for the possibility of nonstate-sponsored justified terrorism.

This allowance accommodates one of Coady's objections, though, at the same time, it makes things worse for some of the others. In particular, Coady wonders whether "the broadening of the potential application of supreme emergency considerations provides a reason for skepticism about the category itself."[18] Part of the issue here is the status of the norms that we plan to make exceptions from and the moral values that those norms protect. Coady identifies two possibilities. The first is "balanced exceptionalism," wherein prima facie obligations reign, though they can be overridden by competing obligations. On this view, noncombatant immunity is one value among many, and, should those other values inveigh against it, then so much the worse for noncombatant immunity.

The second possibility is that of "dirty hands," which Coady traces though Niccolò Machiavelli, Max Weber, and Walzer.[19] The difference between the two is the status of the norms that are excepted such that the dirty hands theorists think that those norms are profound and cannot be casually outweighed. And, furthermore, the moral value is not annihilated in the sense of the balanced exceptionalist, but rather some sort of moral residue persists after the act that violates the norm. This is not to say that the acts cannot be justified, only that the norms they violate cannot be casually overridden; furthermore, regret and guilt are appropriate for the acting agents whose hands are dirty.

I will develop my own—and very different—account of exceptionalism in the next chapter, but some remarks are owed to the choices that Coady offers. The dirty hands approach is one that I reject given the apparent paradox to which it is committed. To my mind, the actions that we choose are either right or wrong, legitimate or illegitimate, justified or unjustified. Appealing to dirty hands creates the odd position of saying that we do what we should do yet nevertheless are supposed to feel badly about it and to acknowledge some persisting moral wrong.[20] If we *should* act in some way—as dirty hands allows—then I simply deny that any negativity carries past the act itself. This is not to say that we should regret *that* there was some situation requiring some certain course of action, only that, if that course of action is, ex hypothesi, the one that we should have chosen, then no moral wrongness persists. It is also not to say that there might be certain situations wherein we have to do something prima facie wrong for which we thereafter owe compensation.

So, for example, imagine that I am justified in stealing your car to get my pregnant wife to the hospital; I could still owe compensation, including, but not limited to, the return of the car after she gives birth.[21] But this is not a case of dirty hands in that what I was justified doing in the first place was stealing the car *given that* due compensation would be made. True dirty hands cases are ones where compensation is impossible, such as when we consider killing innocent civilians. If compensation were possible (e.g., to their families), then this would not be a case of dirty hands at all since fair compensation would cleanse our hands. And, just to be clear, this is not to suggest that we can do whatever we want so long as we "compensate" people, just that appropriate compensation, by definition, makes the transgressed indifferent between the transgression and the compensation.

We are then left with the balanced exceptionalist approach on which there is no residual moral wrongness simply because that moral wrongness was overridden by competing moral features of the case; this is the approach to which I am sympathetic. Part of the motivation for the dirty hands approach, however, has to do with the profundity of the norm that is violated: the reason that moral wrongness persists—that is, that our hands are dirty—is because we have (justifiably) done something *very* bad. How can the balanced exceptionalist preserve the profundity of the violated norm? The answer is quite simply that all norms are not created equally and the violation of some profound norm requires profound countervailing benefits. Furthermore, this is not to presuppose some sort of utilitarianism or even simple consequentialism; such a proposal can be accommodated under, for example, what Thomas Nagel refers to as "threshold deontology."[22] If noncombatant immunity is a tremendously important moral good, then we simply cannot violate it casually and may do so only given even greater moral goods that can be realized only through such a violation.

And, for the balanced exceptionalist, there is no principled reason to restrict the supreme emergency exemption to states; it can also be extended to nonstates. But then Coady worries:

> Any broadening . . . tends to reduce the rarity value of the exemption and hence increase the oddity of the idea that it can be right to do what is morally wrong. Why not allow that the exemption can apply to huge corporations, the existence of which is central to the lives and livelihoods of so many? Or, contrary to Walzer's declared position, to individuals when they are really up against the wall? Yet, the more we move in this direction, the more the currency of supreme emergency is devalued.
>
> These considerations suggest that the category of supreme emergency, in spite of its surface clarity, is conceptually opaque. This opacity is alarming enough in itself since it means that those using the concept may not be making clear sense, even to themselves.[23]

This is an important challenge and one due a reasonable response. I see no reason that corporations could not invoke supreme emergency *if* the stakes were high enough. Which, of course, they would not be. The reason that whatever features could make terror bombing justifiable (e.g., stopping Hitler) would not be present in the corporation case, whatever it is. Allowing that there is an in-principle invocation of supreme emergency to various substate actors falls short of allowing that the invocation would ever (or often) be actually justified.

Nevertheless, this is not going to satisfy Coady, who would thereafter ask what principled reasons we use to adjudicate claims of supreme emergency, licensing such claims in some contexts, and denying them in others. The answer quite simply has to do with what our various values are, including how committed we are to protecting noncombatant immunity. The structure of the dialectic cannot be to ask for some particular number of lives we must be able to save in order to target some other number of noncombatants (e.g., five and two) because doing so commits us to a conclusion that outstrips our theoretical resources. In other words, I maintain only that noncombatant immunity can be justifiably infringed by either states or nonstates given sufficiently low costs and/or sufficiently high benefits. Does this mean that the bombing of Hiroshima was justified? No, because that bombing was not necessary to defeat the Japanese. Were the earlier terror bombings of Germany (i.e., pre-1943) justified? Maybe, so long as it turns out to be true that they were necessary; certainly the stakes were high enough. What does it mean for stakes to be "high enough"? I do not know, but, as above, I disagree that a substantive answer is owed here. There are easier cases and harder cases, and people will disagree on the harder cases. What matters are the structural features of the norms, not what adjudications we make in particular cases. That is not to deny that adjudications must be made in those cases; it is only to say that there is no simple weighting of the values that can be summarily pronounced.

If this is right, can any space be preserved for supreme emergencies? In other words, if we simply weigh the norms against each other and adjudicate in favor of the one bearing the most weight, how does *supremacy* figure into deciding whether to violate noncombatant immunity; have we not just relegated that value to one among others? If its status is diminished, can it still be special in any meaningful way? Or do supreme emergencies—as opposed to more pedestrian situations—still play any critical role in the account? Taking these questions in order: yes, we have relegated that value to one among many, but that hardly need concern us because it is an important value and not one that will be casually overridden. Structurally, there is no problem with making values commensurable as, for example, the weighting of one of those values might be so high that it is never actually overridden. What remains special about such values is that they will be rarely overridden, precisely because they are so important. We have considered very few cases of justified terrorism—primarily restricted to some bombings in World War II—and the reason is simply that the features we care about are not often instantiated. The reason that we need not worry about supreme emergencies becoming casually invoked (cf. Coady's corporation) is, again, simply that the values they threaten are important enough that pedestrian cases will not be able to satisfy the high requirements we have for transgressing against those values.

A final challenge is whether supremacy really matters much in these cases: if we can override various norms given *supreme* emergencies, why can we not override them given (mere) emergencies? One antiutilitarian answer requires not *just* that the costs be outweighed by the benefits but rather that they be *dramatically* outweighed.[24] There are various reasons to reject this conception, not least of which is getting clear about what it is even supposed to mean: what does this dramatic outweighing amount to? Furthermore, if we care enough about the values the emergency threatens such that we can violate other values, why should it be that the former set of values needs to not just outweigh the latter but outweigh them dramatically? I find it hard to motivate this position, which seems to codify some sort of schizophrenic moral philosophy. Furthermore, all of this can be fixed without being some sort of naive utilitarian. To do so, all we need to say is that (mere) emergencies—rather than supreme emergencies—are sufficient but that we really need an accurate accounting of all the values at stake.

For example, imagine that a tyrant is threatening to detonate a bomb and we lack a direct shot on him; we can, however, shoot a passerby in such a way that the passerby falls into the tyrant's lair, thus immobilizing the tyrant before he can detonate the bomb. Imagine two cases: in the first, the tyrant is threatening to kill two noncombatants, and, in the second, he is threatening to kill a thousand. Specifying the rest of the details to forestall irrelevant objections, I am always surprised how many people assent to the intervention in the latter case while rejecting it in the former. And, of course, such intuitions are consistent with the theoretical apparatus that Walzer gives us wherein *supreme* emergency is required instead of (mere) emergency. But, as I argued above, there are reasons to reject this approach. Nevertheless, the rejection of such an approach does not necessarily reject the putative intuitions in these cases; there are other ways to accommodate them. In particular, we could think that there are other values in play other than merely the saving of lives, such as the expressive cost of violating noncombatant immunity. Or else there could be worries about slippery slopes that could be activated by cases wherein the lives saved only marginally exceed the lives taken. To stave off these worries, maybe the number of lives saves needs to be much higher than the number of lives taken. This does not mean that the emergencies need to be supreme, however, only that a proper accounting of the moral values would, illusorily, give that sense. In other words, (mere) emergencies can justify infringement of noncombatant immunity so long as we properly understand what is at stake. And this squares with our moral intuitions insofar as we think that harms could be justified only if they were necessary to prevent worse harms wherein the relevant harms are broadly, as opposed to narrowly, understood (i.e., more than just the number of lives matters).

The point of the aforementioned discussion owes to the fact that terrorism can be justified only if noncombatant immunity can be justifiably infringed; insofar as the moral wrongness of terrorism derives from the targeting of noncombatants, that wrongness is superable only if this targeting can be justified. And, given that the entire locus of this wrongness has been tied to noncombatant immunity, the justified infringement of noncombatant immunity would justify terrorism so long as the associated requirements of imminence, seriousness, and necessity were also met. This conclusion, however, is far more theoretical than substantive. And, in fact, I think that terrorism is rarely justified, at least in part because it is rarely necessary to prevent a serious and imminent threat, but also because it would rarely be the best way to prevent such a threat. The case studies of revolutionary terrorism are decidedly negative, and even supreme emergency cases are few and far between. Coady concludes: "We surely do better to condemn the resort to terrorism outright with no leeway for exemptions."[25] But I reject this insofar as there can be cases where terrorism is the lesser evil. Such a commitment, however, hardly amounts to an endorsement of terrorism simply because of the relative paucity of those cases.

2.3 TERRORISM AND COUNTERTERRORISM

If terrorism is almost always wrong, then we are usually justified in trying to prevent it. Setting aside putative cases of justified terrorism for now, how far are we permitted to go in our efforts to combat unjustified terrorism? Successful acts of terrorism have myriad costs, but counterterrorism has costs as well; surely, we do not want to allow the costs of counterterrorism to be higher than the costs of the terrorism that they prevent. Much of the rest of this book will be specifically about the use of interrogational torture as a counterterrorism technique and whether it can be justified in this capacity. In particular, much attention will be given to the various harms that torture portends and whether, given these harms, it can, nevertheless, be justified. In this final section of this chapter, however, I raise the issue more abstractly and generalize away from any particular counterterrorism techniques to the practice of counterterrorism as a whole, thinking about how it might be justified.

Starting with the costs of terrorism, consider 9/11 as a dramatic example. Following the work of Robert Looney, we might say that costs can be either direct or indirect as well as immediate, short-, mid-, or long-term.[26] Immediate and short-term direct impacts, for example, were that 200,000 jobs in New York were destroyed or relocated out of New York, at least temporarily. Destruction of physical assets was valued at over $16 billion; rescue, cleanup, and related costs have been estimated at approximately $11 billion. Immediate and short-term indirect costs included a slowing of economic activity, with original projections putting the cost at as high as $500 billion; the actual cost probably fell short of this. In the mid- and long term, the costs become indirect but still substantial. Midterm indirect costs include those to the insurance industry ($30–$58 billion), airlines (tens of thousands of jobs and an overall devaluing of the industry), tourism and other service industries (tens of thousands of jobs and lowered equity value for hotels and other facilities), increased military spending (over $80 billion), and so on. Long-term indirect costs include higher operating costs (e.g., increased security), higher risk premium (e.g., from lenders to borrowers), shift of resources from civilian to military forces, shift away from globalization, and so on.[27] Putting dollar amounts on the long-term costs is difficult, and even assessing the midterm costs can be challenging. Nevertheless, we might reasonably assess the economic costs of 9/11 to be somewhere in the vicinity of $500 billion–$1 trillion.

And none of these estimates include the Iraq War. Would this war have taken place had 9/11 not? Assuming that the answer is no, then the price tag for that war gets added as an indirect cost of 9/11, and that price tag is huge. Original estimates were ludicrously low—some as low as $2 billion—with even the more "conservative" ones coming in at $100–$200 billion. The actual cost will be at least ten times that and potentially as high as $3 trillion.[28] Nevertheless, there is something misleading about adding its costs to the 9/11 ledger, especially if that ledger is meant to indicate the costs of terrorism: the Bush administration did not have to pursue Operation Iraqi Freedom, and, regardless, its costs are more appropriately assigned to counterterrorism than to terrorism. (This is not to say that such costs can be neatly assigned to either.) I raise this issue only briefly because the Iraq War—perhaps along with the issue of torture—is an elephant in the room as pertains to the consequences of 9/11; for the discussion that follows, nothing substantive hangs on whether we count it as a cost thereof. Operation Enduring Freedom (Afghanistan) also tallies a significant expense, though probably only about 10 percent that of Operation Iraqi Freedom; estimates for the military efforts in Afghanistan are just under $200 billion from 2001–9.[29]

Included in these costs are the damages of the attacks—both direct and indirect—as well as the counterterrorism measures that they spawned.

These can be usefully separated insofar as such a separation helps us get clear on what we are spending to protect against something else. For fiscal year 2003, additional spending of $48 billion was proposed for national defense as well as $38 billion more for homeland security.[30] The defense budget has continued to rise since 9/11—with the aforementioned wars in Iraq and Afghanistan playing a significant role—and, certainly, some of this can reasonably be said to go to counterterrorism. But the best focus is probably on the Department of Homeland Security (DHS), which was largely created to defend against terrorism.[31] This department serves other functions as well (e.g., security against illegal immigration), but terrorism is a principal focus. A detailed analysis has been carried out elsewhere,[32] but some key results are worth noting. For example, the cost of homeland security spending increased from $56 billion in 2001 to $99.5 billion in 2005. The federal outlays, which are easier to track than the money coming from other sources, are somewhere around half of the total in 2005 ($53.4 billion), which represents 0.4 percent of the gross domestic product; this represents a doubling since 2001 (0.2 percent) and a fourfold increase from the period 1996–2001 (0.1 percent).[33]

Of the fiscal year 2005 spending, approximately 8 percent went directly to domestic counterterrorism, though much of the rest of the budget funds related areas: protecting critical infrastructure and key assets (34 percent); defending against catastrophic threats (15 percent); emergency preparedness and response (11 percent); and intelligence and warning (1 percent). Only border and transportation security (31 percent) is not majorly tied to counterterrorism, reflecting instead the absorption of Immigration and Naturalization Services by the DHS in 2003. Still, even this spending is relevant to counterterrorism insofar as it funds our ability to keep terrorists out of the country in the first place. Given these data, let us therefore conclude that, from 2001 to 2005, the United States was spending somewhere around $50–$100 billion per year on counterterrorism, not including the wars in Iraq and Afghanistan.[34] As the range clearly indicates, this estimate is not meant to be precise; rather, it aims to give us some broad sense—at least within an order of magnitude—of what counterterrorism costs us. And therein lies the question: Is it worth it?

Some people clearly think not. For example, Jessica Wolfendale argues: "We should fear counterterrorism more than we fear terrorism." Her argument has two prongs: she argues, first, that the risk of terrorism simply is not that great and, second, that the costs of our counterterrorism measures are higher than we think. Once we adequately understand the (lesser) costs of terrorism and the (higher) costs of counterterrorism, we will see that the latter are not justified. She takes issue with the hubris exhibited by, for example, President George W. Bush and Colin Powell, who have said, respectively, that terrorism threatens not only our lives but also "our way of life" and our "civilization."[35] But does it? Consider:

> On average only 420 people are killed and another 1249 are injured each year from transnational terrorist attacks. Nevertheless, the public in rich countries views transnational terrorism as one of the greatest threats. This is rather ironic since over 30,000 people die on US highways annually, yet highway safety is not as much of a public concern.[36]

Or more viscerally:

> The estimated 1,000–7,000 yearly deaths from terrorism pales into insignificance next to the 40,000 people who die every *day* from hunger, the 500,000 people who are killed every year by light weapons and the millions who die annually from diseases like influenza (3.9 million annual deaths), HIV-AIDS (2.9 million annual deaths), diarrhoeal (2.1 million annual deaths) and tuberculosis (1.7 million annual deaths).[37]

Or economically:

> Since 2001, the Global Fund to Fight AIDS, Tuberculosis, and Malaria, funded by all willing governments and devoted to combating diseases that kill about 6 million people each year, has committed about $6.9 billion and spent about $4.4 billion. This expenditure comes to roughly $120 per fatality. Between 2001 and 2006, the US Government alone has spent $438 billion on the war on terror. This amount comes to roughly $146 million per US fatality—over a million times more per fatality.[38]

These statistics are meant to show that terrorism poses less of a threat than we think it does or at least that the threat from terrorism pales in comparison to various other threats that we seem to care a lot less about. How, then, can our substantial response to terrorism be justified? If we care so much about whatever terrorism threatens, should we not care less about terrorism and more about these other threats involving higher stakes?

The answer to this question depends on what terrorism threatens. The statistics are, most directly, about the number of lives that stand to be lost, whether through terrorism, highway safety, hunger, war, or disease. But, certainly, terrorism threatens more than just lives; we should not merely observe that terrorism comes up short on the "ledger of lives" and thereafter deprioritize our response to it. As indicated above, the economic costs of 9/11 are staggering, way more than the thirty thousand lives lost to highway accidents. Economic costs are one sort of value, and lives are another; even if one thinks, as actuaries might, that these latter values can be rendered economically, it cannot be denied that there are values *beyond* the mere lives lost that must be put into the calculus.[39]

The non-terrorist-related deaths mentioned above also have economic costs, but they largely take place outside the United States. Without being too cynical, we should admit that it is hardly irrational for American citizens to care more about protecting themselves from terrorism than they do about providing for those at risk outside our borders. This is not meant to take a myopic view of the interrelations among all the world's citizenry, the economic impact of the developing world (on us), and so on or even to deny that we have moral (as opposed to prudential) obligations to much of the rest of the world. Rather, the claim is that the threats of domestic terrorism are to *us*; this, at least to some degree, sets those threats apart from some of the others.

Regardless, the foregoing discussion fails to appreciate other critical costs of terrorism: its symbolic costs. A few thousand people died on 9/11, and the economic impact of that day was catastrophic. Lives and dollars aside, however, that day cost us much more that those numbers could express. The terrorists destroyed the World Trade Center, a central icon of our economic strength. They crashed into the Pentagon, a building that represents our military strength. And, were it not for the brave passengers who helped crash United 93 in rural Pennsylvania, a plane probably would have hit either the White House or the Capitol, buildings that embody the strength of our government. These symbolic attacks against our economy, military, and government were chosen precisely because of that symbolism; as many or more lives—and, perhaps, similar economic damages—could have as easily been exacted through other targets.

While many Americans are personally unaffected by the tragedy of thirty thousand annual highway deaths, few of us could say the same of 9/11. It took away our security. It took away our sense of place in the world. It left us vulnerable at the individual, institutional, and national levels. Even a cynic who belabors the failings of American culture, our national smugness and arrogance, or the way our country conducts itself with regard to the rest of the world must, nevertheless, acknowledge that our collective suffering, even if ill founded, is a substantial moral harm. And, again, this is not to deny that we should care more about, for example, pharmaceuticals in the developing world or even that we have a moral obligation to support poor countries. Rather, the point is simply that terrorism takes more than lives and dollars: it takes things that might matter even more. I therefore reject the position that marginalizes, even comparatively, the threat of terrorism; a proper accounting of its threat demonstrates its significance.

Nevertheless, there is a hazard in developing an account of terrorism or counterterrorism that depends too strongly on 9/11: this is, at least in terms of lives and excluding military bombings during war, perhaps the most spectacular single-day terrorist attack ever.[40] We must be careful not to exaggerate the (ongoing) risks of terrorism by appealing to a singular event and one that will probably not recur, regardless of our counterterrorism strategies. Or, to put it another way, how likely is it that our investment in counterterrorism since 9/11 prevented anything like it from happening since? Or even some constellation of attacks that would collectively approximate 9/11's damage? This is a hard question, and the associated counterfactual reasoning—that is, what would have happened had we not done such and so?—is perilous.[41] Nevertheless, at least a few substantive points can be made.

First, 9/11 was so bad that any individual or constellation of attacks even an order of magnitude off from it would still be heinous. If, for example, our counterterrorism has prevented an aggregated 10 percent of 9/11's losses, this is very substantial. Second, there had been semiregular terrorist attacks against the United States over the two decades preceding 9/11. Marine barracks in Beirut were targeted by two truck bombs (1983);[42] two-thirds of the victims of Pan Am 103 were American (1988); two U.S. embassies were bombed (1998); and then came 9/11 (2001).[43] The bombing of the Alfred P. Murrah Federal Building in Oklahoma City killed 168 people (1995), though this attack was different in the sense that it was domestic—as opposed to transnational—terrorism; regardless, the effects were as real. All told, this is five serious attacks from 1983 to 2001. And, at time of writing in 2010, there has not been a single successful attack since 2001;[44] this is the longest period of safety that we have enjoyed since 1983. The absence of terrorist attacks since the proliferation of our powerful counterterrorism campaign can hardly be a coincidence.

So let us now assume that our counterterrorism campaign is working, without committing ourselves to any substantive view about whether it is optimal; surely, nothing in the real world is. This then brings us to the second of Wolfendale's concerns, which is that the costs of counterterrorism, even if it is successful, are nevertheless high. And these costs are not just the economic ones previously discussed, which we might charitably assume are reasonably justified. Rather, there are all sorts of other potential costs, such as the moral hazards pertaining to the sort of people and nation that we have become in responding to terrorism.[45] We have restricted liberties and undermined due process. We have fueled anti-American sentiment abroad and probably catalyzed more terrorism in the process. All this is bad, no doubt. But the central question is whether these moral harms can be justified given the greater moral benefits that have ensued.

The principal point of this project is to consider interrogational torture as a particular counterterrorism strategy, rather than to consider counterterrorism in its entirety. To that end, we can then ask whether the costs of torture—as an element of our counterterrorism strategy—are greater than the associated benefits. The worries of the preceding paragraphs are important ones, and they must be taken seriously; much of the rest of this book will do just that. As a general proposition, we surely must be careful about the ways in which we combat terrorism, and it is certainly true that some counterterrorism strategies will be inappropriate insofar as they cause more trouble than they are worth. I disagree with critics who allege that our counterterrorism campaign outstrips the threats that it protects against—particularly once those threats are more fully understood—but that line will not be pursued further here. Rather, the goal of this section was to motivate much of what is still to come about utilizing torture in exceptional circumstances. Before moving on to torture, however, it will be useful to develop a more general account of exceptionalism; this will be the focus of the next chapter.

3

The War on Terror and the Ethics of Exceptionalism

Having developed an account of terrorism and its associated moral status, I now consider ways in which terrorism—and our response to it—challenges traditional norms. This chapter serves as a transition to the second part of the book wherein the focus shifts from terrorism to torture; torture is one of the tools that we can consider in our fight against terrorism. (This is not to prejudge whether we should use torture in that fight but only to assert our prerogative to consider it.) While the content of the current chapter largely generalizes beyond torture, it provides a theoretical framework that will be useful to have as substantive arguments regarding torture are developed in remaining chapters.

As a quick locutionary note, the fight against terrorism often goes under the moniker of the War on Terror, though we might wonder about the appropriateness of this tag line. Wars are fought against states—not concepts—and perhaps the War on Terror is more metaphoric (cf. the War on Drugs) than descriptively accurate. Or, as with the War on Drugs, much of the resistance could come from law enforcement rather than the military, thus further attenuating the ascription of *war*. For our purposes, however, none of this matters insofar as nothing of conceptual—if not rhetorical— force hangs on it. With that disclaimer, I propose to follow standard parlance in what follows.

3.1 THE WAR ON TERROR

Since 9/11, we have been told that the nature of war has changed and that our approaches to it must be updated lest we be unable to defend ourselves.[1] Traditional wars, including ones as recent as the first U.S. incursion in Iraq, have tended to be fought on battlefields. The distinction between combatants and noncombatants has been clear, not least of all because combatants wore uniforms and noncombatants did not. Civilians have been largely exonerated from risk during these conflicts: while collateral damage has always been a part of warfare, the risk to civilians was unintended but foreseen. The noninvolvement of civilians was effected, not just by clear identification thereof, but also by the above-mentioned separation between them and the conflict. Wars were fought between state actors with transparent chains of command, a high degree of centralization, and obvious diplomatic and political outlets. To be sure, there are numerous exceptions to these features of conflicts, though it is uncontroversial that they have, historically, been largely instantiated in those conflicts. Not only have we been able to characterize conflicts in these ways, but we have also adopted norms that explicitly require many of them; these have been codified both legally and in the just war tradition.[2]

The contemporary advent of terrorism, however, compromises all these features.[3] Wars are fought, not on conventional battlefields, but rather in urban centers. The combatant/noncombatant distinction has become blurred, at least insofar as combatants are no longer readily identified; certainly, they commonly lack military uniforms. But the distinction has been further blurred insofar as noncombatants often provide material support for combatants through positioning, sustenance, communication, and so on. Can these noncombatants be justly targeted? Are they properly designated as noncombatants? Not only do such people, whether willing or unwilling, become complicit in some of these cases, but noncombatants on the other side also become targets. In fact—and as we saw in §1.3 above—the targeting of noncombatants is one of the hallmarks of terrorism. So, again, the effects that terrorism has on the combatant/noncombatant separation is twofold: terrorists incorporate noncombatants on their side into the conflict while, at the same time, threatening noncombatants on the other side.[4] Finally, terrorists are (usually) not state actors. It is, therefore, often unclear what their command structures—which are usually decentralized—are. And traditional tools, such as diplomacy and other political interventions, are less effective insofar as we often would not even know whom to approach in the first place, and, regardless, the ideological commitments of terrorist groups could render such measures futile. Given that terrorists change the landscape of warfare, we can then ask whether those who attempt to combat these terrorists are justified in changing their tactics as well. Does the fact that terrorists are no longer playing by the traditional rules license the terrorists' opponents to play by different rules as well? If so, what should the new rules be? How do we justify them?

Before moving forward, I should identify some archetypal practices that have catalyzed new discussion vis-à-vis their role in opposing the War on Terror. Interrogational torture is an obvious archetype and one that will occupy us in subsequent chapters. For the purposes of this chapter, however, it is also worth pointing to assassination and enemy combatancy/prisoner-of-war (POW) status; these will also help me develop my account of exceptionalism.[5] None of these is a historically novel issue, but each had a reasonably clear status in pre-9/11 norms (both in the United States and abroad). Since 9/11, however, the associated norms have come under pressure and/or been subject to violation.

While I will consider torture at length in due course, suffice it to say that it has been widely decried as a violation of basic human rights as well as of international law.[6] However, since 9/11, the torture debate has resurfaced. While few have overtly called for the legitimization of torture, the strategy employed by the Bush administration bears notice. For example, §17 of the Third Geneva Convention says that "no physical or mental torture, nor any other form of coercion, may be inflicted on prisoners of war to secure from them information of any kind whatever." By denying suspected terrorists POW status (see below), §17 would seemingly not attach. The Bush administration has also endorsed coercive techniques that, in its estimation, nevertheless fall short of torture.[7] Furthermore, that administration employed counsel, John Yoo, whose infamous "torture memos" sought to give legal grounding to torture or torture-like techniques.[8]

The purpose of this chapter is not to evaluate the policies of the Bush administration, but it bears notice that, after 9/11, proscriptions on torture have been debated, both morally and legally. And, lest we lay this wholly at the feet of an unpopular administration, it is worth noticing that, as recently as 2005, the majority of Americans thought that the torture of terrorists was justifiable in some situations.[9] Why would anyone think this? The putative answer is that, without torture, we leave ourselves more vulnerable to terrorist attacks and more susceptible to the harms that they portend. Whether such an answer succeeds is, for now, beside the point—for more discussion, see chapter 7—which is simply that terrorism puts pressure on existing moral and legal norms, of which those pertaining to torture are an example.[10]

Let me raise two other practices that are similar to torture in the sense that proscriptions against them have been revisited in light of the War on Terror. First, consider assassinations.[11] Historically, these have played an important role in warfare and in thinking about warfare;[12] Sun Tzu mentions assassinations in his *Art of War*, Machiavelli discusses the importance of protecting against them in *The Prince*, and Thomas More wrote about the potential moral advantages of assassination in terms of bringing about a quicker end to hostilities.[13] Before 9/11, however, assassination was clearly not allowed in the United States or by its agents operating abroad. In 1976, President Ford issued Executive Order 11905, which stated (in §5g, "Restrictions on Intelligence Activities") that "no employee of the United States Government shall engage in, or conspire to engage in, political assassination." This apparent ban on assassination was reaffirmed in subsequent executive orders by President Carter in 1978 and President Regan in 1981.[14] However, just weeks after 9/11, President Bush signed an intelligence "finding" that authorized "lethal covert action" against Osama Bin Laden.[15] While the word *assassination* is not explicitly used here, it is nearly impossible to interpret this action from Bush as not relaxing the strictures earlier emplaced by Ford.

As in the torture case, the argument for assassination derives from a post-9/11 climate: terrorists, especially high-impact ones, can effect a tremendous amount of damage and take many civilian lives. Assassination can neutralize the targeted terrorists and, perhaps, save many lives. And, in this climate, the legitimacy of assassination has again become a prominent issue.[16] Why not use regular law enforcement to apprehend and prosecute those terrorists? This is an important question being discussed in the literature, and I do not plan to address it here.[17] Suffice it to say that at least part of the answer has to do with expediency: assassinations might be carried out faster than law enforcement and the judicial process can operate. Furthermore, we also may not always have the diplomatic or jurisdictional avenues that would otherwise empower law enforcement, thus rendering that option moot. It is also worth noticing that the executive orders from 1976 to 1981 were issued during the Cold War, particularly when the Soviet Union thought that we might have been plotting assassinations of Fidel Castro; our presidents' actions had at least as much to do with allaying Cold War hostilities as with any other concern. Therefore, at least part of the historic impetus against assassination lies in antiquated concerns.

Finally, consider the treatment of POWs. The Third Geneva Convention clearly delimits how POWs can and cannot be treated; we have already seen that any sort of coercive interrogation is clearly proscribed, though other issues are addressed as well. The detention facilities at Guantánamo and Abu Ghraib almost certainly failed to live up to these requirements. This was not, however, because of some sort of mere complacency on the behalf of the Bush administration but rather followed from a position that the convention does not apply. As has now become controversial, the administration applied "enemy combatancy"—as opposed to POW—status to the detainees, thus abrogating substantial restrictions on their treatment. However, despite widespread opinion, the Bush administration did not create this status, which was originally proffered in a 1942 Supreme Court case, *Ex Parte Quirin*. The ruling held:

> The law of war draws a distinction between the armed forces and the peaceful populations of belligerent nations and also between those who are lawful and unlawful combatants. Lawful combatants are subject to capture and detention as prisoners of war by opposing military forces. Unlawful combatants are likewise subject to capture and detention, but in addition they are subject to trial and punishment by military tribunals for acts which render their belligerency unlawful. The spy who secretly and without uniform passes the military lines of a belligerent in time of war, seeking to gather military information and communicate it to the enemy, or an enemy combatant who without uniform comes secretly through the lines for the purpose of waging war by destruction of life or property, are familiar examples of belligerents who are generally deemed not to be entitled to the status of prisoners of war, but to be offenders against the law of war subject to trial and punishment by military tribunals.[18]

Under the Bush administration, this legal category effectively allowed foreign detainees to be held indefinitely, without Geneva Convention protections *and* without access to the (civilian) legal system[19]—or at least it did before being eroded by two Supreme Court decisions.[20] As a justification for this approach, we were told by White House counsel Alberto Gonzales that the War on Terror constitutes a "new paradigm" and "renders obsolete Geneva's strict limitations on questioning of enemy prisoners and renders quaint some of its provisions."[21]

Similar sentiments were expressed by Major General Geoffrey Miller, the former commanding officer at Guantánamo, who said: "[Joint Task Force] Guantánamo's mission is to detain enemy combatants and then to gain intelligence from them to be able to win the global war on terrorism. And so we are detaining these enemy combatants in a humane manner . . . and in accordance, as much as we can, with the Geneva Convention."[22] This emphasis on intelligence and the defeasible commitment to the Geneva Convention is endemic of the post-9/11 era.[23] Myriad moral and legal issues are raised by these practices,[24] though their contribution to this discussion is to provide a third example of a way in which terrorism, or at least our response to it, has challenged preexisting norms. Having now sketched how some of those norms—that is, those pertaining to torture, assassination, and enemy combatancy status—have come under pressure after 9/11, I now move on to a more general and theoretical discussion of exceptionalism (§§3.2–3.5) and its ethical upshots (§3.6).

3.2 EXCEPTIONALISM

In this section—and incorporating the above-mentioned and other examples—I will develop a general and theoretical account of exceptionalism. By this I mean that the War on Terror, through its novel face and extreme stakes, suggests to some that we need to make exceptions to traditional norms.[25] In §3.6, I will consider some of the ethical issues that attach to this discussion, but the intermediate sections are largely conceptual. Surprisingly, the literature bears little work on the doctrine of exceptionalism, a deficiency that this chapter aims to ameliorate.[26] In particular, there are four elements that an account of exceptionalism should provide. First, it should tell us what the exception is *to*. Second, it should tell us *what* is being excepted. Third, it should properly delimit the *scope* of the exceptions. Fourth, it should tell us *why* the exception is being made.

Let me briefly expand on each of these elements before moving forward. The semantics of *exceptionalism* mandate that something is being excepted vis-à-vis some category. Consider, for example, some school rule that holds that all students must be in the classroom except those with a hall pass. The exception, then, is to the otherwise inflexible stricture that all students must be in the classroom (element 1). When we talk about what exceptions are to, we are looking for some sort of stricture that would apply in the absence of the exception. The strictures that we are primarily interested in are moral and legal ones, so I will most commonly just refer to *norms*, which we can take to be usefully ambiguous between either of these two classes; nothing in the following analysis hangs on the various distinctions between them.[27] Second, we have to be precise about what is being excepted (element 2), which, in the example given above, is those students who hold hall passes. Importantly, the exceptions have to be granted to a proper subset of whatever the norm binds (including the empty set).[28] So, for example, teachers are not excepted from the norm that all students must be in the classroom since they are, ex hypothesi, not students. Regarding teachers, the norm simply *does not apply*, and that is relevantly different from it having an exception. Therefore, what gets excepted must be something to which the norm otherwise would have applied absent the exception.

The third element pertains to scope, and I think that *scope* can be understood in various sorts of ways. Let me herein mention three; these will be discussed in greater detail in subsequent sections.[29] First, imagine that we can park on the street except on Tuesdays (when street cleaning takes place). In this case, the scope of the exception is *temporal*: the norm applies at all *times* except Tuesdays. Second, consider that Americans can have wine shipped directly from wineries in California, except those who live in Montana (among some other states).[30] In this case, the scope of the exception is *spatial*: people who occupy certain spaces have one set of privileges, while those who occupy some other spaces lack those privileges. Third, consider that all children in Prince George's County, Maryland, were required to be vaccinated against hepatitis B, except those whose families could demonstrate certain religious beliefs.[31] In this case, the scope is *group based* since some groups (namely, those lacking certain religious beliefs) are bound by the stricture whereas others (namely, those having certain religious beliefs) are excepted.

Let me make several other points regarding scope. First, there need not be *single* classes of exceptions, but exceptionalism is, rather, fully consistent with the following: "All X's can/cannot/must φ, except for Y's and Z's." In the wine shipping case, Montana residents are restricted, but so, at the time of writing, were residents of just over a dozen other states. Each of these states is, then, an exception to the norm, and it is irrelevant to their status vis-à-vis that norm what other states' statuses are. In the vaccination case, those with certain religious beliefs were excepted, but so were those with certain medical conditions. And, second, these scopes need not be mutually exclusive: some norm could bind pursuant to two of the above requirements being met and otherwise be excepted. For example, I once lived on a street in Pittsburgh where one could park on only one side of the street (spatial) on Tuesdays (temporal). If it was not Tuesday, or if there was a spot on the permitted side of the street, then the stricture was excepted. The interplay among these different scopes can give rise to more complex norms and exceptions, but, conceptually, such interplay is straightforward.

In addition to the comments offered above regarding scope, there is a further consideration that is more pragmatic than conceptual. To wit, it should be the case that there are fewer exceptions to the norms than cases in which the norms apply. Again, this is not conceptually required, but failing this desideratum would otherwise give rise to poorly specified norms. For example, we could have a "norm" that says that everyone must serve on university service committees, except those who do not work at universities. And, undoubtedly, this is true. But it is not useful, and the problem lies in scope. The proper norm is not this one but rather that all university employees must serve on university service committees: the people who are "excepted" from the first norm never should have been included in its scope in the first place.

Finally, there must be reasons for the exceptions (and for the norms), lest they be arbitrary or capricious. This issue of justification will be deferred until §3.6, when I consider the ethics of exceptionalism, though I certainly take it to be part of the conceptual requirements that we are discussing here. And, in every one of the cases presented above, we can easily supply reasons for both the norms and the exceptions while withholding judgment on their relative merits.

Let us now take the framework outlined above and return to a discussion of exceptionalism as it pertains to the War on Terror in particular. In a recent essay, Jonathan Marks writes about the history that "compartmentalization" has had on various military conflicts; his compartmentalization bears on my group-based exceptionalism insofar as both effect varying treatments for some groups. Marks argues:

> The wars between the city-states of ancient Greece, as well as war waged by Alexander the Great against the Persians, were marked by respect for the life and personal dignity of war victims. Temples, embassies, and priests of the opposing side were spared and prisoners of war were exchanged. Yet both the Greeks and Romans failed to demonstrate similar respect for those regarded as barbarians. . . . More recently, Nazi doctors perceived Jews as *Untermenschen* (or sub-humans) who were, by reason of this categorization, not protected by the 1931 *Reichsgesundheitsrat* regulations prohibiting human experimentation that was fatal, disabling, or conducted without the voluntary consent of the subject.[32]

These are some pre-9/11 examples of group-based exceptionalism: whether the "barbarians" are excepted from certain forms of respect or the Jews were excepted from legal protections, the examples are ones in which group membership changed the norms that were afforded to some population. And, as I will argue below, most of the significant exceptionalisms that are endemic in the post-9/11 era are group-based exceptionalisms, as opposed to temporal or spatial ones.

3.3 TEMPORAL EXCEPTIONALISM

Before turning to that argument, however, let us consider some post-9/11 exceptionalisms that are not group based, as these are worth considering. So, for example, consider the USA PATRIOT Act, which I take as an example of temporal exceptionalism, as does Marks. In this original legislation, there were various provisions—so-called sunset provisions—that were to expire on December 31, 2005, unless they were reauthorized by Congress.[33] In fact, most of these provisions were made permanent by Congress; only §§206 and 215 were left as sunset provisions, now set to expire in May 2011. Some other provisions were slightly modified.[34]

As originally legislated, the gist of the PATRIOT Act was that Americans were to have such and such liberties, *except* for the dates between its being signed into law (namely, October 26, 2001) and its then prospective expiration (namely, December 31, 2005). Since dates are delimiting when the exceptions are in play, this is an example of temporal exceptionalism. However, temporal exceptionalism is not all that significant in the War on Terror. For one, there are very few cases that are overt ones of temporal exceptionalism; probably the PATRIOT Act is the only substantial one. And, of course, the bulk of the PATRIOT Act was made permanent, so it is hardly delimiting temporal exceptions any more. Only §§206 and 215 are still temporally delimited, and they may yet be made permanent. If they are, then none of the sunset provisions will have actually expired.

But it is also unlikely that temporal exceptions are ever what legislators will really be after. In the wake of 9/11, the Bush administration presented controversial legislation that, even in that political climate, would have been hard to make permanent. To my mind, the sunset provisions are more of a test run or political compromise than an end in themselves, as the now permanence of most of the PATRIOT Act indicates. This is probably not always the case for sunset provisions, though the exceptions are strange cases.[35] For example, John Adams and the Federalist Party passed the Alien and Sedition Acts (1798), which were meant to limit political opposition to an undeclared naval war on France.[36] However, this act expired at the end of Adams's presidency such that the Democratic-Republicans (the then political rivals of the Federalists) could not similarly limit opposition to their own agendas. More typical would be something like the Federal Assault Weapons Ban, which was a subtitle of the Violent Crime Control and Law Enforcement Act of 1994, signed into law by President Clinton. This provision was set to expire in 2004 if President Bush did not renew it. He did not, and the provision expired. But, certainly, the advocates of the ban wanted it to be renewed or made permanent, and, as with the PATRIOT Act, the sunset provision on the ban was a political compromise in order to gain temporary legislation as permanent legislation would have been less politically viable.

Of course, there are differences between having sunset provisions and simply repealing laws. Consider, for example, Prohibition in the United

States.[37] The Eighteenth Amendment, which prevented the sale, manu-
facture, and transportation of alcohol for consumption, went into effect
in early 1920. The Twenty-first Amendment then repealed the Eighteenth
Amendment in late 1933, thus restoring the previously precluded practices. However, this is not properly understood as a case of exceptionalism
in the sense that the PATRIOT Act was originally conceived. The latter had
explicit provisions for the cessation of its provisions, whereas the Eighteenth Amendment did not. It is true that Americans have had various
liberties with respect to alcohol *except* during (most of) 1920–33, though
this exceptionalism makes sense only ex post (i.e., once the liberties are
restored). This is importantly different from the PATRIOT Act, which said,
ex ante, that Americans would (not) have certain liberties from part of
2001 until the end of 2005. Or, to put it another way, a repeal just means
that some legislature has changed its mind (or that some new legislature
disagrees with its predecessor and legislates accordingly). Temporal exceptionalism, on the other hand, means that the same legislature is effecting
different legislation at different times and not that that legislature (or
any other) has changed its mind on appropriate legislation. This, then, is
another reason that temporal exceptionalism is not likely to be extremely
prevalent as many of the instances that we might appeal to are, properly
understood, ones of repeal rather than of (ex ante) exceptionalism.

We have, therefore, amassed several reasons to think that temporal exceptionalism will not be common, whether generally or as pertains to the
War on Terror. First, it will rarely be the intent (or, at least, the hope) that
the exceptions are not made permanent. The assault weapons ban is perhaps even more clear in this regard than the PATRIOT Act: it is certainly
not the case that those legislators thought that assault weapons would
be any better in 2004 than they were in 1994, though a different administration intervened against their aspirations. Second, and similarly, exceptions *are* made permanent, at least some of the time (cf. most sections of
the PATRIOT Act). In these cases, there are no temporally delimited exceptions; rather, there is ongoing legislation, though legislation whose
status has changed (i.e., from provisional to permanent). Note, however,
that it hardly matters to whoever would have been affected as there is no
practical difference between a temporary status being made permanent
and a permanent status being assigned from the outset. (This is not to say
that there are not psychological or political differences in these legislative
schemes, just no significant practical differences aside from reauthorization.) Third, many cases that might otherwise look like temporal exceptionalism are better understood as ones of legislative *change* rather than
exceptionalism, strictly speaking.

3.4 SPATIAL EXCEPTIONALISM

As mentioned in §3.2 above, exceptionalism could also occur along some spatial axis: remember our friends from Montana who cannot receive wine directly from California wineries. So here we have some norm that applies to everyone *except* those who occupy some particularly delimited space. And this suggests the generalized conception of spatial exceptionalism: "All X's can/cannot/must φ, except those who are in S (where S is some location)." Unlike temporal exceptionalism, there is undoubtedly a lot of spatial exceptionalism: every time local norms deviate from some more widely held norms, spatial exceptionalism exists. Something would have to be said about how to individuate locations, particularly nested ones, but I shall not pursue that here. For this project, however, the question is whether the War on Terror gives rise to spatial exceptionalism. And I do not think that it does, at least not in the relevant sense. Before seeing the argument for that, let us consider Marks, who argues for the contrary.

Marks points to enemy combatancy status, which was discussed in §3.1 above; we can, therefore, skip the details of that status. Let me say from the outset that this is probably the most plausible example of spatial exceptionalism in the War on Terror and that, if it does not withstand scrutiny, then it is unlikely that spatial exceptionalism is significant in this regard. Marks writes of "*spatial* or *geographic* exceptionalism, in which physical locality is relied upon to justify the nonapplication of protective norms and procedures. A good example of this is Guantánamo, selected by the administration in an effort to keep detainees beyond the *habeas corpus* jurisdiction of federal courts."[38] Marks thinks that this is an example of spatial exceptionalism on the grounds that certain norms (do not) apply, based on location. The norm, then, could be something like: "All those held in U.S. custody have the right to habeas corpus, except those held at Guantánamo (and, perhaps, some other places)."

I do not disagree that this statement is true, nor do I disagree that the Bush administration specifically chose Cuba precisely because it could assign such status to the detainees held there. But this does not seem like an example of spatial exceptionalism, at least once we look at it more closely. Return to the case of the Montanan who cannot directly order Californian wine. In that case, there is nothing about the Montanan *himself* that does any of the motivating work for the legislation. If the Montanan moves south to Wyoming, he can order wine, and this would be of vanishingly little interest to the Montana legislature. The law is precisely designed to govern a *space*, irrespective of whoever occupies that space. If all the residents of Montana and Wyoming traded states, the legislation would continue unaffected. This is, therefore, a perfect example of spatial exceptionalism.

Contrast that case with Guantánamo. The practices at Guantánamo are motivated, not by the space over which they are operative, but rather by the people who occupy that space (namely, the detainees). If the detainees were to swap spots with a couple hundred residents from Florida, the U.S. government, unlike the Montana legislature, would not have any reason to maintain its practices in Cuba. Furthermore, it might have a reason to try to change some of the norms that thereafter applied to those detainees who were now in Florida.

So the appropriate test to distinguish between true spatial exceptionalism and would-be cases is to ask whether it is the *space* that matters or else the *group* that is in the space. Imagine that the Bush administration could deny habeas corpus to suspected terrorists (or allies who might have critical intelligence) *regardless* of where they were. In such a scenario, there would be no reason to create Guantánamo; there is no independent reason to exercise control over that space. Of course, habeas corpus probably cannot be denied in, say, Florida, so the administration has a reason to keep the detainees away from there. Again, the interest is in affecting the status of the *group*, not the space. So, unlike the example with Montana—which is a true instance of spatial exceptionalism—the treatment of the enemy combatants at Guantánamo is effectively group-based exceptionalism masquerading as spatial exceptionalism. This is not, however, to prejudge the morality of the practices, only to identify the proper avenue for that inquiry. Let us now take up group-based exceptionalism directly.

3.5 GROUP-BASED EXCEPTIONALISM

In §3.3 above, I denied that temporal exceptionalism was an important facet of the War on Terror, and, in §3.4, I argued that the War on Terror's most compelling example of spatial exceptionalism was more properly understood as a group-based exceptionalism. In this section, I will argue that the most significant exceptionalisms in the War on Terror are, in fact, group based; in the next section, we will see the ethical implications of this result. Let us now return to the three cases identified as archetypal in the War on Terror: torture, assassination, and enemy combatancy status. The identification of enemy combatancy status as group-based exceptionalism was already made above, but more should be said about torture and assassination in this regard.

Starting with torture, this is clearly an example of group-based exceptionalism. But what is the group that is receiving different treatment? And what is the norm to which the exception is being made? Roughly, it looks something like this: "Do not torture, except when it is necessary to prevent greater harms." Putting aside the associated moral and empirical issues, which will be discussed in subsequent chapters, this is a reasonable approximation of the idealized torture exception as some endorse to fight the War on Terror. Again, this is not to prejudge the morality or efficacy of the exception but rather to try to clarify its proposed structure; let us therefore consider a couple of remarks on this proposal.

First, nobody would seriously argue that torture is justified unless it prevents some greater harm. To foreshadow forthcoming discussion in §4.2, myriad applications of torture are patently impermissible, and there is little to no philosophical merit to having a discussion about these sorts of practices. (There might be practical merits in terms of abrogating such practices where they continue.) Second, this norm seems to be of the right sort insofar as its starting point is *not* to torture and then to allow the exceptions to come in. Alternatively, it could say something like "torture should be practiced, except when . . . ," but this formulation would violate the pragmatic constraint on exceptionalism postulated above insofar as the exceptions should be rarer than the nonexceptions. Even those who defend torture, including me, do so in only limited cases, such that the excepted norm would be one prohibiting torture rather than one allowing it.

Now the question is what the relevant axis of exception is in the above-mentioned norm. It is not spatial: there is no *space* outside of which one norm applies and inside of which a different one applies. Or, if there is, this space delimitation is derivative (cf. the argument offered above regarding enemy combatancy status). Similarly, there is no time at which torture is licensed as against other times, or, if there were, it would again be derivative. For example, we might say that torture is licensed only at *times* during which it would be expedient, but the only reason that those times are relevant is because there are *people*, at those times, who are unwilling to surrender lifesaving intelligence. This proposal, then, is that the exception for torture could be predicated only on there being people from whom we might extract important information. These people, actual or hypothetical, therefore form the *group* that is relevant to the exceptions to our norm against torture: the people from whom lifesaving intelligence cannot be expediently obtained in any way other than torture.

The point of this chapter is not to assess whether such groups exist or, even if they did, whether torture would be permissible; these ideas will be developed in subsequent chapters. Rather, the present objective is to figure out the structure of the exceptions, even if more general comments will be made in the following section regarding some of the moral issues that follow. I take it, however, that torture could be only a sort of group-based exceptionalism, and, as discussed above, the same goes for enemy combatancy status.

Our third archetype, assassination, would be similarly categorized. Starting negatively, the norms against assassination are not tied to specific places: it is not the case that assassination is normalized in place A and not normalized in place B (from the point of view of U.S. agency/involvement, let us say). If we were attempting to assassinate someone, we would not care much where he happened to be, at least not for reasons other than prudence and efficacy. We might care, for example, whether the target was in a crowded place, at an embassy, in some place where the assassin might be noticed, and so on, but all these features are, again, derivative on the class of persons whom we want to assassinate. Temporal exceptionalism is also not appropriate: the would-be assassinated is not off the hook when the clock strikes midnight or at any other time. The circumstances might change such that we no longer pursue assassination at some time, but, in that case, the driving feature is the circumstances themselves, not the temporal features of the case.

Rather, the norm against assassination looks something like: "Do not assassinate, except when it is necessary to prevent greater harms." The exceptions to this norm are going to be *people* who are perpetuating great evils and who cannot be accessed diplomatically or politically. There are probably two classes of people to whom assassination could be the most appropriate—which is not to say that it is necessarily appropriate at all—and those are terrorists and despotic, genocidal leaders. If, for whatever reason, these groups cannot be directly engaged by military action, then there are at least prima facie compelling reasons to target them. Again, this discussion is meant not to render any commentary on the morality of assassination but rather to locate it under the category of a group-based exceptionalism: the putative exceptions to the norms against assassination would be the groups of people that comprise the terrorists and leaders whom the world would be better off without.

Having already discussed enemy combatancy status in §3.4, I will not say more about it, other to reiterate that it was, like torture and assassination, appropriately categorized as group-based exceptionalism. Therefore, *all* the examples that we have considered as archetypal in the War on Terror are of this sort. Furthermore, as argued in previous sections, there are not other examples in the War on Terror where different kinds of exceptionalism are likely to play a significant role. Having now located the sort of exceptionalisms suggested by the War on Terror, let us discuss the ethics of exceptionalism.

3.6 THE ETHICS OF EXCEPTIONALISM

In this final section, let us consider some of the ethical features that are germane to the exceptionalisms presented above. While the most interesting discussion will pertain to group-based exceptionalism, let us start with the ethics of temporal and spatial exceptionalism. From the outset, however, let me say that I consider temporal and spatial exceptionalism more benign than group-based exceptionalism.

Taking temporal exceptionalism first, the idea here was that some norms applied at some times and not at others. Again, this sort of exceptionalism is not particularly relevant to the War on Terror (though, for a discussion of the PATRIOT Act, see §3.3 above). But, even if it were, it could be carried out in a morally sensible sort of way. More generally, imagine that there is some national emergency.[39] This could be war, some infectious disease, a national disaster, or whatever. In these cases, the public good is quite often going to be pitted against the rights of some individuals. We can see this in the public health case, for example, by considering quarantine and forced immunization.[40] In other cases, we might see it in rationing.[41] In all these cases, however, it at least seems reasonable that we might restrict some liberties, so long as such restrictions were necessary, served the greater good, and were lifted when advisable. Certainly, some people might deny this position, though I will not defend it here.[42]

What are debatable, of course, are the sorts of empirical claims that motivate the restrictions on offer. For example, imagine the claim that we need electronic surveillance to conduct the War on Terror, thus violating the privacy rights of at least some. Objections to this line of thought are more often made on the grounds that the results of such surveillance are not likely to be of any use to the War on Terror; such restrictions therefore execute costs without providing countervailing benefits.[43] Civil libertarians certainly like to invoke rights to privacy, but, if they actually believed that, absent such restrictions, our society would be in serious risk of destruction, then it would be unreasonable of them to persist in their objections. Rather, I assert that the empirical basis for restricting liberties is sometimes unsound, not that, in theory, there is any serious moral objection to the sorts of reasonable restrictions that well-founded empirical prognoses would suggest.

Moving on to spatial exceptionalism, I again do not find this to be that worrisome. Or at least I think this insofar as we are considering genuine instances of spatial exceptionalism and not the sorts that are more properly understood as group-based exceptionalism (cf. Guantánamo). Again, return to the example of the Montana legislature excepting its citizenry from norms governing other locales. It seems perfectly acceptable as a premise of self-governance that local legislatures be able to set the parameters by which they govern, and some of these parameters may give rise to spatial exceptionalisms. To be sure, there are constitutional considerations that come into play, such as the Fourteenth Amendment and the Commerce Clause; the Commerce Clause, for example, is being interpreted in ways inconsistent with legislation banning direct wine shipments, which means that the Montana law might soon fall.[44] But there is nothing *in principle* wrong with norms applied to certain geographic zones, so long as those norms do not run afoul of broader considerations (e.g., constitutionality). We certainly do not want it to be the case that local norms are arbitrary or capricious, but, if they were, the problem would be the caprice or arbitrariness and not, intrinsically, the spatial exceptionalism that they characterized.

But what about group-based exceptionalism? Again, this is the most substantial form of exceptionalism suggested by the War on Terror. And, unfortunately, it is the most perilous of all the forms derived in this chapter. Why? There are obvious cases of group-based exceptionalism that are completely immoral and rank among the greatest injustices humanity has perpetuated. I hardly need to catalog these, but consider, for example, slavery or genocide. In both these cases, certain norms applied, except to some group. These norms could range from freedom to vote to even the liberty not to be killed. In the Holocaust, Jews were deprived of practically everything (often including their lives) merely because of their association with some group; the same is true with American slaves and countless other tyrannized groups. The mere fact that some of these horrors are straightforward instantiations of group-based exceptionalism should give us pause when considering the whole category.

Or should it? Just as there are horrible cases of group-based exceptionalism, there are also completely innocuous ones. For example, consider collegiate admissions, which except one group from some outcome (e.g., acceptance or rejection) on the basis of features that it has (e.g., grade point average, SAT scores, etc.). All American citizens can vote, except convicted felons—or at least those not residing in Maine or Vermont—and those under the age of eighteen. This former exception strikes many of us as problematic, but little seems wrong with the latter. We except the group of people who have been in car accidents or otherwise have poor driving records from the car insurance rates to which the rest of us have access. So there certainly seem to be unproblematic group-based exceptionalisms. What, then, is the difference between the acceptable and the unacceptable forms? And, for present purposes, where do our archetypes from the War on Terror fall?

The first thing to say here is that the relevant differential is *not* what norm the exception is from, which might seem an intuitive way to go. Take some norm such as: "None should be enslaved, except those of African descent." The reason that this exception is morally problematic does not, strictly speaking, have to do with allowing exceptions to a particular norm. It might be the case that there are exceptions to the norm (e.g., those who consent to being sold into slavery), or it might not. But it is the *exceptions* that matter, not just the norms, in determining the moral status of the exceptionalism.

To see why this is the case, consider the norm of allowing citizens to vote. As mentioned above, there are and have been exceptions to this norm. In the United States, for example, children cannot vote, and women did not, nationally, gain the right to vote until the ratification of the Nineteenth Amendment in 1920. Consider some time before 1920, when neither women nor children had the right to vote. Granting that one of these exceptions is morally permissible and the other one morally impermissible, it therefore follows that it cannot be the *norm* that drives the permissibility but rather the *group* that is excepted from the norm. I do not deny that it depends on the group *in relation to the norm*, such that some group might be reasonably excepted from some norm (e.g., women's access to men's restrooms) but not reasonably excepted from another (e.g., women's right to vote). However, the norms, independently of the groups to which the exceptions would pertain, are not the proper objects of moral evaluation.[45]

If this is right, we must look at the groups that would be excepted from the norms. Using the suffrage case again, there is no moral reason to exclude women from a political process to which men have access: whatever the morally relevant features are that ground men's claim to voting, they are similarly held by women. As this illustrates, we have to think, not only about the group that is to be excepted, but also about the relationship that a group shares *with the other groups that are not excepted*. We need to treat like cases alike, though we have to specify the dimensions of similarity that matter in each case. Unlike the gender difference in voting, however, we can locate a relevant difference between children and adults, thus grounding the exception made against children's right to vote. Namely, we want our electorate to have a certain level of rationality, capacity for acquisition and processing of information, and so on, and there is no doubt that young children lack this. (I take no position on whether the age of eighteen is the appropriate cutoff.)

Now let us return to the cases presented in the context of the War on Terror, looking specifically at the groups that stand to be excepted and the relationship that those groups bear to the groups that will not be excepted. Furthermore, let us consider whether there are morally relevant differences between these groups that might serve to ground differential moral statuses. Both the groups that are affected by exceptions made for torture and enemy combatancy status are, ideally, those that have critical intelligence.[46] And those that are targeted for assassination are similar insofar as they are assessed to pose threats, whether now or in the future. There might be a difference in these cases insofar as the former groups' crimes could be of omission (i.e., by not revealing the information), while the latter group's crimes would be of commission (i.e., by bringing about the harms directly). I am not sure this is right, however, and, regardless, the distinction is orthogonal to our discussion. Rather, what matters is that all those groups excepted are responsible, actively or passively, for some threat and, through their agency, can abrogate the threat.

An obvious objection to this claim is that it is simply false: many of those subject to detention or torture, in fact, have no critical intelligence, and some are not even terrorists at all (for more discussion, see chapter 7).[47] It might even be the case that those targeted for assassination are not bad people, though I find this less likely: it is more likely that we disagree about what *bad* means and/or whether there are other options available. Regardless, at least this first claim is certainly true. What are its implications for our analysis? To my mind, it does not have important implications for the morality of group-based exceptionalism. The reason is that it just shows that we are applying the exceptions to the *wrong group*: a group that includes, not just the people that we should be excepting, but rather a group that (maybe) includes those people as well as others to whom the exceptions should not apply. That we have our groups delimited improperly says nothing about the status of exceptionalism, *as applied to the proper groups*.

The waiting objection now is that, pragmatically, it is somewhere between hard and impossible to make sure that we have the right groups. First, I do not think that this is completely true: our military intelligence just has to do a good job in classifying people appropriately. There is no doubt that this is a challenge and probably no doubt that it could have been done better than it has been since 9/11. But I certainly think that we can get it mostly right and that, given the complexities of warfare and some of the latitudes that must be therein conferred, this is close enough (cf. collateral damage; see §7.1 below).[48] Second, this really is meant to be a theoretical project, and I need to work out my theoretical commitments before turning to practice in the third part of this book.

Where we now stand is that we have an (idealized) account of exceptionalism wherein we are excepting groups who pose harms from various protections. What is the moral status of such an account? As indicated above, one of the criteria is to compare the moral status of the excepted groups to the nonexcepted groups. In these cases, there is at least one morally relevant difference between those groups, which is complicity or agency in imminent or otherwise future harms. For simplicity, let us just call this something like *(partial) responsibility*. The notion of *responsibility* certainly has hardly gotten a free ride in the philosophical literature, though I will not have anything substantive to say about it here.[49] Rather, I will just observe that we obviously treat responsible parties differently from nonresponsible parties, as evidenced by our systems of praise and blame, and as is codified in our moral and legal systems.[50] And there are certainly good reasons for this.

So there are relevant differences that exist between these would-be excepted groups and their contraries. Are they sufficient to warrant exceptions to the norms? People will disagree strongly about this; I cannot hope to settle the debate but merely to offer the framework in which it should be considered. To my mind what ultimately matters is whether the practices are effective. It either is or is not the case that we gain critical intelligence by holding detainees indefinitely (i.e., without affording them due process) and/or by torturing them. Critics are surely skeptical in both cases, though I am more sanguine vis-à-vis torture than indefinite detention insofar as detention probably offends a higher rate of innocents; escalating the treatment of some within that group to another group subject to torture would, one hopes, be done only with good reason (e.g., reasonable expectation that critical intelligence could be gleaned). This is to suggest, not that torture always—or even most of the time—reveals critical intelligence, but rather that we must discriminate more precisely when we consider torture than when we consider (mere) detention since the former portends a greater and more irreversible moral harm. Finally, assassinations either avert worse harms in the future or they do not, and it is these proclivities by which their merits should be judged.

Note that I have intentionally used vague concepts, such as *effective*, *better*, and *worse*. The reason that I do this is, not to waffle, but rather to appreciate that different people understand these terms differently and that the account offered above is compatible with variable conceptions in this regard. We could make these evaluations in terms of consequences, human rights, dignity, or whatever. The upshot of this chapter, however, is meant to be that there is nothing inherently wrong with group-based exceptionalism. Nor is there anything wrong with exceptionalism merely in virtue of the norms that are being excepted. Both these conclusions, I think, would have been counterintuitive. Rather, we gauge the ethics of exceptionalism by focusing on the *groups* that are excepted and by looking for differentia between those groups and other groups that are not excepted. Ideally, I think that the exceptions that we have considered can be justified. As those exceptions have actually been practiced in the War on Terror, I am less certain. Regardless, I see no in-principle objection to these sorts of group-based exceptionalisms or others that would employ similar strategies.

While the principal focus of this book is the moral status of torture, these first three chapters play an important role in articulating the context of terrorism where we most often encounter questions about torture. In some sense, nothing that follows in the next six chapters hangs on anything that has yet been said. That said, it is more fruitful to situate torture against the backdrop of terrorism than to leave it in a vacuum. To this end, the first chapter articulated a conception of terrorism, the second developed an account of its moral status, and the third explored how the advent of terrorism challenges our traditional norms. The next three chapters introduce the philosophical foundations of torture, though necessarily do so at an abstract level. In the last three chapters of the book, more will be said about how these middle chapters translate into practice.

PART II

TORTURE AND TICKING TIME-BOMBS

4

Conceptual and Moral Foundations of Torture

In this second part of the book—and for the remainder—I consider torture directly. The purpose of the first part was to develop the context of terrorism within which discussions about torture often occur. Much of the argumentation regarding torture that will hereafter be developed has nothing inherently to do with terrorism, though it is that context in which these arguments find their most straightforward application. Nevertheless, it should be emphasized that other contexts—such as kidnapping—bear structural features similar to those that we will consider under the aegis of terrorism. A quick suspicion is that, whatever we think about torture, it would probably be less appropriate in these other contexts than it would be in terrorism simply because the stakes are going to be lower; a standard kidnapping case, for example, might involve a threat to only a single person rather than to many.[1] That said, it is worth acknowledging ways in which the forthcoming arguments may generalize, even if they likely will not.

The aim of this chapter is to introduce the conceptual and moral foundations of torture. To that end, I will begin by considering what torture is. Next, I will consider different kinds of torture before setting the ongoing focus on interrogational torture. Finally, I will consider why, most proximately, torture comprises moral harms. Given that I will, ultimately, go on to defend the morality of torture in exceptional cases, it bears emphasis that I recognize the moral harms of torture; the ensuing argument that torture could be justified despite the moral harms does not deny that such harms exist. In this chapter, we will consider the intrinsic harms of torture, which is to say how torture harms its victims. To be clear, this does not deny that there are other, extrinsic harms perpetuated by torture, and, in fact, many of those will be the focus of subsequent chapters of this book. Perhaps surprisingly, the literature focuses on these latter harms—as well as the issue of efficacy—as much as it does on the intrinsic ones. Nevertheless, it is obvious that some privileged discussion should be afforded to the effects that torture has on its victims.

4.1 WHAT IS TORTURE?

The next section will consider various purposes of torture, but we should first get a working conception of what torture is such that we can see what those various sorts of torture will have in common. A standard starting point in this regard is the UN Convention against Torture and Other Cruel, Inhuman or Degrading Treatment or Punishment (CAT), which is the principal international treaty regarding torture.[2] CAT was adopted by the General Assembly of the United Nations on December 9, 1975, and entered into force once twenty countries ratified it; this happened on June 26, 1987, two days after Canada became that twentieth country.[3] The United States was the sixty-third signatory when CAT was signed by Deputy Secretary of State John C. Whitehead on April 18, 1988. Ronald Regan transmitted it to the U.S. Senate for ratification on May 20, 1988, and the U.S. Senate ratified the treaty six years later, on October 21, 1994. At the time of writing, 146 countries had signed and ratified CAT, with 10 more signatories pending ratification.[4] In the following discussion of CAT, it will also be useful to consider the relationship of the United States to that treaty, insofar as that further clarifies the (legal) understanding of *torture* in the United States as well as provides relevant background for some themes to be considered elsewhere in the book.

CAT has various provisions, but one of its most important is the definition of torture offered in §1:

> Torture means any act by which severe pain or suffering, whether physical or mental, is intentionally inflicted on a person for such purposes as obtaining from him or a third person information or a confession, punishing him for an act he or a third person has committed or is suspected of having committed, or intimidating or coercing him or a third person, or for any reason based on discrimination of any kind, when such pain or suffering is inflicted by or at the instigation of or with the consent or acquiescence of a public official or other person acting in an official capacity.

Two more important provisions are made in §2. For present purposes, the one that matters is §2.1: "Each State Party shall take effective legislative, administrative, judicial or other measures to prevent acts of torture in any territory under its jurisdiction." In other words, signatories to CAT undertake a duty to prevent torture. As a signatory, the United States then absorbs that responsibility. And, while this is less important now than it will be later, §2.2 also precludes torture in emergency situations: "No exceptional circumstances whatsoever, whether a state of war or a threat of war, internal political instability or any other public emergency, may be invoked as a justification of torture."

While this definition, requirement, and lack of exceptions would seem to make the status of CAT quite clear, there are, nevertheless, various ways in which quite the opposite is true. Let us herein focus on two, one on CAT's own terms and one on U.S. obligations under CAT. Starting with the former, consider the full title of the convention, belied by the standard acronym: Convention against Torture and Other Cruel, Inhuman or Degrading Treatment or Punishment. Torture, then, is complemented by another form of nefarious treatment, so-called cruel, inhuman, or degrading treatment (CIDT). In particular, §16.1 states:

> Each State Party shall undertake to prevent in any territory under its jurisdiction other acts of cruel, inhuman or degrading treatment or punishment which do not amount to torture as defined in Article 1, when such acts are committed by or at the instigation of or with the consent or acquiescence of a public official or other person acting in an official capacity.

Two things are noteworthy about §16.1. First is its allowance that there are acts that "do not amount to torture as defined in Article 1." While the point of §16.1 is meant to extend further protections than §1 provides for—that is, protections against CIDT and not just against torture—it almost weakens the protections of §1 by inviting classification under CIDT rather than torture. How could this be true? Whether some act is torture (§1) or CIDT (§16.1), it is, nevertheless, proscribed by the convention, so the section from which the proscription emanates is hardly relevant. But this response now misses the second point and the significance of §2.2, which precluded torture in emergency situations since no such preclusion attaches to CIDT. In other words, CAT prevents torture under emergency situations, but it does not prevent CIDT under emergency situations. And, furthermore, it creates a category—or at least acknowledges one—to which §2.2 does not apply.

Second, the U.S. obligation under CAT is not as straightforward as some of our critics would believe. This comment is not meant to marginalize our commitments, only to motivate clarification as to what they actually are. On ratification, the Senate attached a declaration that the United States "reserves the right to communicate, upon ratification, such reservations, interpretive understandings, or declarations as are deemed necessary."[5] Reservations, understandings, and declarations are standard on ratification of treaties, and the United States is hardly alone in making them: at the time of writing, thirty-five other countries had attached at least some of these to their signing of CAT. The point of allowing them is simply that a "take it or leave it" approach would engender fewer signatories to important treaties, so countries are invited to sign while being able to clarify exactly what it is that they think they are agreeing to. The United States had various reservations, but two of them are critical. First, it said that "provisions of Articles 1 through 16 of the Convention are not self-executing," which means that those articles are effective, not on ratification, but only after associated legislation is passed. By ratifying CAT, the United States undertook a responsibility to pass such legislation in due course, which it did. Second, the United States said that it

> [I.1] considers itself bound by the obligation under article 16 to prevent "cruel, inhuman or degrading treatment or punishment," only insofar as the term "cruel, inhuman or degrading treatment or punishment" means the cruel, unusual and inhumane treatment or punishment prohibited by the Fifth, Eighth, and/or Fourteenth Amendments to the Constitution of the United States.[6]

And furthermore:

> [II.1.a] That with reference to article 1, the United States understands that, in order to constitute torture, an act must be specifically intended to inflict severe physical or mental pain or suffering and that mental pain or suffering refers to prolonged mental harm caused by or resulting from (1) the intentional infliction or threatened infliction of severe physical pain or suffering; (2) the administration or application, or threatened administration or application, of mind altering substances or other procedures calculated to disrupt profoundly the senses or the personality; (3) the threat of imminent death; or (4) the threat that another person will imminently be subjected to death, severe physical pain or suffering, or the administration or application of mind altering substances or other procedures calculated to disrupt profoundly the senses or personality.

So, despite §§2.1 and 16.1 of CAT, what ultimately matters in terms of U.S. obligations under that treaty is these reservations and, more importantly, how we legislated our obligations under CAT into law; not surprisingly, our laws ended up reflecting these reservations. The principal U.S. law in this regard is 118 U.S.C. §2340, which defines *torture* in terms of "severe physical or mental pain or suffering" (cf. CAT's "severe pain or suffering, whether physical or mental") and then goes on to further elucidate these terms, which CAT does not. Consider the first provision from that legislation:

> "Torture" means an act committed by a person acting under the color of law specifically intended to inflict severe physical or mental pain or suffering (other than pain or suffering incidental to lawful sanctions) upon another person within his custody or physical control.

There are various points that could be made about this definition, but, for now, let me just draw attention to the concept of *specific intent*. In legal parlance, this condition is satisfied only when the illegal act was expressly intended. In this case, if severe physical or mental pain or suffering results but was, nevertheless, not the specific intention of the offender, then the action is not torture, even if that pain or suffering was reasonably foreseeable; only "general intent" would be satisfied in this case.[7] Under U.S. law, "negligent torture" is, therefore, a conceptual impossibility, though this is not to deny that negligence might be subject to other sanctions. I suspect that this legislation narrows the scope of torture more than CAT would have preferred. Imagine, for example, that a detainee has a terrible phobia of rats and the guards realize that the detention facility is infested with rats. Furthermore, they could take steps to insulate the detainee's cell from the rats, but they do not. That the rats will make their way into the detainee's cell is far from certain, but it is reasonably foreseeable that they will. In due course, suppose that the rats do make their way into the detainee's cell, and, for expedience, let us just stipulate that "severe physical or mental pain or suffering" thereafter results. Did the guards torture the detainee? My intuition is that they did not and that, under 118 U.S.C. §2340, they will not have satisfied the requirement of specific intent, even if they did possess general intent.[8]

Second, the notion of *severe* in "severe physical or mental pain or suffering" is critical to the definition of *torture* in 118 U.S.C. §2340 as well as its similar usage in CAT. To this end, it is worth looking at John Yoo's well-known memo, which addresses how to interpret *torture* under U.S. law; while his attempt is widely criticized,[9] let us consider the details. First, Yoo acknowledges that the "key statutory phrase in the definition of torture is the statement that acts amount to torture if they cause 'severe physical or mental pain or suffering.'"[10] Certainly this is true. Yoo recognizes that *severe* is not defined in the legislation and quotes a Supreme Court case opinion that holds that, "in the absence of such a definition, we construe a statutory term in accordance with its ordinary or natural meaning."[11] Considering the *Oxford English Dictionary*, we are told that *severe* means "grievous, extreme" or "hard to sustain or endure." Yoo pushed further, however, looking to other statutes wherein *severe* was used. In particular, he finds such usage in statutes having to do with definitions of emergency medical conditions.[12] Quoting Yoo at length:

> These statutes define an emergency condition as one "manifesting itself by acute symptoms of sufficient severity (including *severe pain*) such that a prudent lay person, who possess an average knowledge of health and medicine, could reasonably expect the absence of immediate medical attention to result in—placing the health of the individual . . . (i) in serious jeopardy, (ii) serious impairment to bodily functions, or (iii) serious dysfunction of any bodily organ or part" [42 U.S.C.] §1395w-22(d)(3)(B) (emphasis added). Although these statutes address a substantially different subject from section 2340, they are nonetheless helpful for understanding what constitutes severe physical pain. They treat severe pain as an indicator of ailments that are likely to result in permanent and serious physical damage in the absence of immediate medical treatment. Such damage must rise to the level of death, organ failure, or the permanent impairment of a significant body function. These statutes suggest that to constitute torture "severe pain" must rise to a similarly high level—the level that would ordinarily be associated with a physical condition or injury sufficiently serious that it would result in death, organ failure, or serious impairment of body functions.[13]

Despite the derision that has been foisted on this paragraph, I do not find it ridiculous.[14] Yoo began by trying to ascertain the "ordinary or natural meaning" of *severe* since a definition was not given in the torture statutes. Following that, he went to other statutes to try to further clarify what *severe* meant, noting that the statutes he found "address a substantially different subject."[15] It is hardly his fault that the meaning of the word is unclear, that it appears in only limited statutes, and that, when it does, it sets the bar on *severe* pretty high.

That said, this interpretation probably fails. For example, let us consider some historical forms of torture intentionally selected to make the counterargument. These could be things like whipping, paddling, beating of feet (*falaka*), beating of other parts of the body, slapping, cuffing the ears, dorsiflexing (i.e., overextension of wrists or fingers), violent shaking, eyeball pressing, and so on.[16] It seems to me that all these things could be torture, so long as they were of sufficient intensity or duration (i.e., so long as they were *severe*). But I suspect that the treatments could be classified as torture even if the associated pain was not of a level commensurable with some condition or injury serious enough to "result in death, organ failure, or serious impairment of body functions."[17] This does not deny that some forms of torture—drowning, electrocution, and so on—do satisfy the proffered criterion; it is simply to suggest that the criterion is too narrow. And such is the risk of importing meanings from different sorts of statutes: *severe* could just mean different things to those thinking about emergency medical conditions than it could to those thinking about torture. Those legislations exist for different reasons, were constructed with different framers' intent, and so on. Yoo recognizes this by admitting that they address different subjects but, nevertheless, contends that the health statutes may be "helpful for understanding what constitutes severe physical pain."[18] Maybe they are, but they are helpful in the opposite way that Yoo would have us affirm, namely, in realizing that we mean something different when we use *severe* in torture legislation.

Next, consider that the pain and suffering caused by torture can be mental rather than physical. Unlike with physical pain and suffering, §2340 offers some explanation in this regard:

2. "Severe mental pain or suffering" means the prolonged mental harm caused by or resulting from:

(a) the intentional infliction or threatened infliction of severe physical pain or suffering;

(b) the administration or application, or threatened administration or application, of mind-altering substances or other procedures calculated to disrupt profoundly the senses or the personality;

(c) the threat of imminent death; or

(d) the threat that another person will imminently be subjected to death, severe physical pain or suffering, or the administration or application of mind-altering substances or other procedures calculated to disrupt profoundly the senses or personality.

I think that these provisions accord well with our intuitions about mental abuse. In particular, they accommodate the mental trauma associated with physical pain and suffering (2a) as well as the trauma associated with threats of physical abuse, death, or attacks on others (e.g., one's family) (2a, 2c, 2d). To me, however, this legislation hinges on the word *prolonged*. And, furthermore, remember that this provision is meant to augment language used in the preceding one; that first provision still requires specific intent. So, even if prolonged mental harm were to result but was not specifically intended, it would not amount to torture. Imagine, for example, that a guard threatened a detainee with rendition to a hostile country. Also imagine that the detainee subsequently suffered prolonged mental harm (e.g., following from the trauma of being under that threat). If the guard had meant only to scare the detainee into confession and had not intended the prolonged mental harm, then, insofar as that prolonged mental harm could have been reasonably supposed not to occur, this would not violate the statute against torture.

When someone is interrogated, the infliction of prolonged mental harm will rarely—if ever—be specifically intended. Rather, threats may be issued, and the point of those threats will be to engender the disclosure of some information. Whoever proctors the interrogation has no interest in the detainee suffering prolonged mental harm; all that the interrogator cares about is getting the information. Insofar as the prolonged mental harm would, therefore, have nothing to do with this aim, the interrogator does not specifically intend it. However, this does not completely rule out the possibility of specific intent, so long as it could be shown that the interrogator was unreasonable in failing to recognize that prolonged mental harm would almost assuredly follow from the interrogation. It still seems to me that this would be a hard case to make for the reason that some threats do not lead to prolonged mental harm; surely, whether they do or not has something to do with the constitution of those against whom the threats are wielded, and some have hardier constitutions than others. If not everyone—or not a sufficient number of people—would suffer prolonged mental harm, then it would be reasonable to suppose that such harm was foreseeable but not certain, and this would again go to undermining the establishment of specific intent.

After this discussion, where do we stand? In subsequent sections of this chapter, I will consider some purposes of torture as well as the moral harms that interrogational torture threatens; some of those discussions will further bear on this conceptual issue. But, certainly, some sort of commitment must be made in this regard, despite the challenges therein. Given the comments offered above, I am somewhat skeptical about mental torture, though I certainly do not rule out the possibility. In thinking about physical torture, we must again return to *severe*: Yoo's proposal is too restrictive but gets right that *severe* has to be doing substantial work in the definition. There are certainly easy cases, and the history of torture is rife with them (e.g., beating, drowning, electrocution, and so on).

But there are also less easy cases, like the so-called five techniques used against suspected IRA agents. These were principally used during August 1971 under the aegis of Operation Demetrius and comprised wall standing, hooding, noise exposure, sleep deprivation, and food and drink deprivation.[19] Similar techniques have been authorized in the U.S. War on Terror, going under *stress and duress tactics, torture lite, interrogation techniques,* and other euphemisms. Are they torture? I think not. In *Ireland v. United Kingdom* (1978), the European Court of Human Rights (ECHR) ruled they were inhuman and degrading but stopped short of calling them torture.[20] This makes them in violation of CAT but leaves them open to emergency invocations denied to torture. Even setting aside the ECHR ruling, are such techniques severe? Return to the dictionary definitions, which held that severe treatment must be either "extreme" or "hard to sustain," depending on the selected definition. Now take hooding. Is this really either extreme or hard to sustain? Certainly, it is unpleasant, but I think that it falls short of these other metrics. Stress positions are not hard to sustain so much as uncomfortable to sustain: if they were hard to sustain, they could not be sustained for hours (or indefinitely), as they sometimes are. What if these techniques are all applied simultaneously? Certainly, that exacerbates the discomfort of the recipient. But I am still reluctant to think that they are severe. To make this point another way, consider something that, by any reasonable conception, is severe, like drowning.[21] There are obvious differences between drowning and these other techniques, and it seems to me that severity is what sets them apart.

A fallacy looms here such that we might, for example, be dissuaded from thinking a 100-degree day is hot just because it is not as hot as a 120-degree day: both days are hot even if one is hotter than the other. Similarly with *severity,* the mere fact that one treatment is more severe than another does not preclude the latter from being legitimately characterized as *severe.* Rather, what it comes down to is how we calibrate our usage. Should we call stress and duress tactics severe, acknowledging that there can be greater severity? I am not inclined to, for the reason that, to me, doing so deprives *severe* of its intended force. Certainly, others will disagree, allowing *severe* to be used at levels of pain and suffering short of where I would license the ascription. Perhaps the fact that reasonable people—should someone charitably count me as such—disagree on this matter is sufficient to undermine ascriptions of *severe* in these cases.

None of this is to deny that stress and duress tactics are far from pleasant. Or even that they can give rise to extreme consequences, such as psychosis[22] or death.[23] But what follows from this? For example, consider Jessica Wolfendale's ambitious claim that "the widely held assumption that torture lite methods do not *generally* produce as long-lasting and severe harm as other forms of torture is without merit."[24] This has to be false, for the simple reason that the anecdotal evidence to which she adverts does not show that such methods "generally" do anything. Whether a greater percentage of people are killed by electrical torture or wall standing is an empirical question, and these statistics are not readily available. Suffice it to say, however, that I am pretty confident which way the answer goes.

Regardless, the point of this section has been to explore what torture is, and I have clearly wanted to draw a distinction between torture and CIDT. This should not be surprising, however, as even CAT makes such distinctions. Why do they matter? Legally, they matter insofar as §2.2 of CAT—which denies torture in emergency situations—does not apply to CIDT. Philosophically, however, the distinction does not matter much at all. For the account that I will develop in later chapters of the book, even torture can be morally permissible if it prevents greater harms; I certainly do not want to draw the line at CIDT. That said, such a conclusion has obvious legal obstacles, though I will return to this issue in chapter 8. In the meantime, it should simply be acknowledged that the requirements of morality and law can diverge (cf. laws allowing slavery), and maybe this is one of those cases. Or maybe not; the important moral work remains to be done. For now, let us move forward and consider purposes under which torture has or could be practiced.

4.2 WHY TORTURE?

There are various purposes of torture, and discussions about the moral status of torture commonly begin by making various distinctions in this regard. This might seem to put the cart before the horse in the sense that partitioning various purposes of torture before elucidating why torture is bad forsakes the opportunity to show what all these different purposes of torture have in common. While this section will, nevertheless, limit the scope of discussion for the remainder of the book, much of the moral discussion to follow in subsequent sections of this chapter—if not following chapters—largely does generalize across the distinctions that will be made. So why make the distinctions up front? The reason is that nobody seriously defends torture across a broad swath of these purposes, so we might as well just set such purposes aside from the outset and proceed more precisely with our discussion.

Let me start by saying that torture could be characterized in at least the following ways: sadistic, confessional, punitive, terroristic, and interrogational. Perhaps this list is not exhaustive, but it at least captures the principal distinctions that are worth making.[25] And, certainly, these characterizations are not mutually exclusive insofar as some particular act of torture could cut across them. Imagine, for example, that some convicted criminal is tortured (punitive) but, at the same time, that this scares other would-be criminals from committing their would-be crimes (terroristic). Further imagine that the act could be conducted as some sort of well-received public spectacle (sadistic) that was intentionally provided for by the authority who issued the torture. So, while acknowledging that individual acts of torture could be multiply characterized, let me nevertheless try to say more about each individual characterization.

A useful way to proceed is to take these in increasing order of sophistication, starting with those that have the least going for them and winding up with the ones that have the most surface plausibility. Or at least this might give us a rough ordering; quite a few of these really have quite little going for them and few to no defenders. First, consider sadistic torture, which is torture perpetuated merely for the enjoyment of the torturer. Such torture can be rejected out of hand if you believe in rights: the fact that one person derives pleasure from someone else's pain is irrelevant if that pain is achieved by violating a right. Maybe some person would be really happy if he stole someone else's television, but most of us hardly see this as any reason to justify the theft. Rights, such as those against torture, are trumps against other nonrights considerations: it does not matter how much pleasure someone would derive from violating a right because the right is incommensurable with and lexically prior to considerations of utility.[26]

But imagine that rights do not (directly) occupy a central part of one's moral theory, such as in utilitarianism. The utilitarian can talk about rights—and, in fact, John Stuart Mill did[27]—but rights are valued only insofar as they promote utility; as soon as they cease to, those rights are derogable.[28] Still, the utilitarian is going to be hard-pressed to justify sadistic torture, despite the fact that such putative commitments are often wielded as an embarrassment against the theory. The reason is that the pleasure of the torturer is only part of the hedonic calculus: the pain suffered by the torture victim must be accounted for as well. Is it really plausible to think that the sadist derives so much pleasure from watching torture as to outweigh the pain of the victim? I think that this is radically implausible. Maybe our naughty sadist smiles a little, giggles some, but it hardly seems possible to go into the sort of paroxysms of pleasure that would be the mirror image of our poor victim. And this says nothing of other important parts of the hedonic calculus, most notably duration:[29] our victim will certainly remember and continue to suffer from his torture, whereas we might expect the sadist's pleasure to be comparatively short-lived.

Surely, the utilitarian—or else his critic—can get this to work out somehow. A single sadist might, indeed, be insufficient to tip the balance, but round together a bunch of these sadists such that the pleasure borne from their collective sadism is enough to overwhelm the pain caused to the torture victim. Give the victim some fantastic pill that prevents any memory being formed from the torture and, therefore, precludes long-lived disutility. Should knowledge of this temporal anesthesia diminish the pleasure of the sadists, do not tell them about it. Find the right sorts of sadists, namely, the ones who really do go into pleasurable paroxysms rather than those who experience less dramatic enjoyment. And find the right sort of victim, preferably someone reasonably stoic; again, modulo the effects this might have on the sadists' pleasure. Ensure that this will happen only once and that there will not be any sort of societal ramifications, perhaps such as these events being practiced in less rigorous adherence to the hedonic calculus. Or, to make it even easier, just take a pass on the details and stipulate that the torture will maximize total aggregate happiness.

Could this sort of sadistic torture be justified? Presumably not to anyone other than the utilitarian, and probably even then only to the most naive sort of utilitarian and the one who has the fewest theoretical resources. But the embarrassment for the theory is still elusive because these imagined cases have so little to do with reality that no utilitarian actually needs to worry about them. As we will see in the next chapter, Jeremy Bentham actually wrote about torture, but it is revealing that even he was not concerned with his theory justifying sadistic torture; his discussions are more suggestive of interrogational or punitive torture.[30] We can draw a distinction between justifiable in theory and justifiable in practice and acknowledge that there are theoretical cases wherein utilitarianism may justify sadistic torture while, at the same time, denying that those cases would ever be realized. To my mind, this counts as no reason at all to think that anything is wrong with utilitarianism, but that is neither here nor there at present. Rather, the point is just that sadistic torture could probably be justified only by a single moral theory, and even that theory is not likely to ever end up justifying it. If such a case were realized, it is not clear to me that torture would not be justified, though I am more sympathetic to utilitarianism than most. For now, let us rest by acknowledging that even the theory most likely to support sadistic torture—if not the only one—is highly unlikely to do so in practice.

Now consider judicial torture, which can come in two variants: confessional and punitive. The term *judicial* is commonly associated with these sorts of torture insofar as judiciaries are the bodies that authorize it, but there is no necessary connection in this regard. A mob, for example, could practice confessional torture just as readily as some sanctioned judiciary, though, as well will see, confessional torture does have deep historical roots through sanctioned judiciaries. Similarly with punitive torture, one individual might torture another punitively in light of some (perceived) transgression; surely, some abusive relationships bear these hallmarks. Since confessional and punitive torture can, therefore, transcend judicial emanations, and since *judicial* conflates these different purposes, I shall present them individually.[31]

Taking confessional torture first, its purpose is, obviously, to elicit confessions, generally of some crime. This confession would, then, be used as evidence against whoever gave it and would, therefore, aid in conviction. Confessional torture had a long history in continental Europe, a history that is eloquently described in John Langbein's *Torture and the Law of Proof*;[32] the details are interesting enough to warrant quick discussion. Roman-canon law of proof applied to cases in which blood sanctions—execution or severe maiming—were potential sentences. There were three fundamental rules that were relevant to this law of proof. First, the court could convict if there were two eyewitnesses to the crime. Second, lacking two eyewitnesses, the court could convict only on the basis of confession. A corollary of this second rule is the third, which holds that circumstantial evidence (*indicia*) could not form an adequate basis for conviction, no matter how compelling. As Langbein writes: "It does not matter . . . that the suspect is seen running away from the murdered man's house and that the bloody dagger and the stolen loot are found in his possession. [Without eyewitnesses or a confession, the] court cannot convict him of a crime."[33]

Because circumstantial evidence could not secure a conviction, and because two eyewitnesses were often hard to come by, there would have been few convictions without confessions. And here is where torture came in: suspects were questioned under torture in order to secure their confessions, with thumbscrews, legscrews, the rack, and stappado being preferred techniques.[34] Lest torture be prescribed indiscriminately, there were various safeguards in place. First, "half proof" against the suspect was required before torture could occur, and this requirement was satisfied by having either one eyewitness or else circumstantial evidence of sufficient merit; in the aforementioned example, the dagger and the stolen loot might each count as quarter proof, thus summing to the requisite half proof. Second, the questions asked under torture were not supposed to be suggestive and should have been ones to which only the guilty person would know the answer.[35] So an appropriate question might be, "What color was the victim's clothing?" rather than, "He was dressed in all black, right?" An innocent person could readily assent to the latter—designed by the prosecutor for just that purpose—yet be unable to answer the former. The content of the confession was, thereafter, to be verified in order to ensure that the confessor actually had intimate knowledge of the crime. Furthermore, the confession was to be repeated after torture, such as the following day. Unfortunately, if the suspect recanted, the proof for conviction would be eradicated, and the judicial proceedings would continue, almost assuredly under torture to reelicit the confession. The suspect would then be faced with either confirming the confession or else being indefinitely returned to torture.

What was wrong with this system? On its face, it seems to have some things going for it. Torture was not issued indiscriminately since the half-proof requirement had to be met. And, because suggestive questions were disallowed, confessions were really supposed to be impossible for the innocent. Torture was allowed only for severe crimes—namely, the ones for which blood sanctions were at stake—and disallowed for petty crimes (*delicta levia*). Also, this law of proof was objective in the sense that judiciaries were not forced to try to assess the merits of circumstantial evidence for conviction; circumstantial evidence was used only to authorize the torture.

But, even setting moral objections aside, the safeguards were woefully inadequate to ensure the integrity of the confessions. As a practical matter, suggestive questioning could not be wholly eliminated. An innocent person would, presumably, have been apprehended for bearing some proximity to the crime and, therefore, might have been able to recount some of its relevant details without being the actual perpetrator (e.g., when and where it happened). For some crimes, such as hearsay and witchcraft, it was not clear what objective evidence could be used to verify the confession. And, in various jurisdictions, the confessions were not subjected to very exacting scrutiny; sometimes the claims made under torture were accepted without any verification at all.[36]

By the second half of the eighteenth century, confessional torture had been abolished throughout most of Europe, but Langbein argues that moral outrage was not the principal catalyst for abolishment. The standard version of the story points to moralists such as Cesare Beccaria and Voltaire who derided the aforementioned safeguard failures.[37] Langbein, however, finds this implausible insofar as the dangers of the system were echoed since Roman times and elaborated by the British jurist John Fortescue in the fifteenth century, to say nothing of other writers from the sixteenth through the eighteenth centuries.[38] In short, Beccaria and Voltaire came too late and only repeated what had already been said. The downfall of confessional torture owed, not to a moral outcry at the end of the eighteenth century, but rather to developments in penology. Galley sentences, workhouses, and, ultimately, the emergence of prisons made blood sanctions less necessary—that is, there were now places to put convicts—as well as less desirable since the dead or maimed could not perform labor in the service of the state.[39]

This historical context is important, but what can we say of confessional torture philosophically? The thing not to say—as many critics will—is that it is ineffective, that, under torture, someone will confess to anything. The reason that this is the wrong thing to say is, simply, that the safeguards could be better enforced. Questions could be vetted to ensure that they were not suggestive, they could be issued without the prosecutor present, the confessions could be verified, and so on; if these were properly handled, then the ready yet innocent confessor would be unable to avail himself of reprieve. Rather, the problem with confessional torture is, simply, that it is unnecessary given our current standards of proof. Remember that confessions were necessary insofar as circumstantial evidence could not convict, but our jurisprudence has evolved such that this is no longer the case. Confessions are not required for conviction, and, therefore, neither is torture.

The second important point is that confessions do not necessarily serve any important moral good. Given that something is wrong with torture, it could be justified only if this moral wrong were somehow compensated. Whether some would-be convict confesses to a crime has no obvious moral upshot. The only way that it could be morally relevant is if the subsequent conviction forestalled his future crimes, but, as we have already seen, conviction no longer requires confession.[40] Whatever moral ends are served by confessions can be accomplished by adjusting our standards of proof rather than by practicing torture; it turns out that this is exactly what we have done. So, in addition to confessional torture being a nonstarter owing to various legal principles (e.g., due process), it is also hard to motivate philosophically.

While confessional torture aims at a confession and, thereafter, a conviction, punitive torture is issued as a punishment after conviction. Again, this is going to be a legal nonstarter for various reasons (e.g., the Eighth Amendment), even if it has historical precedent. Stocks, for example, were used since medieval times to immobilize the ankles or wrists of a prisoner; pillories were more severe in that they also isolated the head. Used primarily in Germany, prangers tied the victim's neck to his shackled ankles by a chain that barely reached them, thus ensuring a hunched and uncomfortable position. These sorts of restraints are worth mentioning insofar as they are the forerunners of some of the stress and duress tactics (e.g., forced positions) that have been practiced in places like Guantánamo and Abu Ghraib. But punishments could be far more severe than this. Consider, for example, whipping, which was practiced at least from biblical times through the French Revolution and into the nineteenth century in Europe and North America; it is even still practiced today in some countries (e.g., Singapore). Stoning—a form of execution—is even more brutal, yet it still takes place in various Islamic and African countries.[41]

As mentioned above, none of these is going to happen in the United States. Among other judicial and legislative developments, the Eighth Amendment has been interpreted as increasingly prohibitive over its history, taking many things off the table, and putting few back on; for example, far from allowing stoning, it has ruled out comparatively humane gas chambers, hangings, and firing squads.[42] These currents portend an eventual total ban on execution, which has already been made illegal in much of the country. Again, however, let us set aside the legal issues and consider the philosophical ones. What would be the point of punitive torture, whether it ultimately led to death or not?

Starting with what the answer is not, consider recidivism. Torture may make the torture victim less likely to commit future crimes, but so would other means, like detention. In fact, detention would work even better insofar as someone tortured and then released *could* commit a crime—even if he were wary of doing so—whereas someone detained could *not* commit a crime in virtue of his detention.[43] What about detention coupled with torture? Then the torture is just redundant. We could be asked to imagine cases wherein detention was impossible, say, because the detention facilities were already at their capacity. But it hardly follows that the answer is, then, to start torturing, as opposed instead prioritizing an expansion of the detention facilities.

Rather, the only way that punitive torture could be justified would be in terms of the deterrent value that such punishment would have for future crime (by *other* would-be criminals). But this just wades right into many of the stock criticisms of utilitarian theories of punishment, which we might quickly rehearse. First, it is simply not clear that deterrence is effective, as is evident from the relationship between the existence of capital punishment and murder rates.[44] Critics of executions find deterrence to fail, but a more reasonable conclusion to draw is that the relationship is simply equivocal. At any rate, it is simply not clear that this sort of deterrence works. Would there be a stronger deterrence relationship with torture than with execution? I am not inclined to hazard an a priori guess on this one, other than to say that the answer is not obvious either way; furthermore, we will never have the empirical data about punitive torture that we would need to resolve it.

Second, even on the utilitarian's own terms, torture would be unnecessary: all that would matter would be the appearance of torture and not the torture itself, so long as the illusion were believed. In other words, to deter would-be criminals, we do not need to actually torture convicted criminals but rather only to lead those would-be criminals to believe that they would be tortured were they to commit some (sufficiently serious) crime. Given all the pain that actual torture would create, it would surely be worthwhile to seek alternatives, even at the risk of those alternatives being exposed (i.e., so long as that risk were low enough but the pain caused by torture high enough, the hedonic calculus would still tell us not to torture). And there are various other curiosities to the deterrence theory of punishment; one of these is that we need not punish a guilty person at all but rather someone we could hold up as a guilty person. Regardless, whether one is a utilitarian or not, there are myriad reasons to think that punitive torture is not justified.

Turning to terroristic torture, consider Argentina's so-called Dirty War (Guerra Sucia), which took place during the late 1970s and early 1980s. Following the return from exile of Juan Perón in 1973 and his death the following year, his wife, Isabel Martínez de Perón, ascended to the Argentinean presidency. She was deposed two years later and replaced by a military junta—led by Jorge Rafaél Videla—that took the previous government's anti-left-wing policies to an extreme, directing particular hostility toward trade unionists and other activists. Torture against Videla's opponents was widespread, as was their disappearance and execution; estimates hold that somewhere in the vicinity of fifteen thousand people were killed under his regime.[45] Even more expansive was the torture that took place in Augusto Pinochet's control of neighboring Chile from 1973 to 1990. Pinochet quickly deposed Salvador Allende, the previous president of Chile, a mere twenty days after Allende had appointed Pinochet head of the Chilean army. Over the years of Pinochet's rule, a comparatively low three thousand people were killed,[46] but torture was widespread, being practiced against thirty thousand citizens.[47] The report that documented the extent of torture also revealed over eight hundred clandestine torture centers as well as eighteen different kinds of torture that were deployed.[48] Pinochet was certainly less discriminating than Videla, though again trade unions and political opposition bore specific animus.

Surely more could be said about the details of the atrocities that took place in Argentina and Chile—as well as myriad other places[49]—but these are sufficient for developing our concept of *terroristic torture*. In particular, we have cases wherein a dictator perpetuates torture against his own population in order to terrorize would-be opposition. This opposition is most ostensibly political, but it could be any sort of opposition, including economic or cultural. What moral argument could possibly be advanced in favor of this sort of practice? Deferring that question for now, let me offer several against it.

First, almost by necessity, terroristic torture has to be used indiscriminately. If it were used more discriminately, then at least some of the opposition would get away unscathed, thus mitigating the terror that was meant to be generated; in other words, some of the opposition might reasonably think that it could evade the torture, thus undermining its efficacy. Rather, the net must be cast too widely rather than too narrowly in order to achieve the intended aim. But then the obvious problem is that, even by his own lights, the dictator is torturing (at least some of) the wrong people. Surely, this issue will recur in my subsequent discussion of interrogational torture, when I consider torturing someone without any intelligence value. For now, however, suffice it to say that the issue in this context is that in the other writ large, insofar as thousands or even tens of thousands of people are being tortured as opposed to, say, a few hundred who have been treated far less worse at Guantánamo, at least on average.

Second, there is not even anything prima facie morally wrong with opposing a government, at least insofar as such opposition is carried out nonviolently. Under these South American regimes, even voicing displeasure with the leadership would have been sufficient to invite sufficiently unpleasant treatment or death. Yet there is no presumptive moral authority of a government against its critics and certainly not one that would extend to torture or execution. Even sadistic torture has more going for it than terroristic torture insofar as some positive moral good (namely, pleasure) is served by it. Terroristic torture, by contrast, can appeal only to the status quo since it aims at forestalling the dissension that could undermine the extant government. And, absent some independent argument (e.g., about continuity, stability, etc.), there is no reason to think that the status quo should inherently be protected. As those governments were practiced, it is unlikely that any sort of independent argument could be on offer.

Returning now to the question of the defense to which terroristic torture could appeal, the principal answer is the self-interest of those who perpetuate it. They might try to offer something else, like a greater good argument, but it would almost be laughable when, for example, Pinochet's regime sent upwards of 80,000 citizens to jail and 200,000 more into exile; these are huge numbers and not ones that some positive good of his government could plausibly absorb. And, in fact, the self-interest claim is often borne out in practice, such as through Pinochet's tax evasion and embezzlement. Self-interest—even of an inner circle, if not some particular individual—cannot come close to justifying the harsh treatment of thousands on thousands of others; the obvious thing to say in these cases of terroristic torture is simply that it was morally wrong.

Could terroristic torture ever be morally permissible? I am inclined to think so, though I am extremely skeptical whether the requisite conditions could be manifest in practice. Return, for example, to the discussion of justified terrorism in §2.2 above: if the only way to defeat a tremendous evil is to terrorize its citizenry, and if such attacks against the citizenry are less of a moral affront than the evil that would otherwise result, then I think that the attacks are justified. But there will be only exceptional circumstances that satisfy these conditions, such as, perhaps, some of the earlier Allied bombings of Germany in World War II. Imagine now that the only way to stop Hitler would have been to torture German citizens rather than to bomb them; let us suppose that such torture would, as the bombings did, terrorize the population and undermine his core support. In this case, would torture be permissible? Probably, but the imagined hypothetical is so fanciful that little hangs on it.

The more interesting cases are not the widespread sorts of terroristic torture that we have heretofore countenanced wherein thousands are tortured such that governments either retain their power or, in our imagined case, lose it. In these cases, either torture is patently unjustified, or, at best, it is very dubious that it would be justified in practice (i.e., in actual cases). Rather, the interesting cases are ones, for example, that would contemplate the torture of Eva Braun such that Hitler relinquish power and dismantle his army and government. But is this a case of terroristic torture? I am not sure, but it might be. In particular, it probably has to do with Braun's moral status and whether she is properly recognized as a noncombatant; her complicity in Hitler's activities might nullify or compromise her immunity. Assuming that she does retain her immunity, this presents a tough case. Structurally, however, it is similar to other supreme emergency cases. And, even if this designation opens the door for morally justified terroristic torture, I nevertheless think that the availing cases will be somewhere between vanishingly and negligibly few. I will return to this issue somewhat in my discussions of interrogational torture as well as in the last chapter of the book.

Finally, let us consider interrogational torture directly. This discussion can be somewhat shorter than some of the others insofar as the rest of the book will be about it, but there are some important preliminaries to establish from the outset. Interrogational torture aims at the retrieval of information; some detainee would be interrogated under torture because of actionable intelligence that he is presumed to have. Again, more will be said about this later, but there are at least some obvious things to say up front. First, there must be some reasonable expectation that the detainee actually has the information for which he will be interrogated. Second, there must be good reason to believe that the intelligence is actionable, which is to say that, if we were able to acquire the information, we might (or, more strongly, would) be able to do something important with it, such as save lives. Third, the torture must be reasonably thought to be the least offensive way to elicit the information, modulo issues of expediency. If there were some less problematic way to get the information within an appropriate time frame, there would be no reason to torture. Fourth, whatever torture is administered should be that which is minimally necessary to acquire the information. Fifth, the moral harms of the torture must be less egregious than the harms the torture aims to prevent.

There are myriad epistemic worries with all these conditions, and I will address them in detail in later chapters; the point of mentioning them here is simply to circumscribe some sort of minimal conditions under which interrogational torture could be reasonably countenanced. The fifth condition, in addition to having an epistemic component—that is, we have to know what the harms are—also has a metaphysical one: we have to be honest and comprehensive about the harms that derive from interrogational torture and to think critically about whether these can be outweighed by the benefits. Whatever proposal we develop should also seek to minimize those harms and to maximize those benefits as surely there are better and worse ways to go. Furthermore, more needs to be said about the whole aggregative framework to which this proposal is committed; some moral theorists will reject it out of hand. This is a lot to do, but all these challenges must be taken seriously.

However we circumscribe the appropriateness of interrogational torture, we should acknowledge from the outset that this form is morally different from the other forms that we have previously considered. In particular, interrogational torture aims at a positive moral good, namely, the disarming of some threat. In ticking-time-bomb cases—the subject of the next two chapters—a terrorist is tortured such that an imminent threat is forestalled, thus saving the lives of potential victims. In these cases, the point of the torture is, therefore, to save lives, and lives have moral significance. And this moral significance only increases as more lives hang in the balance. Whatever else one thinks about torture, it has to be said that saving lives is, all else equal, a good thing. In this sense, interrogational torture largely stands apart from sadistic, confessional, punitive, or terroristic torture, none of which offers much moral promise. So, while there are many open questions about the moral status of interrogational torture, it at least offers a compelling question. That said, there is no denying that interrogational torture perpetuates various moral harms. If the case can be made for it, that case has to be made against a recognition of these harms, and a full accounting therein is owed. It is to that discussion that I now turn.

4.3 WHY IS TORTURE (INTRINSICALLY) BAD?

In this section, I consider why torture is bad. As I said in the opening paragraph of the previous section—and despite all the other purposes of torture previously discussed—the focus shall henceforth be on interrogational torture. These other purposes are simply not morally plausible in a way that interrogational torture might be, so they were presented in order to set them aside. Regardless, much of this following discussion still generalizes even if other purposes will no longer be of particular interest.

Torture exacts two basic sorts of moral harms, which we can designate as *intrinsic* and *extrinsic*. The intrinsic harms are those that lie at the very nature of torture; they are the harms without which torture would not be torture. Extrinsic harms, on the other hand, are not inherently part of torture but, nevertheless, (might) result from it. For example, torture could not be torture without severe pain or suffering. Pain and suffering are, therefore, intrinsic harms of torture. In addition to pain and suffering, torture can lead to various moral harms. For example, torturing terrorists might embolden more terrorists to attack us, but there is nothing intrinsic to torture that leads to those attacks; torture might just as well not have such an effect, depending on the circumstances. As discussed in the previous section, there are myriad purposes of torture. Sadistic torture, for example, would not embolden terrorists to attack us since it has nothing to do with terrorists at all. But even the torture of terrorists would not necessarily lead to more terrorist attacks; maybe the torture is done in secret, maybe these are timid terrorists who are not emboldened, maybe all the terrorists were apprehended, and so on. Torture therefore could be torture without leading to more terrorist attacks, which means that those attacks are not intrinsic to torture. This is not to deny that, under certain conditions, torture would lead to more attacks; the point is just that those attacks are extrinsic to the torture itself.

Another way of couching this distinction is to say that extrinsic harms can be mitigated, at least in principle.[50] By contrast, intrinsic harms cannot be mitigated since those harms are inherent to torture. This gives another motivation for the distinction, which is one of presentation. The intrinsic harms to be discussed in the remainder of this chapter are not up for debate, whereas the various extrinsic harms are. In particular, we can have substantive debate about whether those extrinsic harms are likely to result from torture, and we can consider ways in which torture might be practiced to mitigate those harms. Much of the rest of this book will be about extrinsic harms, and much of that discussion will be highly contentious. For now, however, let us focus on common ground.

Intuitively, we can conceive of the intrinsic harms as being of two principal sorts. The first, and easier to understand, is the pain and suffering that torture engenders; the history of torture is rife with brutal examples in this regard.[51] While pain and suffering explain part of why torture is bad, they do not obviously set torture aside from other practices. For example, imagine a beating that is perpetuated for either of two reasons, as torture or as a general assault. Certainly, assaults are bad, but I submit that our moral intuitions hold torture in even worse regard than assault, even if the physical intervention is identical. For the remainder of this section, my focus will be on a second class of intrinsic harms, namely, those that go beyond pain and suffering. Just for emphasis, this is not to deny that torture can effect tremendous pain and suffering or that pain and suffering are significant moral harms. Rather, pain and suffering are less in need of philosophical elucidation than the other features of torture that we will now consider.

In pursuing this discussion, let us consider an elegant essay by David Sussman. Sussman's discussion is admittedly framed to emphasize interrogational torture as opposed to other variants,[52] but there are two things to say about that. First, interrogational torture is, henceforth, my focus, so such an emphasis is fine. Second, much of it still does generalize, though I shall not pay too much attention to what generalizes and what does not.

As above, Sussman contends that the harms of torture go beyond the pain and suffering that it portends. Quoting his strategy at length:

> I defend the intuition that there is something morally special about torture that distinguishes it from most other kinds of violence, cruelty, or degrading treatment. Torture is all of these things, of course, and is morally objectionable simply as such. What I deny, however, is that the wrongness

of torture can be fully grasped by understanding it as just an extreme instance of these more general moral categories. I argue that there is a core concept of what constitutes torture that corresponds to a distinctive kind of wrong that is not characteristically found in other forms of extreme violence or coercion, a special type of wrong that may explain why we find torture to be more morally offensive than other ways of inflicting great physical or psychological harm.

He then goes on to argue:

> Torture forces its victim into the position of colluding against himself through his own affects and emotions, so that he experiences himself as simultaneously powerless and yet actively complicit in his own violation. So construed, torture turns out to be not just an extreme form of cruelty, but the pre-eminent instance of a kind of forced self-betrayal, more akin to rape than other kinds of violence characteristic of warfare or police action.[53]

Subsequently, Sussman characterizes the relationship between the torturer and the torture victim as distinctive: the torture victim is completely defenseless against the will of the torturer, and the power asymmetry between them is absolute. Unlike a simple assault, the torture victim cannot offer any resistance—for example, by raising his hands to shield himself—because of restraint or immobilization. Similarly, the torture victim poses no threat to the torturer, which is different from other attacker/attacked dynamics: not only can the torture victim not defend himself, but he also cannot do anything to the torturer.[54]

Furthermore, the only assurance that the torture victim has that the torture will ever end are the assurances of the torturer. So the torturer might say something like, "Just give me the information that I need, and I will stop," but the torture victim really has no reason to believe that this is true. Contrast this dynamic with that of a soldier under attack by opposing forces: all that the soldier has to do to end the threat is surrender. Or he can fight back. The victim of torture, however, is not a threat—at least in the sense of being a physical threat to his attacker—yet is still subject to attack without being able to return that attack. Note that this also betrays a connection to just war theory insofar as noncombatants are owed immunity from attack; if the torture victim is a noncombatant, then it violates the war convention to assault him.[55]

One response here is that the torture victim can simply disclose whatever the relevant information is, thus eradicating whatever reasons the torturer would have for continuing the torture. Henry Shue considers this line in his classic essay and remains skeptical. For Shue, torture could be permissible only given that "the victim of torture must have available an act of compliance which, if performed, will end the torture." He uses this "constraint of possible compliance" to dismiss terroristic torture but allows that such a constraint might be satisfied in interrogational torture. Nevertheless, he thinks that it probably will not be because the torturer will never know whether the torture victim has fully disclosed all the information that is being sought.[56] For example, imagine that a terrorist confesses to some terroristic plot. Should the torturer stop torturing? Maybe the terrorist knows about another terrorist plot, despite his assurances that he does not. What would it take for the torturer to stop? As Sussman writes:

> Even if the victim is willing to supply the information or confession that seems to be wanted, she has no reason to believe that her tormenter will accept it as accurate and complete. Perhaps she will continue to be tortured "just to make sure," or for some other reason entirely, or for no reason at all. She can neither verify any claims her tormentor makes, nor rely on any promises or assurances he offers.[57]

So the worry is not just that torture constitutes an attack on a defenseless person but also that the attack could be perpetual.

Sussman thinks that Kantian moral theory elucidates some of the core moral harms of torture above and beyond those that the utilitarian can identify. In particular, there is a "profound disrespect [torture] shows the humanity or autonomy of its victim." While being more sanguine about utilitarianism's ability to accommodate these harms, I agree that torture is extremely compromising in this regard. The pain and suffering generated by torture lead to a further worry about the dissolution of one's autonomous agency: it is, as Sussman puts it, "almost impossible to reflect, deliberate, or even think straight when one is in agony."[58]

Continuing with Kant, torture clearly violates the second formulation of the categorical imperative, which directs us to treat each other as ends and never merely as means. Through torture, we use the torture victim as a means to our end (e.g., the acquisition of some information) and fail to respect him as an end in himself. But torture is even worse than this insofar as it forces the victim to conspire against himself and his projects. For example, imagine that I torture someone sadistically, thus failing to respect his autonomy. Contrast this case with one wherein a terrorist has invested considerable time in the development of some terrorist plot and is passionately committed to that plot. Through torture, we acquire information that destroys that plot, thus frustrating his plans. The violation is worse in the second case than in the first, even though both constitute violations of autonomy. The reason is not that the terrorist's plans have any sort of positive moral weight in and of themselves—they surely do not—but that they have value *to the terrorist* and that value has to fit somewhere within our normative framework.

Sussman further thinks that torture pits the victim against himself, making him complicit in his own abuse and suffering. For example, he discusses a common element of torture, which is the denial of toilet facilities. The problem

> is not just the infantilizing and dehumanizing disgrace of soiling oneself, but the futile struggle against one's own body not to do so. The victim confronts the question of whether she was simply forced to soil herself, or whether she allowed herself to do so, discovering herself to be willing to purchase some comfort at the price of public or personal humiliation.

He continues:

> Torturers often force their victims to stand or maintain contorted postures ("stress positions") for prolonged periods of time. In these cases, the victim's own efforts to remain in a particular position serve as the immediate source of his suffering. One of the most common forms of contemporary torture is "the submarine," a technique that involves repeated partial drowning. I take it that the torture here is not just the agony of inhaling water, but the hopeless struggle against one's own desperate urge to breathe that precedes it. Not only does the victim find himself hurt by his body, but he also finds himself to be the one hurting his body as well, in some way pushing it against itself.[59]

This discussion further elaborates the differences in autonomy violation postulated by the two cases presented above and also helps set apart what is unique about interrogational torture, namely, how it forces the victim to conspire against himself. In principle at least, the torture will end whenever the victim compromises his own projects. Given that, in practice, it might not, this only makes everything worse.

In introducing the various harms that torture comprises, I suggested that we focus on harms other than the pain and suffering in order to figure out what sets torture apart from some other sorts of treatments. This proposal was meant to be useful and to follow common thinking, but, now that it has been presented, let me go back and briefly challenge it. As a utilitarian, I do not think that there are moral harms beyond pain and suffering, but I nevertheless think that Sussman introduces important considerations for thinking about why torture is bad. Despite his obvious sympathy to Kant, he acknowledges that utilitarian thinking is important in understanding torture, namely, insofar as "the Kantian seems unable to do justice to what we would normally take to be a clearly nonaccidental truth: the fact that torture *hurts*."[60]

So, for Sussman, the utilitarian and Kantian analyses are complementary; neither tells the full story on its own. We agree, then, that utility matters. But does Kant matter? Return to my earlier example that was meant to frame the torture of the terrorist as worse than sadistic torture on the grounds that the former's interrogational torture would, if successful, lead to the betrayal of his own commitments and values; assume that nothing similar was going on in the sadistic analogue. It seems to me that the thing to say is that being complicit in one's own betrayal would, in and of itself, exacerbate one's pain and suffering. The more one cares about the project, the more pain and suffering would be associated with contributing to its demise. Or, to put it another way, if there were no more pain and suffering, then the terrorist case would not be any different than the sadism case.

Many people will surely prefer a different analysis. I make these comments, not to be convincing, but rather to preclude any accusations of inconsistency as I move forward. My principal problem with Kantian approaches will not even be the moral values that they identify; rather, it will be their absolutism. I will return to this issue in §6.5. For now, there is no disagreement about the moral importance of the values that Sussman identifies, even if we disagree about how to accommodate them. As a last remark on Sussman, it is worth noting that even he does not "contend that torture is categorically wrong, but only that it bears an especially high burden of justification."[61] So, again, there need not be a disagreement.

An approach similar to Sussman's—and with similar Kantian sympathies—comes from Michael Davis.[62] Davis proposes to draw a distinction between "agent-centered" and "victim-centered" conceptions of torture; he is concerned with defining torture (cf. §4.1 above), though his discussion is equally at home in this section about why torture is (intrinsically) bad. According to Davis: "The agent-centered approach seeks to develop a conception of torture by considering torture (primarily) from the torturer's perspective. . . . In contrast, the victim-centered approach seeks to develop a conception of torture by considering torture (primarily) from the victim's perspective." Davis characterizes Sussman's account as victim based since Sussman is concerned with torture being a "violent overwhelming of the victim's agency," such as through collusion against himself. Davis, on the other hand, prefers agent-based accounts, characterizing torture as "the intentional pushing of a sentient, helpless being to the limit of its ability to suffer—against the being's will and indifferent to its welfare."[63]

Is this a useful distinction, and, if so, is there anything to be said for one conception over the other? Davis has three arguments for the agent-based account over the victim-based account. First, he thinks that Sussman cannot distinguish between the "ordeal" of torture and "torture proper"; these concepts are not illuminated in the associated discussion, but Davis maintains that there are compromising ordeals other than torture. His examples including caning and branding, but these miss the point of Sussman's argumentation insofar as they do not manifest the self-betrayal that Sussman emphasizes. Or else maybe they do, and there is something deeply compromising about these practices; then Sussman would be able to categorize them as torture. Either way, Davis's challenge is dissolved since the putative counterexamples are either rejected or else accommodated under Sussman's account.

Second, Davis complains that Sussman's analysis of the phenomenology of torture is "from the perspective of a relatively sophisticated victim" and says nothing about "the torture of animals, young children, the mentally infirm, or others who lack full moral autonomy but who can be tortured."[64] My own intuitions are that this latter sort of torture is actually impossible, so long as the associated autonomy is substantially lacking. For example, I doubt that it is possible to torture insects, even if we sometimes (mis)speak that way; their lack of sufficient cognition simply precludes anything other than basic battery. To put it another way, I do not see Davis's account as being usefully broader than Sussman's. Rather, the challenges that Davis offers come at the margins such that—and as in the preceding paragraph—Sussman can either reject them as being relevant or else accommodate them under his own view.

Alternatively, this could be the wrong analysis, but then Davis and I would be working at cross-projects insofar as he is trying to tell us what torture *is* and I am trying to figure out why interrogational torture is *bad*. While I doubt it, maybe Davis is right and Sussman's account is too narrow. Even if this were true, Sussman's account still captures the wrongness of interrogational torture since the sorts of people therein subjugated to it would all share similar phenomenal experiences. If they did not—for example, if they were not sufficiently sophisticated and autonomous—then they would not be the sorts of people that would be complicit in the sorts of projects that interrogational torture seeks to compromise. It is important to figure out what different sorts of torture have in common (e.g., see §4.1 above), but my current task is to figure out what is bad about interrogational torture; Sussman's account is particularly elucidating in this regard.

Davis's third argument against Sussman is the most compelling:

> Morality is primarily about agency (what we should do) rather than victimhood (what we suffer). . . . What is primarily wrong with any victim-centered approach—not only Sussman's—is precisely that it is victim-centered, that is, that it focuses on what the victim suffers . . . whether a disintegration of personality, sense of betrayal, loss of dignity, or something else, rather than on what the victimizer (the torturer) intends (whether he succeeds or not).[65]

If his preferred account is any stronger than Sussman's, I take it to hang on the plausibility of the distinction that Davis purports to draw between the agent- and the victim-centered conceptions. So what are we to make of this distinction? To me, these conceptions are just opposite sides of the same coin and are, therefore, inextricably bound together. Someone cannot cause pain and suffering (agency) without someone being caused pain and suffering (victim), and vice versa, at least in cases of moral evaluation (cf. someone being caused pain and suffering by a falling hailstone). Talking agentwise is not to add any information over and above what we get by talking victimwise, but it is rather only to present the same information from a different perspective. Does the perspective—independent of the content—matter?

Consider saying that one sports team won or else that its adversary lost: this is just to relay the same thing differently. Davis would presumably say that this is a bad analogy because "morality is primarily about agency"[66] whereas winning and losing in sport can be mutually translated; there is not a reason to privilege winners or losers as there is to privilege agents over victims. Again, however, we do not gain useful content by using one perspective rather than the other. And, regardless, I do not share Davis's view about the priority of agency, particularly if that is supposed to have some upshot in terms of intentional action (i.e., the moral metric by which Kantians assess agency). If someone intended to torture yet failed to achieve the desired pain and suffering (e.g., because some torture device failed), I think that would be morally preferable than someone causing pain and suffering unintentionally (e.g., because some torture device was merely meant to serve as a threat and inadvertently deployed). Davis, pace Kant, would have to say the reverse.

At any rate, I do not think that the agent-centered conception is any worse than the victim-centered conception, just that they are not usefully distinct. Certainly, interrogational torture is bad because it leads to pain and suffering. It is bad because it threatens self-betrayal and because it proffers a torturer whose precise design is to elicit that self-betrayal. The prospects of this self-betrayal undoubtedly exacerbate whatever pain and suffering would otherwise have been on offer (cf. merely sadistic torture), and we can either accommodate this exacerbated pain and suffering into a utilitarian framework—as would be my preference—or else introduce nonutilitarian considerations to accommodate these moral harms. And, returning to a distinction that I made at the beginning of this section, these are only the intrinsic moral harms of torture; there are still myriad extrinsic harms that we will encounter in subsequent chapters. Given all these harms, how could interrogational torture possibly be justified? In the following two chapters, I answer that question.

5

Ticking-Time-Bomb Methodology

In thinking about putative justifications for interrogational torture, we are commonly asked to imagine exceptional cases wherein such torture is necessary to save some significant number of lives. These cases are generally referred to as ticking-time-bomb cases, which invites us to think of the relationship they bear to terrorism: some terrorist has planted a bomb in a crowded metropolitan center that will kill many noncombatants unless the terrorist is tortured. But, as I suggested in the first paragraph of the last chapter, terrorism need not have anything to do with these cases, nor, really, do bombs. Rather, what matters is that there is some threat to many people that can be avoided—and that, in most formulations, certainly will be—only through the torture of someone already in custody. The locution *ticking time-bomb* is, therefore, somewhat narrow, but not in any drastically misleading way. Furthermore, most of the contexts worth considering—by which I mean the real-world ones most closely approximating these hypothetical constructs—probably will be those involving terrorists and weapons, if not necessarily bombs. And, for purposes of engagement, there is merit in following the standard usage. Having thus registered these disclaimers, I shall hereafter revert to that usage.

The purpose of this chapter is methodological rather than normative: by this distinction, I mean that I will consider the logic and deployment of ticking-time-bomb cases rather than what follows from them (i.e., whether they justify interrogational torture in exceptional circumstances). My contention is that, despite their simplicity, these cases have been misunderstood, whether in terms of what they claim, what role they are should to play in our moral thinking, or even whether they should play any role at all. The next chapter, by contrast, will be normative: having thought about how to properly understand ticking-time-bomb cases, I shall then use them to derive normative conclusions. But it is important to first get clear on the methodology so that these subsequent discussions can be situated on the requisite foundations.

5.1 ORIGINS OF THE TICKING TIME-BOMB

Let us start by considering the origins of ticking-time-bomb cases; in doing so, we will also start to see some of the different formulations that these cases assume. In terms of the philosophical literature, an early formulation owes to a seminal essay by Henry Shue:

> Suppose a fanatic, perfectly willing to die rather than collaborate in the thwarting of his own scheme, has set a hidden nuclear device to explode in the heart of Paris. There is no time to evacuate the innocent people or even the movable art treasures—the only hope of preventing tragedy is to torture the perpetrator, find the device, and deactivate it.[1]

But not only have these cases appeared in academic journals; they have also crossed over to popular media outlets and, thereafter, into public consciousness; this is noteworthy. For example, consider the following, which comes from an essay Michael Levin wrote in *Newsweek*:

> Suppose a terrorist has hidden an atomic bomb on Manhattan Island which will detonate at noon. . . . Suppose, further, that he is caught at 10 a.m. . . . , but preferring death to failure, won't disclose where the bomb is. What do we do? If we follow due process, wait for his lawyer, arraign him, millions of people will die. If the only way to save those lives is to subject the terrorist to the most excruciating possible pain, what grounds can there be for not doing so? I suggest that there are none.[2]

While less often acknowledged, Anthony Quinton had, over a decade earlier, briefly entertained a similar scenario in the *Listener*, a now-defunct weekly magazine established by the BBC:

> I do not see on what basis anyone could argue that the prohibition of torture is an absolute moral principle. . . . Consider a man caught planting a bomb in a large hospital, which no one but he knows how to defuse and no one dare touch for fear of setting it off. It was this kind of extreme situation that I had in mind when I said earlier that I thought torture could be justifiable.[3]

Before that, Jean Lartéguy fictionalized an episode from the French occupation of Algeria in his 1960 *Les centurions*.[4] But, despite these formulations of ticking-time-bomb cases in the second half of the twentieth century, Jeremy Bentham had been writing on the morality of torture almost two hundred years earlier, dating from the late 1770s.[5] (He also provided one of the earlier characterizations of torture.)[6] Bentham probably had the first formulation of a case that looked anything like a ticking-time-bomb case, though this came later—in 1804—and was not otherwise attached to a systematic treatment of torture. Consider what he wrote:

> Suppose an occasion, to arise, in which a suspicion is entertained, as strong as that which would be received as a sufficient ground for arrest and commitment as for felony—a suspicion that at this very time a considerable number of individuals are actually suffering, by illegal violence inflictions equal in intensity to those which if inflicted by the hand of justice, would universally be spoken of under the name of torture. For the purpose of rescuing from torture these hundred innocents, should any scruple be made of applying equal or superior torture, to extract the requisite information from the mouth of one criminal, who having it in his power to make known the place where at this time the enormity was practicing or about to be practiced, should refuse to do so? To say nothing of wisdom, could any pretense be made so much as to the praise of blind and vulgar humanity, by the man who to save one criminal, should determine to abandon [one hundred] innocent persons to the same fate?[7]

The principal difference between Bentham's case and the others previously presented is simply whether the harm that the torture aims to dispel is already active (namely, the current torture of innocents) or else prospective (namely, the future explosion of a bomb). Morally, there need not be any difference between these cases: what matters is whether the torture is necessary to prevent the harm. If that harm is temporally distant, then that would undermine the need to torture insofar as there might be other—and less morally offensive—ways to dispel it. But, so long as the torture is necessary, then whether the harm is ongoing, imminent, or even temporally distant is irrelevant, at least so long as *necessary* really means what it says. I will return to this below, but, for now, the point is merely that Bentham's case is structurally similar to the others.

Aside from this more casual presentation of a single case, Bentham also offered a more extended treatment of torture, as recorded in two manuscript fragments. It is worth considering these fragments for at least three reasons, only one of which is historical. The second is more philosophical in that Bentham starts to elucidate some of the key logical elements of ticking-time-bomb thinking, even if that discussion floats free of a particular ticking-time-bomb case. And the third bears on the relationship between ticking-time-bomb methodology and utilitarianism, a relationship that is more complicated than usually acknowledged. With these three reasons in mind, let us now look at some of Bentham's writings on torture.

First, Bentham asserts that torture may be applied in two cases: "The first is where the thing which a Man is required to do being a thing which the public has an interest in his doing, is a thing which for a certainty is in his power to do." And he continues that torture is otherwise permissible

> where a man is required what probably though not certainly is in his power to do; and for the not doing of which it is possible that he may suffer, although he be innocent; but which the public has so great an interest in his doing that the danger of what may ensue from his not doing it is a greater danger than even that of an innocent person's suffering the greatest degree of pain that can be suffered by Torture, of the kind and in the quantity permitted to be employed.

Then he asks: "Are there in practice any cases that can be ranked under this head? If there be any, it is plain that there can be very few."[8] That Bentham was reserved about the extent to which torture can be justified bears notice: being a utilitarian hardly commits one to the promiscuous use of torture as there are myriad utilitarian reasons to oppose it.[9] I will discuss some of these below and throughout the rest of the book, but I want to get early purchase on the concept of *exceptional*—as opposed to *normalized—torture*.[10]

After these introductory remarks, Bentham goes on to offer a series of moral rules that have to be satisfied for the legitimate application of torture. While the details of those rules need not concern us here, suffice it to say that they are precisely the sorts of principles that undergird contemporary ticking-time-bomb cases. For example, torture should not be applied without (near) certainty that the would-be tortured has the relevant knowledge (rule 1); that torture is appropriate only as a last resort in "cases which admit of no delay" (rule 3);[11] that minimal means should always be preferred to extreme ones (rule 4); that the prospective benefits are greater than the prospective costs (rules 5 and 7), and so on.[12]

Importantly, many of these rules were effectively codified in Bentham's hedonic calculus, published shortly thereafter.[13] Bentham predicated his utilitarianism on seven factors, all of which are at least implicitly manifest in the ticking-time-bomb cases: intensity, duration, certainty (or uncertainty), propinquity (or remoteness), fecundity, purity, and extent. While intensity and duration are rarely emphasized in the cases, they certainly *could* be, and such invocations would seemingly make the cases only more compelling: imagine that the terrorist need be subject to only a "comparatively minor and brief" form of torture to disclose the location of the bomb.[14] (Note that this is to suggest not that torture could ever be minor—which some might argue to be incoherent—but rather that it most certainly comes in degrees and could be *comparatively minor*.)

The other features, however, are at least near explicit in the cases. Certainty is perhaps the most conspicuous feature of ticking-time-bomb cases: *everything* is certain. It is certain that the detainee is a terrorist. It is certain that he has information regarding the location of the bomb. It is certain that the torture will produce the information. It is certain that the information will lead to the timely deactivation of the bomb. And many critics of the cases promptly seize on all this certainty, which undoubtedly represents a departure from (at least almost all) actual cases;[15] I will return to these criticisms below and in following chapters.

Next come fecundity and purity, which are opposite sides of same coin: when we torture, we will get good things (fecundity), and we will not get bad things (purity). This fecundity is, thereafter, magnified by the invocation of extent, the last of Bentham's elements, which holds, not that a single life will be saved through the torture, but rather that *a lot* of lives will be saved (cf. Levin's "millions"). The purity condition comes through insofar as no bad consequences—aside from the pain and suffering of the tortured (see §4.3 above)—are postulated. And, while it is open to the critic to say that such cases do not preclude such consequences, it is equally open to the proponent to merely issue such a stipulation, at least at this stage of the dialectic.

Critics nevertheless do complain about ticking-time-bomb cases precisely on the issue of purity. They assert that torture would have to be institutionalized,[16] including the implementation of training programs for the torturers;[17] that such institutionalization portends harms for liberal democracies;[18] that our torturing our enemies makes it more likely that our enemies will torture us;[19] that torture makes it more likely for us to perpetuate other wrongs;[20] and so on.[21] I will return to these issues in the next chapter, but, for now, I just want to mention some of them.

Regardless, the proponent of ticking-time-bomb methodology is still free to say, "Look, that just *is not how the case goes!*" The critic cannot load conditions into the case that are patently excluded by presupposition.[22] To do so is simply to change the case and to ask a different question altogether—and precisely not the one that we currently care about. Rather, the question at hand is whether torture is permissible given features either stated or implied in the ticking-time-bomb cases, and this is a question to which moral philosophy owes an answer. Following that inquiry (chapter 6), we can then think about what implications it has vis-à-vis (real-world) cases that relax some of the idealizations and abstractions (chapter 7). But, as the dialectic goes, the aforementioned complaints are completely irrelevant.

To return to a distinction from the introduction to this chapter, the present aims are methodological rather than normative: I purport, not to have even asked questions about the morality of torture in the real world, but rather to be defending a certain methodological approach to those questions. This approach is one in which ticking-time-bomb cases figure prominently, regardless of the relationship that they bear to real-world cases. The next chapter will be normative, though will stay within the realm of this philosophical construct; the third part of the book will then move to the real world. But, for now, let us first get clear about how ticking-time-bomb methodology is meant to work lest we not properly understand its application. In the remainder of this chapter, I first consider objections against this proposal and then further articulate the logic and underpinnings of ticking-time-bomb methodology.

5.2 INTUITIONS AND THOUGHT EXPERIMENTS

Having seen some of the origins of the ticking-time-bomb cases as well as their putative grounding in classical utilitarian thinking, we can turn to the role these cases are meant to play in the torture debate. Despite the frequency with which the cases are invoked, their purpose has often been misunderstood. The most obvious point is that they are constructed such as to elicit intuitions about the moral permissibility of torture in rarefied situations. Or, to put it another way, they are meant to propose sufficient conditions for torture's permissibility: *if* we had a scenario in which ticking-time-bomb conditions were met, then torture is permissible.

For this reason, it hardly follows that ticking-time-bomb cases provide too stringent requirements for the application of torture—that is, that they "[set] the bar too high"[23]—or that torture will never be allowed in the real world because these stipulated conditions will never be met. These interpretations commit the fallacy of denying the antecedent: given the conditional that, "if ticking-time-bomb conditions are met, then torture is morally permissible," nothing follows about the permissibility of torture when those conditions are not met in just the same way that, "if today is Tuesday, then I am wearing a green shirt" says nothing about the color of my clothing on days other than Tuesday. To say this another way, ticking-time-bomb cases must be providing sufficient—as opposed to necessary—conditions for the permissibility of torture since, if the conditions were (merely) necessary, then that permissibility would never follow insofar as there might be additional necessary conditions beyond those specified.[24] Clearly, ticking-time-bomb cases invite us to think that torture is morally permissible under the appropriate conditions, so the logic of these cases has to be one of sufficiency rather than necessity.

Unlike some other authors, I think in terms of ticking-time-bomb *cases* as opposed to ticking-time-bomb *arguments*.[25] Arguments have premises and conclusions, and ticking-time-bomb cases do not. Rather, such cases are thought experiments that are meant to elicit our intuitions in regard to some proposed scenario. They tend to be framed in terms of things we should "imagine" or "suppose," rather than in terms of premises. The difference between these two is that premises have truth values whereas "imagine that P" and "suppose that Q" do not (i.e., these are imperatives, like "close the door"). Looking at the formulations by Shue, Levin, and Quinton introduced above, I read them all as cases, though Levin and Quinton go on to say what they think about the permissibility of torture given the relevant suppositions. And this is as it should be: the cases invite moral reflection.

Importantly, ticking-time-bomb methodology does not encourage us to infer the permissibility of torture from our intuitions alone. "I intuit P, therefore P," is a bad argument because our intuitions are (morally) fallible; or, to put it another way, we should not read off normative conclusions from descriptive premises (namely, ones about our intuitions). Rather, ticking-time-bomb cases reveal our deepest moral commitments—in the specified cases only—and those commitments then figure into our moral theorizing. Sometimes those commitments can be sustained through this process, but sometimes they are rejected given conflicting moral principles, other moral commitments, and so on.[26] This is the normative—as opposed to the methodological—project that will occupy us in the next chapter. But, for now, I propose that ticking-time-bomb cases are meant to offer conditions under which we are invited to countenance the moral permissibility of torture.

When critics have properly understood the logic of ticking-time-bomb methodology, they have taken a range of responses, ranging from dubious to downright hostile (cf. David Luban's allegations of "intellectual fraud").[27] Still, very few authors actually engage the cases on their own terms, instead offering empirical critiques of the presuppositions. These will have to be dealt with in later chapters, but, again, the purpose of the current chapter is wholly methodological. One of the few purely methodological critiques is offered in an ambitious paper by Michael Davis, whose ideas we also met in §4.3 above. For present purposes, one reason that Davis's paper is so useful is that he analyzes ticking-time-bomb methodology in the same way that I do, though we reach different conclusions: I think that this methodology is useful, whereas he thinks it should be discarded. In particular, we both agree that the cases are meant to elicit intuitions, as opposed, for example, to thinking that they are meant to constitute arguments. Davis then has three objections to the intuitions that the cases supposedly elicit, all of which threaten their role in some broader sort of moral theorizing. He summarizes these from the outset, then expands on them later:

> The intuition [that torture is permissible in those cases] is not as widely shared as necessary to constitute the required demonstration. Second, the intuition is not as reliable as necessary for such a demonstration. We lack the experience that would vouch for it. And, third . . . what we are intuiting . . . is an excuse rather than a justification.

Suffice it to say, I think that all these objections are misguided. Regarding the claim that the intuition is not as widely shared as necessary, there are simply no empirical data to back up his claim; he merely offers passing allusions to "good Kantians" and "some Catholics."[28] In §5.3, I will present some empirical data about intuitions in ticking-time-bomb cases, and the data flatly controvert Davis's claim. But my presentation of those data is not really even meant to have normative implications, precisely for the reason mentioned earlier: the fact that some people intuit P does not necessarily mean that P is true. Perhaps out of charity, Davis seems to consider the idea that a widely shared intuition would have justificatory power, though I reject this idea. And, furthermore, he seems to think that, if that intuition is not universal, it cannot have justificatory power. Even if I did think that intuitions had the justificatory potential that he entertains, I would reject this requirement: the fact that racists, for example, have certain moral intuitions does not mean that the intuitions of the rest of us are any less likely to track moral truth, even if intuition alone is insufficient to identify that truth. Regardless, I reject the idea that widely shared intuition is necessary for moral justification. (As a philosopher whose views bear little intuitive popularity, I had certainly better.)

The second objection, however, really threatens: it alleges that the intuitions we have in ticking-time-bomb cases are irrelevant because these cases fall so far from our experience. This objection is importantly different from those of other critics who simply deny the empirical plausibility of ticking-time-bomb suppositions since those objections allow for the legitimacy of ticking-time-bomb intuitions yet deny their relevance. Moves are available to the proponent of ticking-time-bomb methodology here, such as to argue for that relevance. Davis's objection, however, cuts deeper by threatening to take those intuitions off the table altogether. My reply to this takes two parts: first, I question whether his claim is true, and, then, granting it, I argue that it is problematic.

Is it true that we lack whatever experience could support ticking-time-bomb intuitions? For the sake of argument, let us grant that none of us has had the experience of torturing a terrorist in order to prevent a threat; maybe some of the readers have been less fortunate, but that need not concern us here. Nevertheless, I submit that we do not need experience of ticking-time-bomb cases in order to have whatever experience is relevant. Consider, for example, the following thought experiment:

> *Lost Wallet*. One Tuesday, you are walking home and see a brown wallet sitting on the sidewalk. You pick it up and find $240 inside as well as the driver's license of its owner. It turns out that the owner lives two houses down and he happens to be sitting on his front porch. He seems well enough off, however, and you have just lost your job, thus threatening the well-being of your family. The $240 could be used to buy groceries for a week as well as to purchase important medicine for one of your ailing children, none of which you can otherwise afford.

Should you return the wallet? For this discussion, the answer is irrelevant; the point is to question whether we have the necessary experience to legitimize our intuitive responses to the case, whatever they are. Strictly speaking, no: this *exact* situation has almost certainly never befallen any of us. Does that mean that the informativeness of our intuitions is somehow compromised? Absolutely not. Those intuitions are still morally informative, despite the fact that they are not narrowly grounded in experience. Consider that some of us have found wallets but it was Wednesday, the wallet was black, or whatever. Those experiences share the *relevant* moral features insofar as days of the week, color, and so on are morally irrelevant. But what if some of us have never found a wallet at all? Or had ailing children? For example, I do not even have children, yet it certainly seems like hunger and sickness are things that I can understand. The morally relevant features of this case are things like property rights, honesty, suffering, and so on; however they are instantiated is unimportant. All of us have experience with those things, so therefore our intuitions are useful. It is actually hard for me to think of any thought experiment that postulates morally relevant features with which none of us could identify, but this difficulty is precisely to make the point: we all have rich moral lives and experiences that comprise myriad moral features. If we did not, there would be something oddly obscure about those proposed moral features.

I take all the above to be straightforward, so, for the objection to have any plausibility, it would have to hold that ticking-time-bomb cases are so "radically different" from our experience as to significantly distinguish them from the lost wallet case; that latter case would have to be pedestrian or quotidian by comparison. But how would this line be motivated? In a straightforward sense, the cases bear the same moral features. The owner of the wallet has a right to have it back, and, let us suppose, the terrorist has a right not to be tortured. By violating that right, some greater suffering is alleviated. So what is the difference? It could be pragmatic insofar as ticking-time-bomb cases portend some sort of practical abuse, but that is irrelevant to philosophical methodology. Is it that there is a *lot* of suffering (cf. thousands of lives) and all these lives are somehow distortional (i.e., that the number of lives somehow "messes up" our intuitions)? This cannot be right for the simple reason that the number of lives *matters*: torture is morally better (or less morally bad) if it saves thousands of people than if it saves two people.[29] At any rate, I doubt that ticking-time-bomb cases are radically different from those in our experiential repertoire or, if the difference is only a matter of degree, that degree is insufficient to invalidate the intuitions.

But suppose that one remains unconvinced. Consider some of the greatest thought experiments in moral philosophy. Start with Judith Jarvis Thomson's famous violinist case, which is so fantastic that it is worth quoting at length:

> Let me ask you to imagine this. You wake up in the morning and find yourself back to back in bed with an unconscious violinist. A famous unconscious violinist. He has been found to have a fatal kidney ailment, and the Society of Music Lovers has canvassed all the available medical records and found that you alone have the right blood type to help. They have therefore kidnapped you, and last night the violinist's circulatory system was plugged into yours, so that your kidneys can be used to extract poi-

sons from his blood as well as your own. The director of the hospital now tells you, "Look, we're sorry the Society of Music Lovers did this to you—we would never have permitted it if we had known. But still, they did it, and the violinist is now plugged into you. To unplug you would be to kill him. But never mind, it's only for nine months. By then he will have recovered from his ailment, and can safely be unplugged from you." Is it morally incumbent on you to accede to this situation?[30]

Thomson's case is meant to be analogous to pregnancy due to rape, and our intuition in this case that it is permissible to disconnect the violinist is meant to similarly suggest that it is morally permissible to terminate rape-induced pregnancies.

Or else take Peter Singer's shallow pond case, which asks us to imagine whether we are obligated to save a child drowning in a shallow pond even if it would be inconvenient and lead to the muddying of our clothes.[31] Singer proposes this case as analogous to that of our obligations vis-à-vis easily preventable deaths of the world's poor and takes our intuitions in the shallow pond case to inform those obligations. Or, finally, consider Philippa Foot's trolley case—used to motivate the doctrine of double effect— retold to greater effect by Thomson:

Suppose you are the driver of a trolley. The trolley rounds a bend, and there come into view ahead five track workmen, who have been repairing the track. The track goes through a bit of a valley at that point, and the sides are steep, so you must stop the trolley if you are to avoid running the five men down. You step on the brakes, but alas they don't work. Now suddenly you see a spur of track leading off to the right. You can turn the trolley onto it, and thus save the five men on the straight track ahead. Unfortunately . . . there is one track workman on the spur of the track. He can no more get off the track in time than the five can, so you will kill him if you turn the trolley onto him. Is it morally permissible for you to turn the trolley?[32]

Whatever else we want to say about the success of these thought experiments, they all countenance scenarios far different from our experience. Of them, Singer's is really the only one that is even empirically *plausible*; the other two are almost farcical. Again, my contention is that these cases instantiate moral features with which we do have familiarity, but let us set that aside for now. If the problem with ticking-time-bomb cases is that they outstrip our experience, then all these thought experiments will surely have to be jettisoned as well, along with countless others. And, depending on what we mean by *experience*, so will hypotheticals such as "imagine that you come home next Tuesday, and [whatever]"; even such a simple hypothetical outstrips our experience, at least in a trivial way. I proposed above that the difference might have to do with morally relevant and morally irrelevant features, but I do not see what the argument would be to include these hypotheticals and yet to exclude the aforementioned thought experiments.

Regardless, there are various possibilities. The first is that ticking-time-bomb cases are excluded from our moral thinking, but violinists, shallow ponds, and trolleys get to stay. This seems implausible to me, but more will be said about it below. The second is that *everything* that even minimally outstrips our experience gets jettisoned, including simple hypotheticals. This cannot work as it would completely impoverish our moral thinking. The third proposal would be some sort of compromise wherein simple hypotheticals get to stay but ticking time-bombs, violinists, shallow ponds, and trolleys are all out. I suspect that this is the sort of idea that Davis has in mind, but I want to saddle his critique of ticking-time-bomb cases with an indictment of these other cases as well. And, while not as impoverishing as the second proposal, this third one still substantially impoverishes moral philosophy. Leaving aside ticking time-bombs for now, violinists, shallow ponds, and trolleys have played critical roles in helping us think about abortion, our duties to the poor, and the doctrine of double effect; without these constructs, those inquiries would be much worse off. And this is true even if the thought experiments fail as those failures are important for catalyzing discussion and developing alternative ideas. The same holds true for ticking-time-bomb cases.

My reply to Davis—or anyone else of similar spirit—therefore has various prongs. First, I deny that ticking-time-bomb cases outstrip our experience in any morally relevant way. Second, even if they did, this criterion threatens to undermine a broad and important swath of moral philosophy, perhaps even crippling the discipline. Third, even if that challenge can somehow be mitigated, various other useful thought experiments would be in at least as much trouble as ticking-time-bomb cases; moral philosophy would be worse off without these. The costs of jettisoning these cases is too high, especially since nothing even stands to be gained. Therefore, we should keep these thought experiments as part of our moral methodology. Of course, none of this is to say anything about particular normative conclusions; rather, it is just to allow esoteric thought experiments as part of our philosophical tool kits.[33]

Let us now turn to Davis's third objection. It will be useful to say more than is minimally required in response here given that this objection raises issues to which I will return in §§8.3–8.4. Davis thinks that we are intuiting "an excuse rather than a justification" when we reflect on torture in ticking-time-bomb cases.[34] This thought is motivated by something that Shue wrote: "[If] the situation approximates those in the imaginary examples in which torture seems possible to justify, a judge can surely be expected to suspend the sentence."[35] Davis thinks that this indicates that we find the torturer "guilty but excused," which "suggests doubts about moral justification."[36] These various comments invite us to think about an important point: What is it that we are meant to intuit in ticking-time-bomb cases? As I said above, the answer needs to be moral permissibility—or justification, this difference not being important here—for ticking-time-bomb methodology to work. If we are intuiting excuse rather than justification, that would, indeed, be a problem for this methodology.

So, first, what is the difference between an excuse and a justification? Or, even before that, let us start with a suspended sentence. Suspended sentences have nothing to do with either excuses or justification: a suspended sentence is a form of judicial discretion that can be issued to show leniency, often to first-time offenders or as part of a plea bargain. Shue suggests that a suspended sentence might be appropriate for someone who tortured under ticking-time-bomb-like conditions. But a suspended sentence means that such a person would have to be *convicted*, and I do not think that the ticking-time-bomb torturer should be convicted. I will take up that issue in chapter 8; for now, back to Davis. Justification and excuse are means to *acquittal*: a suspended sentence comes after an ascription of guilt, which is exactly what justification and excuse are meant to forestall. In other words, Davis's "guilty but excused" is not a proper category since excuse precludes guilt (cf. *not* guilty by reason of insanity).

To see this, let us now return to the difference between *justification* and *excuse*. While these concepts are important hallmarks of our criminal law—and moral thinking—they are somewhat more complicated than might be expected.[37] Consider, for example, Joshua Dressler: "A justification claim . . . seeks to show that the act was not wrongful, an excuse . . . tries to show that the actor is not morally culpable for his wrongful conduct."[38] Or Sharon Byrd: "An excuse . . . not only presupposes the violation of a legal or moral norm, but also the wrongful or unjustified nature of this violation."[39] Or, finally, Michael Moore: "A justification shows that *prima facie* wrongful and unlawful conduct is not wrongful or unlawful at all . . . by contrast, an excuse does not take away our prima facie judgment that an act is wrongful and unlawful; rather, it shows that the actor was not culpable in his doing of an admittedly wrongful and unlawful act."[40]

One of the principal differences between justification and excuse is that, if someone is justified, then he did not do anything wrong; if he is (merely) excused, then he did something wrong, but it is not his fault. Self-defense and necessity are justifications: when these are adequately established, we acknowledge that the accused did not do anything wrong.[41] Excuse, however, goes to incapacity, such as would be manifest through duress or insanity. If the accused kills someone but can establish insanity, then we do not hold him (morally or criminally) liable since it was not his fault. But, in excusing him from legal punishment, we do not say that the killings were justified.

To further elucidate this distinction, consider that justifications attach to acts whereas excuses attach to actors.[42] If, for example, someone were justified in killing one person to save five others (cf. the necessity defense; see §8.3 below), then some other person would have been also. In other words, what matters is the act of preventing the greater harm, not who perpetuates that act. Excuses, on the other hand, are different: the incapacities that they portend—like duress or insanity—are personal and attach to individuals. Second, claims of justification rest on a balancing of interests and considerations of the greater good, while excuses do not. Killing one to save five could be justified, but killing however many could still be excused if the killer lacked capacity (i.e., the numbers do not matter). Third, legally speaking, justifications acknowledge exceptions to prohibitions on criminal law, whereas excuses do not.[43] While the distinction between justification and excuse can be complicated, blurred, or attenuated in practice,[44] this basic presentation is sufficient for my purposes.

Let us now return to ticking-time-bomb cases: Which is it that we are meant to intuit, justification or excuse? Contra Davis, the answer is unequivocally justification. Remember that excuse has to do with incapacity, but that is not at stake with the ticking-time-bomb torturer. Return to the three criteria outlined above. First, our moral evaluation of the torture would not change whether the torturer was one person or another; the assessment is on the act of averting the egregious harm. Second, the balancing of interests is precisely what is it stake, and, should that balance not come out properly, then the torture was inappropriate. And, third, to endorse torture in those cases is to acknowledge that a universal prohibition on torture is misguided (if expedient). It bears emphasis that the most plausible legal justification for torture is necessity; I will return to this discussion §8.3.

The goals of this section have been to articulate and defend some of the central features of ticking-time-bomb methodology as well as to consider some objections to that methodology. As I proposed earlier, we should separate these methodological issues from the empirical ones: ticking-time-bomb cases do not make empirical claims, so empirical objections miss the point. Those objections loom when we try to figure out how to apply ticking-time-bomb cases to the real world, but we have various stops before getting to that project. For the rest of this chapter, I propose to accept ticking-time-bomb methodology as philosophically legitimate and to further explore some of the central features of these cases.

5.3 TICKING-TIME-BOMB CASE VARIANTS

If ticking-time-bomb methodology is defensible, then we can look more closely at the details and logic of ticking-time-bomb cases. As discussed in §5.1, at least two features of these cases are (allegedly) conspicuous: their dependence on utilitarian thinking and their high degree of idealization and abstraction. In that discussion, I did not say much about what *idealization* and *abstraction* were, so let us briefly consider those here. I take these terms from a recent essay by Shue; in this essay, Shue complains about the ticking-time-bomb methodology that I defended in §5.2. In doing so, he invokes a distinction between idealization and abstraction that owes to Onora O'Neill:[45]

> Why are imaginary examples like ticking-bomb hypotheticals so badly misleading about how to plan for real cases? They mislead in two different ways that compound the error: idealization and abstraction. Idealization is the addition of positive features to an example in order to make the example better than reality, which lacks those features. Abstraction is the deletion of negative features of reality from an example in order to make the example still better than reality. Idealization adds sparkle, abstraction removes dirt.[46]

As examples of idealization, Shue points out various assumptions built into ticking-time-bomb cases: that we have apprehended the right person, that torture will lead to prompt and accurate disclosure, and that torture will be practiced in rare and isolated cases.[47] There are actually even more idealizations than these, some of which I discussed in §5.1. For example, it is also implicit, not only that will we get the right information from the right person, but that the information will actually be used to disarm the threat. The bomb squad is infallible, time constraints are superable, the bomb is readily accessible, and so on. Shue's principal abstractive feature has to do with the institutional features that torture requires: he thinks that we simply could not have (effective) torture—even in one-off cases—without various institutions supporting it. And, following from this, Shue is skeptical about whether we could have one-off torture at all, that torture could be "conducted by wise, self-restrained angels."[48] Rather, he thinks that torture is inherently subject to abuse and nefarious spread.

Unfortunately for me, this all sounds quite compelling. Nevertheless, it runs together various issues that can be usefully separated. First, Shue thinks that ticking-time-bomb cases need to be reasonably similar to real-world cases in order for the former to inform the latter; I am dubious about this. Regardless, I will talk more about torture and the real world in the third part of the book. (I should also say that I am more sanguine than Shue about how empirically plausible ticking-time-bomb circumstances are.) Second, Shue's claims about abstraction make substantive claims about torture that I simply think are false: I think that torture can be (successfully) practiced without extensive institutional structures and, furthermore, that safeguards could be put in place to prevent the abuses that he worries about. For present purposes, we just need to agree that these are open questions; they will receive more discussion in subsequent chapters.

This then leaves idealizations, and I actually am sympathetic to the idea that ticking-time-bomb cases are highly idealized, both in the ways that Shue suggests and in the others that were already mentioned. But there are two things to say here. First, whether they are idealized has to do with empirical circumstances that we have yet to consider; one cannot simply label the cases as idealized without looking at actual cases. Presumably, the critic agrees, which gives rise to his contention that, by looking at actual cases, we will realize how idealized ticking-time-bomb cases are. But I worry that this gets the quantifiers wrong: surely not *all* actual cases are like ticking-time-bomb cases, but nobody ever said they were. If the ticking-time-bomb proponent could even come up with a *single* real-world case that bears the alleged idealizations of ticking-time-bomb cases, then ticking-time-bomb methodology is at least vindicated in that case.

But, second, let us grant that ticking-time-bomb cases are idealized. Why would idealization make those cases less philosophically useful? The concern is that ticking-time-bomb methodology elicits intuitions about some cases (namely, the idealized ones) and then presumes to transfer those intuitions uncritically to different cases (namely, nonidealized cases). Or, in other words, ticking-time-bomb cases elicit different intuitions than less idealized variants, and, therefore, these former intuitions are not useful in thinking about the latter cases. I actually suspect that this is false in both regards, but the former is a claim that we can test experimentally. If it can be shown to be false, then the worry about idealizations can be forestalled; more on this shortly.

We can further use the experimental approach to gather data about the relationship between intuitions in ticking-time-bomb cases and simple utilitarian thinking. As we will see, some of the critics of ticking-time-bomb cases have alleged that such cases codify some sort of naive utilitarianism, and, as they quickly reject utilitarianism, they can similarly reject ticking-time-bomb methodology. I think that the intuitions ticking-time-bomb cases elicit are actually more subtle than this and include important nonutilitarian considerations; if this is correct, then the antiutilitarian critique of ticking-time-bomb methodology fails. We can gather empirical data about intuitions regarding ticking-time-bomb cases and their putative utilitarian bases that will help us adjudicate this issue.

To test these ideas, I designed four thought experiments that manipulated two variables in standard ticking-time-bomb cases.[49] In these cases, the torture is effected against a *terrorist* who is *guilty* of perpetuating some terrorist plot. The first variable, *guilt/innocence*, trades on this feature by proposing torture on an *innocent* (namely, the terrorist's daughter)[50] with the effects otherwise being the same (namely, the terrorist giving up the location of the bomb). Also, in standard cases, the torture is *certain* to lead to the saving of many people: as mentioned in §5.1, we are certain that the terrorist possesses material knowledge of the location of the bomb, that the torture will generate the release of that information, and that the information will lead to the timely deactivation of the bomb. As against this certainty, we might postulate *uncertainty*: these cases offer a 1 percent chance of saving the lives rather than certain saving in their converses, giving us the second variable, *(un)certainty*.[51]

It is worth offering two notes on the cases with uncertainty. First, these cases are silent as to *why* there is uncertainty: maybe the terrorist does not know the location of the bomb; maybe the torture will not work; maybe the information will not lead to the deactivation of the bomb. The uncertainty cases can accommodate any of these sources of the uncertainty since any of them could lead to a reduced likelihood of saving lives. Second, in the uncertainty cases, the number of lives saved (ten thousand) is higher than the number of lives saved in the certainty cases (one hundred). This is to keep the expected numbers of lives saved through torture the same since the lower likelihood of success in the uncertainty cases (1 percent) as against the certainty cases (100 percent) renders the expected outcomes identical. Were the outcomes not to be identical, it would not be clear whether the (un)certainty or the number of lives alone was driving the moral judgment, which would then preclude the proper analysis.[52]

These two variables—guilt/innocence and (un)certainty—can be combined in the following ways:

	Guilt	Innocence
Certainty	Case 1	Case 3
Uncertainty	Case 2	Case 4

Here are the cases, along with the prompts that were included on the surveys:

Case 1: Guilt/Certainty. Imagine that you have just apprehended a terrorist who is responsible for planting a bomb in a crowded metropolitan center. The bomb squad has been unable to defuse the bomb, and, unless the terrorist provides the deactivation code, it will detonate and kill one hundred people.

You have exhausted all other possibilities and must now contemplate more extreme measures. If the terrorist is subjected to moderate torture, then he will surely provide the deactivation code for the bomb in time for its safe deactivation.

It is morally permissible to torture the terrorist.

Case 2: Guilt/Uncertainty. Imagine that you have just apprehended a terrorist who is responsible for planting a bomb in a crowded metropolitan center. The bomb squad has been unable to defuse the bomb, and, unless the terrorist provides the deactivation code, it will detonate and kill ten thousand people.

You have exhausted all other possibilities and must now contemplate more extreme measures. If the terrorist is subjected to moderate torture, there is a 1 percent chance that he will provide the deactivation code for the bomb in time for its safe deactivation. However, there is a 99 percent chance that the torture will accomplish nothing and that all the lives will be lost.

It is morally permissible to torture the terrorist.

Case 3: Innocence/Certainty. Imagine that you have just apprehended a terrorist who is responsible for planting a bomb in a crowded metropolitan center. The bomb squad has been unable to defuse the bomb, and, unless the terrorist provides the deactivation code, it will detonate and kill one hundred people.

You have exhausted all other possibilities and must now contemplate more extreme measures. The terrorist has been trained to resist torture, so torturing him to get the code will not be effective. You have learned the location of the terrorist's young daughter, who is completely innocent and knows nothing of her father's terrorist activities. Psychological profiling of the terrorist reveals that, if his daughter is subject to moderate torture, then he will surely provide the deactivation code for the bomb in time for its safe deactivation.

It is morally permissible to torture the terrorist's daughter.

Case 4: Innocence/Uncertainty. Imagine that you have just apprehended a terrorist who is responsible for planting a bomb in a crowded metropolitan center. The bomb squad has been unable to defuse the bomb, and, unless the terrorist provides the deactivation code, it will detonate and kill ten thousand people.

You have exhausted all other possibilities and must now contemplate more extreme measures. The terrorist has been trained to resist torture, so torturing him to get the code will not be effective. You have learned the location of the terrorist's young daughter, who is completely innocent and knows nothing of her father's terrorist activities. Psychological profiling of the terrorist reveals that, if his daughter is subject to moderate torture, there is a 1 percent chance that he will provide the deactivation code for the bomb in time for its safe deactivation. However, there is a 99 percent chance that the torture will accomplish nothing and that all the lives will be lost.

It is morally permissible to torture the terrorist's daughter.

These cases were administered to 833 students, all of whom consented to participate in the research project. In order to preclude order effects,[53] each subject randomly received one of the cases; therefore, there were just over two hundred responses to each case. The response was on a seven-point Likert scale, the standard sort of scale for such questionnaires.[54] On this scale, they were asked to indicate the degree to which they disagreed or agreed with the sentence that concludes the case; "strong disagreement" was indicated by a score of 1 and "strong agreement" by a score of 7. Subjects were further asked to report their gender.[55]

A 2×2 ANOVA, with guilt/innocence and (un)certainty as the between-participant variables, revealed a significant independent effect for guilt/innocence, $F(1,829) = 90.9$, $p < .001$, $\eta^2 = .10$, but not for (un)certainty,

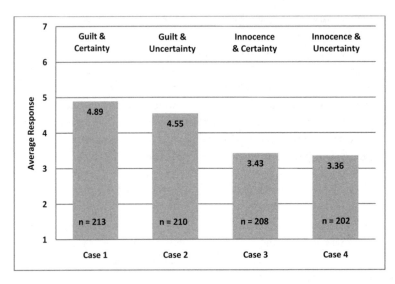

Fig. 1. Mean Response by Case

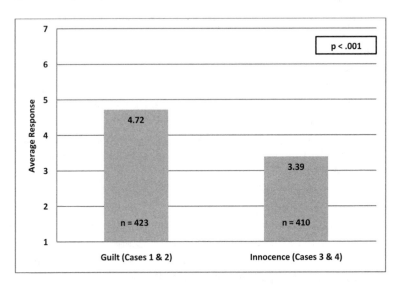

Fig. 2. Guilt and Innocence Mean Responses

$F(1,829) = 2.1$, $p = .14$. In addition, there was no interaction between the two variables, $F(1,829) = .90$, $p = .34$.[56] The mean results for each case are displayed in figure 1. Recall that, in case 1 and case 2, the torture would be effected against a *terrorist* and that, in case 3 and case 4, it would be effected against the terrorist's *innocent daughter*. The mean results for the guilt/innocence variable are displayed in figure 2. There is a substantial difference between the moral judgments in these categories and, indeed, one that is statistically significant.

The second variable, (un)certainty, can also be studied independently of the overall case averages. In case 1 and case 3, the torture was *certain* to save lives, and, in case 2 and case 4, saving the lives was far less certain (only 1 percent likely). The mean results for the (un)certainty variable are displayed in figure 3. In this instance, there is also a difference in responses depending on whether the outcomes are (un)certain, but the response is *not* statistically significant.

Both these results—that is, guilt/innocence and (un)certainty—have direct implications for the use of ticking-time-bomb cases. First, ticking-time-bomb cases do not trade wholly on utilitarian considerations, as is made clear by the guilt/innocence axis: it *matters* whether the subject of torture is a guilty terrorist or his innocent daughter. In each of these cases, the hedonic calculus comes out the same, yet the moral judgments are relevantly different.[57] This large literature, then, which focuses on the negative consequences of torture, misunderstands at least one central feature of the cases, namely, that the fact that we would torture a guilty terrorist is of primary moral importance.[58] Since guilt is a deontic notion, the cases invoke nonutilitarian features, and criticisms that direct their animus toward utilitarianism are missing at least part of the story. Furthermore, notice that the critics of these cases have either criticized the cases' alleged

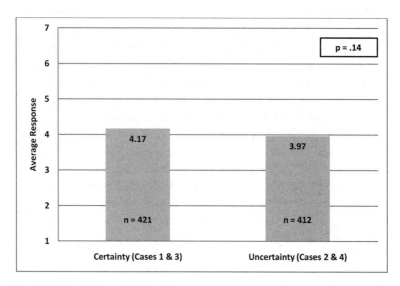

Fig. 3. Certainty and Uncertainty Mean Responses

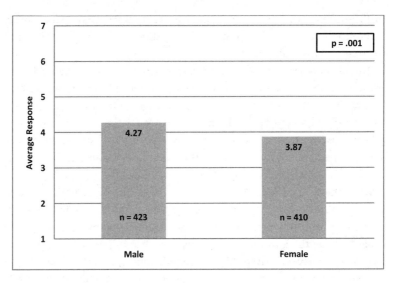

Fig. 4. Mean Responses by Gender

utilitarian underpinnings as morally myopic (cf. invocations of dignity, inhumanity, rights, etc.)[59] or else have tried to show that the conclusions do not follow on utilitarian grounds alone; this was mentioned above and will bear more extensive treatment in the next chapter. Either of these criticisms, however, is compromised if nonutilitarian features help drive our intuitions, which they do.

The implications of the (un)certainty results are less straightforward, but my contention is that they mitigate worries about the idealizations. As already discussed, traditional ticking-time-bomb cases suppose us to have various epistemic certainties, many of which we might (usually) expect to lack in the real world. Rather, the situation is far more likely to be that we have apprehended someone who may or may not be a terrorist, may or may not know the location of the bomb, may or may not give up (correct) information during torture, and so on. Furthermore, such information may or may not lead to the saving of lives. In the cases designed to reflect uncertainty, there was a 1 percent chance that the torture would, ultimately, lead to saving lives. But—and this is critically important—there was no statistically significant difference in responses *regardless* of whether the outcomes were certain or uncertain. The certainty in standard ticking-time-bomb cases, then, has not been shown to be psychologically efficacious regarding judgments as to the permissibility of torture. Or, to put it another way, the idealizations in these cases were not shown to affect the responses that we have to them. There is no evidence that our intuitions are getting messed up by idealizations since they turn out, statistically speaking, to be the same whether idealizations are present or not.

As a final point, consider that survey data also reflected the gender of the subjects. The means analyzing gender as a covariate—$F(1,828) = 10.6$, $p = .001$—are displayed in figure 4. Note that males were more likely to think that torture was permissible, and this difference was statistically significant ($p < .001$). The mean responses for individual cases are displayed in figure 5.

In all but the third case, men were, on average, more likely than women to think that torture was morally permissible.[60] I do not want to lean on this result too heavily, but there have been studies that investigated differences in moral development and moral intuitions between men and women; part of this literature developed in response to Lawrence Kohlberg's work on stages of moral development.[61] Critics held that this account, which was undifferentiated between sexes, was incomplete since, even if there are insignificant sex differences in moral development, the sexes might differ in some aspects of moral reasoning.[62] For example, Carol Gilligan has argued that males and females differ in their "orientations": men typically have a justice/rights orientation, whereas women have a care/response orientation.[63] In subsequent work, Anne Kolby and Kohlberg suggested that this care/response orientation would manifest utilitarian thinking,[64] though the response has been critical.[65]

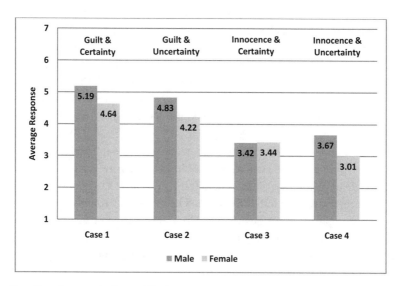

Fig. 5. Mean Responses by Case and Gender

Of course, what is interesting about our results is that men are more likely to find torture permissible than are women, both overall and in three of four cases. To the extent that Kolby and Kohlberg are right—that is, that women are more likely to be utilitarians—then it would follow that, in these ticking-time-bomb cases, (wholly) utilitarian considerations are *not* the only ones present in the thought experiments since men were more likely to find torture morally permissible. Again, I do not want to place too much weight on this analysis, but the differences in gender response were striking: if the links between gender and moral orientation hold up, this is another reason to think that ticking-time-bomb cases incorporate nonutilitarian considerations. It is not necessarily clear what those considerations would be, however. If the guilt of the terrorist was driving the reactions, then we would expect the men to have a higher average response in guilt/certainty and guilt/uncertainty, which they did. But then men and women should have the same responses in innocence/certainty and innocence/uncertainty, yet men were still more likely to support torture in innocence/uncertainty, if not innocence/certainty. Regardless, the stronger support for the nonutilitarian considerations is still the (ungendered) guilt/innocence results.

This chapter has covered much ground, so it might be useful to tie together various themes that have been herein developed. In §5.1, we considered the origins of ticking-time-bomb cases and also looked at some of the features that various formulations of these cases share. In that discussion, we saw the work of Bentham as well as the consonance between ticking-time-bomb cases and classical utilitarian thinking. In §5.2, we considered various methodological objections to the use of ticking-time-bomb cases. I defended the use of the cases against those methodological objections, arguing that they play a legitimate role in our moral theorizing.

In §5.3, we considered variants of ticking-time-bomb cases in the aims of reaching two substantive conclusions. First, I argued that our moral judgments in these cases are responsive to nonutilitarian features; this is important given the affinity that Bentham's hedonic calculus bears to the cases as well as allegations that have come from critics. Second, I presented evidence that moral judgments in idealized ticking-time-bomb cases are statistically indistinguishable from less idealized cases. This result goes against objections that traditional ticking-time-bomb cases are ill formed since the idealizations were not shown to be cognitively efficacious. Therefore, it is simply not a strike against ticking-time-bomb cases that they are idealized—if, in fact, they are.

As the title of this chapter indicates, the issues that have been herein discussed were methodological, as opposed to normative. Ticking-time-bomb cases play such a central role in the debate about interrogational torture that this methodology deserves extended consideration. And, since the use of the cases has come under fire, a defense was needed if we are to proceed with them in our arsenal. It is my hope that I have delimited a legitimate purview for their incorporation and articulated some of the bases of the cases. Having now offered this methodological foundation, I turn to its normative upshot.

6

Should We Torture in Ticking-Time-Bomb Cases?

In the last chapter, I defended the use of ticking-time-bomb cases in thinking about the moral status of interrogational torture. That chapter, however, was wholly methodological and had no (direct) normative implications. In the present chapter, my investigation will be normative; to wit, is it morally permissible to torture in ticking-time-bomb cases? This question is trickier than it looks for the simple reason that there are myriad moral theories and different theories may yield different answers. An ineffective strategy of amelioration in this regard would be to try to defend one moral theory against its rivals, both because that would take us too far afield and regardless, because such a defense would not be very convincing; no matter how well I defend utilitarianism against my deontologist friends—or vice versa—none of us ever seems swayed. Rather than stake my chances on those prospects, I propose something else.

This other strategy is to recognize that all moral theories can be categorized into one of two groups: absolutist or nonabsolutist. Absolutist theories posit moral rules that can never, under any circumstances, be justifiably violated, whereas nonabsolutist theories deny the existence of such rules. It seems to me that every moral theory—on pain of logic—has to fall into one of these two categories. Absolutist theories can be subdivided into two types: absolutist in principle and absolutist in practice. This distinction is meant to acknowledge that some theory could deny that, even in fanciful cases, some moral rule could be justifiably violated, or else it could hold that such violations might be justified in theory, if never in practice. These are importantly different theories, and different things should be said in regard to them vis-à-vis the moral status of torture. Absolutism in principle will be discussed in §6.4, and absolutism in practice will be discussed in §6.5; I treat absolutism in practice second because of its contiguity with chapter 7.

I will, therefore, begin with nonabsolutist theories, though this is hardly a monolithic group. Again, I am hardly sanguine about being able to convince a deontologist to be a utilitarian, so my strategy will be less (or more?) ambitious: to show that any nonabsolutist moral theory can accommodate the moral permissibility of torture in ticking-time-bomb scenarios. In other words, whether we care about utility (§6.1), rights (§6.2), or anything else (§6.3), the case for torture can be made.[1] Or, if it cannot, the theory is more properly regarded as absolutist (§§6.4–6.5). Lest this chapter overwhelm the rest of the book, I will have to sacrifice comprehensiveness for judiciousness, but the argumentative strategy in §§6.1–6.3 should be readily apparent and straightforwardly extended. Necessarily, §6.3 will be the most overdrawn, though I will register appropriate comments and disclaimers in that regard. As a final methodological note, this chapter is concerned with the ethics of torture in ticking-time-bomb cases; the third part of the book will be about torture and the real world.

6.1 TORTURE AND UTILITY

In §5.1, we considered the congeniality between classical utilitarian thinking and ticking-time-bomb cases, though I ultimately challenged that link in §5.3. Regardless, there is little doubt that torture in ticking-time-bomb cases could be justified by utilitarianism; this is true even if those cases commonly trade on the guilt of the terrorist, a moral feature with no straightforward utilitarian upshot. In other words—and separating the methodological and the normative projects—utilitarianism can justify the torture of a guilty terrorist as readily as it can the torture of his innocent daughter, so long as the utilitarian calculus comes out right. The methodological point of §5.3 was simply that our moral judgments about the permissibility of torture distinguish between these two configurations but utilitarianism need not; in fact, that was precisely the point.

Of all the major moral theories, utilitarianism probably offers the most direct justification of interrogational torture.[2] In subsequent sections of this chapter, I will make the case that other moral theories need not be opposed to torture, but making that case plausible certainly requires more work than it does in the case of utilitarianism. For example, we might think that people—terrorists or otherwise—have a right against being tortured, and being able to take rights seriously while still being able to license torture therefore faces an obvious obstacle (cf. §6.2). For the utilitarian, however, no such obstacle exists: so long as the hedonic calculus comes out right, torture is readily justified. Opponents of torture therefore can go either of two ways. First, they can reject utilitarianism, whether for more general reasons or else because it could support torture. In doing so, they must adopt some sort of moral theory in its place, and, therefore, we will have more to say to such positions in the following sections. Second, they can deny that utilitarianism would justify torture (in practice), even if it could (in theory). This line has the merit of being responsive to utilitarian commitments and, therefore, is able to say something to the utilitarian; the first line simply does not engage the position. For this reason, I have a lot of respect for critics who advance utilitarian arguments against torture insofar as those arguments are responsive to the dialectic: a convincing response to the utilitarian should be, not that his theory is wrong—presumably he has already thought about this—but rather that his theoretical commitments are different than he might have suspected.[3] In this section, let us engage the second sort of opponent, deferring the first for later.

As already mentioned in §5.1, the basis of a utilitarian argument for torture is straightforward: it could prevent the deaths of many noncombatants. Their noncombatancy status does not really (directly) matter from the utilitarian perspective, so long as the aggregated value of those otherwise forfeited lives is sufficiently high to cover the costs of torture. For the utilitarian, torturing one terrorist to save a thousand other terrorists could even be justified, at least if the thousand to be saved were not going to sow too much suffering in the world. It is worth noting that the utilitarian calculation here is about preventing a utility loss rather than effecting a utility gain: it is not that torture brings more utility into the world but rather that it prevents its longitudinal exit. This distinction, however, is not of much use to the utilitarian, who cares only about maximizing total aggregate happiness; whether that quantity turns out to be positive or negative is beside the point, so long as it is maximal. In other words, torture could manifest a utility loss yet still be justified so long as that loss is less than what would be realized without torture.

Again reprising §5.1, there are several desiderata that the utilitarian would require torture to satisfy. First, torture should be the least harmful remedy applied, and, similarly, some insufferable form of torture should not be deployed when a lesser one would elicit the valuable information. If the information that would save lives could be gleaned through some less offensive means (e.g., simple questions), then those means should be pursued. And, presumably, they would be: there is little reason to torture before otherwise asking the location of the bomb. Furthermore, there should be some expectation that the torture will be efficacious, be it against someone whom we can reasonably expect to have the intelligence, against someone with the appropriate vulnerabilities, not against someone who will hopelessly deceive us with misinformation, enacted on a timetable commensurable with the extant threat, and so on. There is no doubt that, in the real world, all these requirements can get messy, but, in the land of ticking time-bombs—where we currently are—they are straightforwardly stipulated.

While these stipulations are often challenged, such challenges radically misunderstand the state of play. For example, consider an ill-named paper by Vittorio Bufacchi and Jean Maria Arrigo, "Torture, Terrorism and the State: A Refutation of the Ticking Time-Bomb Argument," which is anything but. Bufacchi and Arrigo think that the ticking-time-bomb argument takes its premises to be that a terrorist is captured and that, if he is tortured, he will reveal information regarding the location of a bomb. From this, the conclusions are meant to be that torture is permissible, that information about the bomb is retrieved, and that lives are saved. But then they argue that this formulation has suppressed premises (e.g., that it is almost certain that the terrorist has information about the bomb) and, more to the point, that "all the premises in the argument are contentious from an empirical point of view": intelligence is never infallible, torture is not guaranteed to work, torture is not efficacious in short time periods, misinformation is revealed under torture, and so on.[4] Ultimately, they maintain that the ticking-time-bomb argument fails by its own (utilitarian) lights. And this sort of strategy has been repeated elsewhere by others, be it about the institutional costs of torture[5]—including the costs of training programs for torturers[6]—or various other negative consequences.[7] Assuming that all these objections can be developed in utilitarian currency, where does the utilitarian argument for torture stand?

As discussed in §5.2, I look at ticking-time-bomb cases, not as arguments, but as cases. The upshot of these cases is some sort of moral judgment about the permissibility of torture, and those judgments somehow figure into our moral methodology (e.g., through reflective equilibrium). That said, we can make ticking-time-bomb cases figure into an argument that looks something like the following: In all cases (and all else being equal), if we can choose a lesser harm to a greater one, we should. In ticking-time-bomb cases, torture is the lesser harm. Therefore, we should torture in those cases. I take the first premise to be self-evident, the second is the key kernel encoded into ticking-time-bomb cases, and the conclusion deductively follows. Bufacchi and Arrigo's formulation seems clunky by comparison, though maybe they aim to break out my second premise. Regardless, their strategy is just to deny some presuppositions of the cases on empirical grounds. This move, however, misses the point of the dialectic since the realm of discourse at this stage is nonempirical; rather, it is about the hypothetical cases. Their response is a red herring insofar as they change the question from being about ticking-time-bomb cases to being about the world. Ultimately, their position has to do with torture policy,[8] but ticking-time-bomb cases are not about torture policy; they are about one-off applications of torture.[9]

What matters to the utilitarian is how the hedonic calculus plays out in the cases under consideration. For the purposes of this chapter, we are still concerned with ticking-time-bomb cases, and those straightforwardly license the moral permissibility of torture on utilitarian grounds. In the next chapter, I shall incorporate empirical considerations, but they are not yet upon us. And, regardless, it registers an important concession when opponents of torture turn empirical, at least to my sensibilities. The empirical turn presumably allows that torture *could* be justified; otherwise, there is no need—save, perhaps, dialectical expedience—to make that move. If the allowance that torture could be justified is, nevertheless, tightly followed by the contention that it *would* not be justified, then we just have to look at the cases and see how it comes out. By even getting to the cases, however, the opponent to torture has lost ground.

As a final note in this section, let me suggest that these arguments generalize to other (or all) forms of consequentialism. Utilitarianism is one form of consequentialism, of which there are many others. What these theories have in common is a commitment that consequences are the ultimate arbiter of moral good, though they differ in how they assess consequences. Utilitarianism—the most renowned consequentialist theory—takes utility (i.e., pleasure and pain) to be all that matters, but other things might matter, such as welfare, desire satisfaction, and so on; these other values are what individuate the theories. While I prefer utilitarianism to its brethren, any of them could return similar verdicts in favor of torture in ticking-time-bomb cases. Or, if there were some aberrant consequentialist theory out there—that is, one that did not straightforwardly license torture in ticking-time-bomb cases—it would have to be true that, qua consequentialism, the consequences of ticking-time-bomb cases could be somehow adjusted such that torture came out permissible under the theory.

6.2 TORTURE AND RIGHTS

Many of those working in ethics want little to do with utilitarianism: this is a theory that (supposedly) lets the sadists abuse their victims, cares more about total aggregates than fair distributions, and so on. For our purposes, however, it is this first concern that matters insofar as utilitarianism makes no provisions for deontological constraints, such as the right not to be tortured. But is there such a right, and, if so, is it absolute? Even if it is, does it follow that torture is categorically impermissible? These pivotal questions inveigh against cavalier proclamations of a right against torture. In this section, let me try to untangle some of the issues that such questions portend in order to understand where a commitment to rights takes us with regard to the moral justifiability of torture.

To get the proper point on the first question, consider this: does the terrorist responsible for threatening many lives and unwilling to end that threat have a right against torture?[10] I am not sure. Certainly, there are things that we can do to forfeit our rights. A negligent parent forfeits his right of custodianship to his child. A drunk driver forfeits his right to operate a motor vehicle. A murderer forfeits his right to freedom (e.g., through incarceration). There are various distinctions that could be drawn about types of rights (e.g., positive, negative, etc.), legal versus moral rights, qualified and unqualified forfeiture,[11] and so on, but some extensive typology is not important here.[12] Rather, the point is merely that at least some rights are not absolute.[13]

However, even if some rights are not absolute, it does not follow that none are; perhaps the right against torture is one of those. Stepping back from that for a moment, however, are there any less contentious examples? The right to due process is a strong candidate and one that the negligent parent, drunk driver, and murderer certainly retain. In §3.1 above, I discussed prisoner-of-war status—as well as associated due process protections—and how the War on Terror challenged this status. But it is an open question whether the Bush administration got that wrong; merely because some protections were suspended, it hardly follows that they should have been. Nevertheless, suspension of due process protections (namely, the right of habeas corpus) is directly built into our Constitution—and for good reasons.[14] It is also dubious that the most important rights—including the right to due process—are the ones that are absolute insofar as, for example, many of us think that capital punishment can be justified.[15]

One of the tests for whether a right cannot be justifiably infringed is whether we owe restitution after transgressing against it. So, if someone has a right not to be battered, then the assailant owes compensatory damages for that battery and maybe punitive and criminal sanctions as well. The negligent parent, drunk driver, or murderer, however, is not owed compensation for the rights against which we infringe since those infringements are justified. Is torturing a complicit terrorist like this or like the battery case? Imagine that, through torture, a terrorist's arm was broken but that he ultimately provided the information that led to lives being saved. Do we have an obligation to pay for his medical care? I do not have a strong intuition here and can see arguments going either way. Regardless, it ultimately does not matter so long as torture can be justified *even* if the right against torture can be asserted. In other words, there are two ways to justify torture vis-à-vis rights: the first is to argue that the right against torture is somehow compromised, and the second is to argue that, even if it is not, torture can be justified nonetheless. Dialectically, this second strategy is superior insofar as it is against a stronger position; if the first strategy were well articulated, it would still be ineffective against someone who simply denied its premise. The second strategy is more ambitious, but it covers more argumentative space and is, therefore, the strategy that I will pursue. As a reminder, we are presently considering nonabsolutist approaches in general and rights-based deontologies in particular. There are, certainly, other forms of deontology, and some of those come out to be absolutist; I will return to absolutist theories more generally in §§6.4–6.5.

For now, let us suppose that the terrorist has a right against being tortured and, furthermore, that he does not relinquish this right in virtue of his complicity in terrorist activity. Does it follow that he cannot be tortured? I think that the answer is quite clearly no. The reason is simply that his rights are not the only ones in play: the victims of the bomb stand to have their rights violated as well (e.g., their right to life). However we approach this issue, it cannot be through some myopic (mis)accounting of the rights at stake. In this thread of the dialectic, the point is that someone's rights are going to be violated *regardless*: either the terrorist's right against torture or else the noncombatants' collective rights to life. Therefore, just trotting out the terrorist's right against torture misses the central point of ticking-time-bomb cases, even from a rights-based perspective.

Setting the torture context aside for simplicity, imagine that there are three people, A, B, and C, all of whom have a right to life. Further imagine that A is getting ready to shoot B and C and that these executions can be prevented only if D shoots A. What should D do? The deontologist can now say one of two things. On the one hand, he could say that D cannot shoot A because rights are, to use some well-known locutions, trumps[16] or side constraints[17] (e.g., against social goods). Such a line holds that we may not infringe against some right even if such a violation will engender fewer overall rights violations. Alternatively, the deontologist might adopt some sort of aggregative approach that would hold that the right actions are the ones that either maximize or minimize whatever features he takes to be morally relevant (e.g., rights preservations or rights violations, respectively). For this latter sort of deontologist, D should shoot A: if he does, there is one rights violation (namely, A's), and, if he does not, there are two (namely, C's and D's). Rights violations are minimized through the shooting, thus making it morally required. (A similar story could be told for maximizing rights preservations.)

Which is the more plausible view? I maintain that the aggregative approach makes a lot more sense. Ronald Dworkin has argued that, in cases of rights conflict, we should look, not at the explicit formulation of the right, but rather to the values that suggested the right in the first place.[18] So, if individuals have a right to life, it is because life itself is something that is valuable and worth preserving. Given a conflict where the violation of one person's right (e.g., to life) could prevent the violation of five other person's right to life, the values that led to the creation of the right to life would suggest violating the one in order to prevent violation of the five.[19] By considering why we would endorse rights in the first place (namely, because we value the objects of those rights), it would be permissible to act such that the underlying values and their associated objects are preserved to the highest degree possible. This approach sometimes goes under the aegis of "rights-based utilitarianism," though utility really has nothing to do with it.[20]

Some people have objected to such a view, most notably Robert Nozick. As I implied above, someone who really took rights seriously might think that some aggregation procedure is more attractive than rights fetishism, but Nozick does raise a legitimate concern against aggregation. In particular, he asks: "Why . . . hold that some persons have to bear some costs that benefit other persons more, for the sake of the overall social good?"[21] Instead of our earlier example, imagine the following: A is preparing to execute B and C but will refrain if B executes D, where D is some innocent third party. The aggregative deontologist would, presumably, have to say that B should execute D since then we have only one rights violation (namely, D's) instead of two (namely, B's and C's). If we agree with Nozick that this commitment is problematic, then that would be a strike against the theory.

However, there are at least two available responses. First, in a note, Nozick expresses concern with the application of his theory to "cases of catastrophic moral horror," which are precisely what ticking-time-bomb cases model.[22] So, ultimately, it is unclear whether even Nozick would object to minimizing rights violations in these cases. Second, Nozick's objection to aggregative deontology is, effectively, that innocent third parties might absorb all the burdens such that unrelated parties derive all the benefits. But this concern is obviously rendered moot in the ticking-time-bomb cases since the terrorist is, ex hypothesi, not an innocent third party: he planted the bomb and is withholding the information that could be used to disarm it. To be sure, there are cases when Nozick's fear could be realized, such as the ticking-time-bomb case variants we saw in §5.3 above wherein the terrorist's innocent daughter was tortured so that he would disclose the relevant information. I will return to this issue in §9.2 below, but, for now, it is irrelevant insofar as we are talking about standard ticking-time-bomb cases in which the guilty terrorist is the one to be tortured.

Let me now integrate various threads from this section. The key is to recognize ticking-time-bomb cases as ones of rights conflicts rather than as merely involving the rights of the terrorist and, furthermore, to recognize that the cases are constructed such that torture minimizes overall rights violations. We can acknowledge that not all rights violations are of equal moral significance and even, for the sake of argument, suppose that the right against torture counts more than the right to life. While I suspect that this latter supposition is false, the rights of a substantial number of people who would otherwise die militate in favor of torture. To put it another way, even if the right against torture is five times more morally valuable than the right to life, the rights of the thousands that the terrorist threatens swamp his right against torture. On a straightforward rights aggregation, torture comes out to be morally permissible. And, even if we were to acknowledge that there could be problems with such an approach in general—such as those suggested by Nozick—they simply do not apply to ticking-time-bomb cases in particular. Therefore, they fail to indict the moral permissibility of torture in such cases.

The critic could object to the argumentation of this section by claiming that I have considered a peculiar version of rights-based deontology and not the one that he wanted. But the strategy was fair: I considered a general rights-based account and explored what commitments such an account would have. Surely, a view could be constructed with different commitments, even including ad hoc restrictions against torture. Ultimately, however, any deontology has to be either absolutist or nonabsolutist. If it is nonabsolutist, then there has to be some way to extract concessions about the permissibility of torture; such is a conceptual requirement of nonabsolutist theories. In other words, if someone has a nonabsolutist view sufficiently different from the considerations that I have entertained in this section, then it is true that my arguments have not committed *that* theory to the permissibility of torture. But, insofar as the theory is nonabsolutist, it must license torture in at least *some* cases, and, whatever those cases could possibly be, ticking-time-bomb cases have to be plausible approximations. The best retreat is, therefore, to some absolutist account, and that discussion will ensue in §§6.4–6.5.

6.3 OTHER MORAL THEORIES

There are many moral theories other than utilitarianism and rights-based deontology; the risk of the present dialectic is that, even if §§6.1–6.2 were convincing, someone might say that his preferred moral theory nevertheless would not allow for torture. Since I surely cannot cover every moral theory, what is the best way to cover the available logical space? In an earlier paper, I tried to catalog various moral theories: the idea was to show either that all the major ones would license torture in ticking-time-bomb cases or else that they were absolutist. I then went on to argue that absolutism was implausible, which left the theories committed to torture. Given their shared commitments, and without adjudicating among them (i.e., by application of separation of cases), it follows that torture in ticking-time-bomb cases is morally permissible.[23] Nevertheless, the dialectic can be made more sophisticated, and I hope to improve on that previous work. As we will see in subsequent sections, absolutism can come in two sorts: absolutism in principle and absolutism in practice. I still think that absolutism in principle can be rejected out of hand, but absolutism in practice cannot, and my previous argumentation left this base uncovered. The last two sections of this chapter will, therefore, recognize these different types of absolutism and offer separate arguments in regard to each.

But the second improvement can be made in regard to nonabsolutist theories, and, in particular, the logical space can be more thoroughly exhausted. The earlier work considered utilitarianism, rights-based deontology, virtue theory, social contract theory, and moral pluralism and moral particularism. Some of those treatments bear repetition, but a better strategy than this separation of cases is just to make more comprehensive remarks; it is better to be overarching than piecemeal. So, in this section, I will consider some other moral theories and then offer more general comments about nonabsolutist theories. This first project is so transparent given the broader plan that my discussion can be brief, but stating the case will be useful.

Let us start with virtue theory, the theory of Plato and Aristotle.[24] After a hiatus for two millennia—with the notable exception of the Scottish Enlightenment—virtue theory again became popular in the late twentieth century, perhaps especially toward its end.[25] Ironically, that time period also saw the advent of situationism, which proponents take to inveigh against the psychological plausibility of virtue theory.[26] Nevertheless, we can wonder what those committed to some virtue theory would say about ticking-time-bomb cases. These theories are a little tricky insofar as they tell people how to *be* (namely, virtuous) rather than, directly, what to *do*. It is, presumably, the case that we can at least render this directive adverbially, thus saying that we should act virtuously, though the cultivation of virtue requires a long-term habituation that belies simple questions about individual acts. All that aside, assume that we find a sufficiently virtuous person; would this person torture? Is torture compatible with virtue?

First, let us think about what the virtues are. Plato postulated wisdom, courage, temperance, and justice.[27] Aristotle kept these (albeit with slight taxonomic emendations) and added generosity, pride, good temper, truthfulness, modesty, wittiness, friendliness, modesty, and righteous indignation.[28] Which are relevant to our case? Or, in other words, if the virtuous person has all these character traits, which will influence his decision whether to torture? Probably more than one will come into play. For example, torturing someone is presumably demonstrative of the vice of unpleasantness (which opposes friendliness). Conversely, letting many people die preventable deaths is not very friendly. If the virtuous person wanted to *maximize* his display of friendliness, should he not torture? Similar conflicts probably exist with other virtues.

Maybe the most obvious virtue to invoke is justice. Which conception should we use? Plato proposes that justice is a harmony of the tripartite soul, which is to be governed by the rational element. Aristotle offers a plurality of justices, differentiating the general from the particular, and subdividing the particular into distributive justice and rectificatory justice. I do not see how either Plato's or Aristotle's conceptions are of much use in settling the question before us. If we jump ahead a little more than two thousand years, there might be some promise in the Scottish Enlightenment. Francis Hutcheson, for example, thought that justice consisted in being motivated by universal benevolence.[29] If this is right, we might expect the just person to perform torture for reasons similar to those expressed in §6.1 above. David Hume criticizes Hutcheson's account and provides his own, which is roughly (and perhaps controversially) that justice is an artificial virtue ultimately motivated by self-interest.[30] On Hume's conception, we could refine the example such that the agent was one of the people who would perish in the bomb detonation (e.g., we could stipulate that the bomb was at an unknown location within the building and that the terrorist was willing to become a martyr). Then torture would be in his self-interest, so justice would require that he perform it.

But maybe we are making this too hard by trying to determine which conception of justice is the proper one here or even by assuming that justice would be the principal virtue at stake (whatever that would mean). So let us retreat to the original question: would the virtuous person torture in ticking-time-bomb cases? If this person does not perform torture, many people will die. And the torture of the terrorist will alleviate all these deaths. I do not see any plausible line that could hold that our virtuous person would not engage in this torturing. To be sure, he will be evincing at least some vice through the torture; virtue ethicists sometimes refer to such situations as "tragic dilemmas" (i.e., ones in which vicious behavior will result *regardless* of what the virtuous person chooses to do).[31] We might reasonably suppose that, in such cases, the virtuous person should pursue the least vicious path available, and we might further reasonably suppose that it would be less vicious to perform a single act of torture than to allow many deaths.

To be sure, this conclusion follows from a highly generic virtue ethic, but I take that to be part of its strength. In other words, because it is not following from any idiosyncratic conceptions of individual virtues, it has more power. So I think that this is the right conclusion to draw: the virtue ethicist should allow that the virtuous person should torture in the ticking-time-bomb case, though we can, perhaps, acknowledge that such a case is a tragic dilemma and that complete virtue cannot be displayed regardless of what the virtuous person does. Or else the virtue ethicist could deny this conclusion, thus propounding a virtue ethic that never, under any circumstances, admits of torture. But then this is an explicitly absolutist position and one to which I shall return in the last two sections of this chapter.

Another candidate moral theory is that of the social contract. Despite the recent appeal of the works of John Rawls, David Gauthier, T. M. Scanlon, and others, social contract theory has a rich tradition with roots in Thomas Hobbes, John Locke, David Hume, Jean-Jacques Rousseau, and so on. What stance would social contract theorists take on torture? To be sure, it would depend on the version of the theory that one adopted, and there are substantial differences among competing versions. Nonetheless, social contract theories all share some set of central features, of which the most notable might be "the idea that morality is deeply implicated in the very notion of agreement, and vice versa, so that whether an action is right or wrong must depend on whether the act accords with or violates principles that are, or would be, the object of suitable agreement between equals."[32] Following a distinction proposed by Stephen Darwall, we might broadly categorize social contracts into two broad families, contractarianism and contractualism, depending on how they understand the notion of *equality*: for the contractarian, the equality of the contracting parties is "merely *de facto* and their choice of principles rationally self-interested"; this can be contrasted with contractualism, which proceeds from "an ideal of *reasonable* reciprocity or fairness between *moral equals*."[33] Hobbes offers the classic statement of the contractarians' notion of de facto equality:

> Nature hath made men so equal in the faculties of body and mind as that, though there be found one man sometimes manifestly stronger in body or of quicker mind than another, yet when all is reckoned together the difference between man and man is not so considerable as that one man can thereupon claim to himself any benefit to which another may not pretend as well as he. For as to the strength of body, the weakest has strength enough to kill the strongest, either by secret machination or by confederacy with others that are in the same danger with himself.[34]

Alternatively, contractualists postulate some moral norms that exist antecedently to the contract; these norms often have to do with justice, mutual respect, and/or fairness, norms that Hobbes denies his state of nature.[35]

Since these two families of views have such different commitments, we should look at them individually. Start with contractarianism, in which the parties to the contract will be motivated by nothing other than self-interest and there are no antecedent restrictions in their pursuit of this goal (save for similar motivations by everyone else). On this scheme, there are various ways in which we might approach ticking-time-bomb cases. First, I know that I am not a terrorist, and I know that I might stand to suffer by the terrorist's bomb if torture were not exacted on him. Therefore, it would be in my self-interest to torture the terrorist in the ticking-time-bomb case, and I would push for such provisions in the covenant. Since, as the cases have been stipulated, there are more would-be sufferers from the terrorist's bomb (namely, many) than there are terrorists (namely, one), the popular will would condone torture. Even if, at the time of legislation, I did not *know* that I would not become a terrorist, any sort of reasonable probabilistic projection would sanction my endorsement of torture in the cases under consideration.[36]

This line of reasoning would not be popular among everyone, particularly the contractualists. For one thing, it permits the tyranny of the majority, which contractualists might deem *unfair* (a word lacking in the precontract vocabulary of the contractarian). For another, even if some contractarianism lacked this feature, the contractualist might, nevertheless, object to the dominance that self-interest plays in the theory, whether by imparting some other normative end or else by placing some restriction on pursuit of this one. A standard contractualist move is to introduce some further motivation (e.g., justification of one's reasons to others; cf. Scanlon) or else some further construct, such as Rawls's veil of ignorance and its resulting principles of justice. Given the popularity of Rawls's version, let us focus on it as a plausible contractualist view. The veil of ignorance deprives the contracting parties of any idiosyncratic features that they might use to differentially bias the outcomes of the bargaining process in their favor. For example, Rawls thinks that, if I did not know whether I were male or female, I would be unwilling to legislate in a way that might benefit one group at the expense of the other. The reason, according to Rawls, is the "maximin rule," by which I should try to maximize the position of the worst well-off because I would not want to occupy that position.[37] From behind the veil of ignorance, Rawls holds that we will adopt two principles of justice that will restrict all other substantive legislations we might make for our society. The first principle is that "each person is to have an equal right to the most extensive scheme of basic liberties compatible with a similar scheme of liberties for others," and the second is that "social and economic inequalities are to be arranged so that they are both (a) reasonably expected to be to everyone's advantage, and (b) attached to positions and offices open to all."[38]

There is no reason, in principle, that torture in ticking-time-bomb cases would be impermissible on Rawls's view. His two principles are ordered, which is to say that applications of the second principle are restricted by the first principle. Therefore, we need not worry about the difference principle (namely, 2a) if a case can be made for the permissibility of torture on the first principle. In ticking-time-bomb cases, someone is going to deprived of his right not to be tortured, or else a lot of people are going to die, thus violating their right to life and whatever associated liberties those lives would have otherwise empowered. Rawls asks us to adopt the most extensive scheme of basic liberties consistent with similar extension to all, but we must now choose which liberties are going to be prioritized: the liberty against being tortured or the liberty to life (and whatever other liberties this liberty preserves). Given the conflict, we cannot grant all these liberties to everyone, so we must make choices. Obviously, Rawls rejects utilitarianism,[39] but he clearly wants to maximize the number of liberties afforded to members of society, so long as such liberties can be afforded to all. It is preferable to extend liberties associated with continued life to many even if doing so deprives the terrorist of various liberties (i.e., those of which torture deprives him).

This strategy need not even be motivated by some sort of rights-based utilitarianism; rather, it could take its motivation from a conception in which the liberty to life is, to use Rawls's word, more *extensive* than the liberty from torture. In preserving the liberty to life, we preserve a tremendous number of other liberties, whereas the abrogation of the liberty from torture is more "localized" insofar as it does not deprive the victim of *all* other liberties that he might have otherwise had; death is, surely, maximally deprivational on any liberty calculus. Prioritizing life and its associated liberties need not even violate Rawls's concern about respecting the "separateness of persons" since we could view this decision, not as a sacrifice of the terrorist to the collective, but rather as a conceptual point about what our commitment to maximally extensive liberties requires. Therefore, torture can be justified under at least some contractualist theories. Without even looking at a particular contractualist view (e.g., Rawls's), the point could be made more generally that, whatever precontractual norms exist, they invoke terms (e.g., equality, respect, fairness, etc.) that could license torture over the deaths of many. Or else torture is always incompatible with some particular view, be it contractualist or contractarian. If this latter, then the view is absolutist and will be considered in §§6.4–6.5.

As mentioned at the outset of this section, there are myriad different moral theories; surely, they cannot all be considered in a single chapter. In §§6.1–6.3, we have been concerned with nonabsolutist moral theories, and it would be useful to make a few general remarks about what these all have in common. This is useful, not just as a summary, but rather because it also goes to staving off objections about other (or other versions of) nonabsolutist theories not herein considered.[40] In fact, this simple point almost makes all the preceding discussion extraneous: nonabsolutist theories, *by definition*, do not absolutely prohibit torture. The reasons why they allow torture in some cases and the details that delimit those cases can vary, but such reasons and such cases necessarily exist. Aside from very curious nonabsolutist theories,[41] I assert that any plausible one will license torture in ticking-time-bomb cases. We have already gone through four broad families of views, and all of them led to the same conclusion. Furthermore, there is no good reason to think that, were those views to be slightly different, the conclusion would have changed. And, if it did, we could just adjust the details of the case. The point of these three preceding sections has not done anything to rule out moral theories that categorically oppose torture; rather, it is to see how much of the moral landscape is perfectly compatible with torture in ticking-time-bomb cases.

Absolutist views start to look marginal and radical when compared with this broad swath of moral theory, as, indeed, they are. Let us now consider them directly.

6.4 ABSOLUTISM IN PRINCIPLE

As mentioned in the introduction to this chapter, absolutism with regard to torture can come in two different forms: absolutism in principle and absolutism in practice (henceforth let us designate these *a-principle* and *a-practice*, respectively). The difference between these two is modal: a-principle holds that torture never *could* be justified, whereas a-practice holds that it could, but never *would*, be justified. In other words, a-practice allows that torture could be justified but denies that whatever circumstances are sufficient for this justification—perhaps including those of ticking-time-bomb cases—will be manifest in the real world.[42] By contrast, a-principle denies that such circumstances could even be imagined. In this section, let us consider a-principle, saving a-practice for the next.

First, it bears emphasis that comparatively few people explicitly defend a-principle; even those who do defend absolutism with regard to torture overwhelmingly advance arguments against a-practice.[43] The limited advocacy for a-principle is not surprising given that it is a very extreme position, effectively the most extreme that one could possibly advocate. To wit, a-principle postulates some class of actions that, regardless of circumstances—whether real or imagined—is always impermissible. No view could be more extreme insofar as it is logically impossible to allow torture in any fewer cases. Regardless, some people do defend something like this. For example, consider Kim Lane Scheppele: "I do in fact believe that torture is always and absolutely wrong, given the position we should accord to human dignity, even of terrorists."[44] Or Ben Juratowitch: "Torture is so barbaric that the right to be free from it is never defeasible. However desperate the countervailing circumstances, torture is always wrong and should never occur."[45] Anyone of a sufficient Kantian bent would also defend a-principle since torture treats its victim as a means to our end, operates on a maxim that generates a conflict in will, fails to respect autonomy, and so on; any act with these commitments is categorically impermissible. Even if a-practice is more common than a-principle in the literature, a-principle has its defenders and, therefore, deserves serious consideration.

Second, it is worth noting that one can oppose torture while, at the same time, thinking that a-principle is the wrong way to go. In other words, the forthcoming problems with a-principle hardly result in the permissibility of torture, especially given the availability of a-practice. So, for example, consider Jeff McMahan, who begins his essay by throwing himself in with the camp of "those of us who oppose torture" but continues:

> I believe that the case against torture cannot plausibly take an absolutist form and that effective opposition to torture is ill-served by appeals to unexplicated and ultimately unserviceable notions such as that torture violates human dignity and undermines the perpetrator's humanity. We fail to take the problem of torture sufficiently seriously if we treat it as a simple matter of civilization versus barbarism, or as a choice between respect for human dignity and a collapse into moral degradation and defilement.[46]

It is, therefore, important to recognize the distinction between a-principle and a-practice, and the arguments in this section go against only a-principle; a-practice will be considered in §6.5.

While I will consider deeper theoretical problems with a-principle below, a few more preliminary observations bear interest. First, few—if any—people defend a-principle with regard to anything other than torture.[47] For example, consider killing: who would think that killing is absolutely, under all circumstances, morally wrong? As McMahan points out, such a position is almost incoherent insofar as we can imagine cases where, whatever someone does, an innocent person will be killed.[48] So imagine that person A is dropped onto a panel such that, if he stays on the panel, a blade will be deployed to decapitate person B and that, if A steps off the panel, a gun will fire to kill person C. To say that A acts wrongly by staying on (or getting off) the panel implies that he could have otherwise done better than he did, which is false. Perhaps the incoherence allegation is too strong, and quibbles could be made about this hypothetical. But, even if it is possible not to kill, only extreme pacifists think that killing is absolutely wrong; the rest of us allow for killing in self-defense, out of necessity, in a just war, and so on. Assuming that killing is sometimes justified in practice—and, a fortiori, in principle—then why would torture have such a different moral status?

Certainly, it is not logically inconsistent to think that some acts could be justified in principle while others cannot. But how would this distinction be motivated vis-à-vis killing and torture? Killing is bad, yet there are times when it is, nevertheless, justified. This sounds right. According to a-principle$_{torture}$, torture is bad, and there are no times in which it is justified.[49] Given our endorsement of the statement about killing, the prohibition on torture is curious. One way this could go is to say that torture is (always) worse than killing. If φ is morally justifiable but Ψ is worse than φ, the permissibility of φ tells us nothing about the permissibility of Ψ.[50] Less formally, suppose that it is morally permissible to kill ten people in order to save one hundred others. Killing twenty people is worse than killing ten people, and the permissibility of killing ten people does not directly tell us anything about the permissibility of killing twenty. Perhaps the cutoff for permissibility lies at fifteen killings, thus making the killing of twenty morally impermissible. Or maybe the cutoff is twenty-five lives, thus making the killing of twenty morally permissible. The point is simply that one cannot read off the (im)permissibility of doing something worse given some datum about the permissibility of doing something less bad.

This stratagem offers a way to set a-principle$_{\text{torture}}$ apart from a-principle$_{\text{killing}}$: if torture is always worse than killing, then the rejection of a-principle$_{\text{killing}}$ tells us nothing about the status of a-principle$_{\text{torture}}$. But such an invocation is only as plausible as its supposition that torture is always worse than killing, and this supposition is certainly false. Take a young person with a valuable future and ask whether it is worse to kill this person (painfully) or else to exact some comparatively minor degree of torture (e.g., pull out a single fingernail). Build in whatever psychological features you like such that this person is constituted to recover quickly, not to hold grudges, and so on. Or even stipulate there to be some pill that makes the victim completely forget about the torture and, instead, form some false yet blissful memory of whatever would have been happening during the time he was tortured; the lack of such pills in practice is wholly irrelevant to a-principle. This person's death constitutes a great moral wrong, while his forgotten torture and subsequent pleasure are certainly a lesser moral wrong, if not a moral good.

But we really do not even need the fantastic cases, even if they are open to us in responding to a-principle. Rather, all we have to consider is a comparatively minor case of torture as against a terribly grievous death; fill in these details however your intuitions and moral theory suggest. I submit that it is completely implausible that no instance of torture is less wrong than the worst death.[51] If this is true, then torture is not always worse than death, and our nonabsolutism regarding killing comes into conflict with a-principle$_{\text{torture}}$. It is possible to resolve this tension by jettisoning the former, but that one is so well entrenched in our moral sensibilities, laws, and so on that we should have a lot of confidence in it. Torture, on the other hand, is such a sensationalized, emotionally driven, and current debate that endorsement of a-principle$_{\text{torture}}$ quite probably owes to various affective and other biases. Regardless, apart from independent consideration of a-principle$_{torture}$, we already have reasons to find it dubious given its relationship to some of our other moral commitments.

That said, there are independent reasons to think that a-principle$_{torture}$ is implausible, and these reasons attach more generally to any a-principle. Consider any candidate moral value by which to construct a moral theory. Suppose that there is some act, φ, that (maximally)[52] promotes its preeminent value V in some case C. Every moral theory other than a-principle treats this supposition in a straightforward way and endorses φ. A-principle, however, needs it to be the case that φ is ruled out a priori (i.e., without consideration of the details of C). There are two ways this exclusion could go. First, a-principle could deny that φ promotes V (in C). So the idea would be that, necessarily, φ is incompatible with whatever value undergirds our moral theory. Or, second, a-principle could say that, even if φ promotes V (in C), φ is, nevertheless, impermissible.

This second response borders on the nonsensical insofar as some theory's commitments preclude action to promote its own preeminent value. It even seems contradictory insofar as the theory espouses V while, at the same time, obstructing its realization (i.e., disavowing φ, which promotes V). This is not to object to there being *other* theoretical commitments that φ might compromise, but that just forces us to elaborate the argument. For example, maybe φ promotes V_1 while, at the same time, diminishing V_2; imagine that these are both values of some particular a-principle. Now there are theoretical resources to oppose φ, namely, its impact on V_2. But all this shows is that our first example was overly simplistic since it postulated only a single value for the theory. If we allow that φ promotes $V_1, V_2, \ldots,$ V_n (i.e., all the values of a-principle), then it will still be curious that φ is prohibited.

However, the first response—that is, the denial that φ promotes V (in C)—cannot be rejected out of hand. We could even create a moral theory such that this response comes out right. For example, suppose that human dignity is our highest value, and suppose that torture violates human dignity. Furthermore, imagine that quick and painless deaths by a terrorist's bomb do not violate human dignity. We could imagine that these deaths are not conducive to overall happiness, do violate their victims' rights, and so on but, nevertheless, do not force them into a sense of self-betrayal—whether mental or physical—that is undignified (cf. §4.3 above). On this account, torture would be ruled out. But now let us change the details of the case. Imagine that the deaths would not be quick or painless but rather that the bomb deploys a debilitating—but nonlethal—biological agent that compromises the dignity of its victims.[53] Still, a-principle cannot allow torture even if it ultimately promotes the retention of dignity.

The response that torture could never promote dignity is now forestalled by the stipulations of the case. (Remember that, on a-principle, it is completely beside the point whether the case is empirically plausible, though this one certainly seems to be.)

Ultimately, a-principle needs to be predicated on some value that torture necessarily cannot promote; it is virtually impossible to think of what such a value would be, save "unexplicated and ultimately unserviceable" Kantian values like those that McMahan indicted above.[54] About the only other things that would clearly work are completely ad hoc, such as some value to minimize torture. But why would *that* matter? Either torture is wrong because it transgresses against some fundamental moral value(s), or else it *represents* that fundamental moral value. This latter proposal cannot work insofar as it precludes any substantive answer of the form "torture is wrong because *P*," where *P* is anything other than circularly about torture. And nobody holds anything like that regardless. Rather, torture is (prima facie) wrong because it causes pain, violates rights, assaults dignity, or whatever. On any of these accounts, there are at least in-principle justifications for torture, thus making a-principle untenable. Having now seen various problems with a-principle, let us turn to its less ambitious complement, a-practice.

6.5 ABSOLUTISM IN PRACTICE

A-practice, unlike a-principle, makes substantive claims about the world. While a-principle holds that there are no circumstances under which torture *could* be justified, a-practice holds that there are no circumstances under which torture *would* be justified; this former claim is true or false a priori, whereas the latter is true or false a posteriori. In other words, to argue that torture is never actually justified requires some engagement with the world, or at least it does to the extent that a-practice means to be saying anything different from a-principle. To wit, a-principle also holds that torture is never actually justified, though this *actually* is redundant insofar as torture never could have been justified, whether actually (i.e., in the real world) or in imagined cases.

Various people defend a-practice, but a useful formulation is that by Daniel Statman, who argues that "the moral danger of torture is so great, and the moral benefits so doubtful, that in practice torture should be considered as prohibited absolutely."[55] I choose this formulation among others because it usefully sets his view apart from a-principle insofar as the conclusion pertains to the implementation of torture *in practice*. It is perfectly consistent with Statman's thesis that there are fantastic cases wherein torture could be justified but that none of those cases would ever attain in the real world. Henry Shue writes something similar, slightly taking himself to task for his earlier work: "I now take the most moderate position on torture, the position nearest the middle of the road, feasible *in the real world*: never again."[56] Per the observation above, it is possible that Statman and Shue actually endorse a-principle, but then why do they talk about "practice" and the "real world" in their papers? Given their choice of language, a-practice is the more suggested reading. Regardless, this section is not necessarily about either of their views in particular; rather, it is about a class of views that emphasize practice instead of theory, and theirs are merely likely candidates.

I think of a-practice as making empirical claims about the world as opposed to being committed to any particular moral principles more generally. In other words, a-practice does not have any moral commitments other than the one that torture cannot be justified in the real world; such a view tells us nothing about the moral permissibility of, for example, abortion or euthanasia. This is in contrast with the views considered in §§6.1–6.3, which were independent moral theories whose commitments we could evaluate vis-à-vis torture. Utilitarianism, for example, says that we should maximize total aggregate happiness: we can ask whether torture (in some particular case) does so. Not so for a-practice, which does not tell us anything other than that torture will never be justified in the real world. Aside from this sole moral commitment of a-practice, it is otherwise compatible with a wide range of moral theories. For example, there are utilitarian defenses of a-practice,[57] and there could be myriad other defenses of it as well: torture will never promote rights, virtues, the social contract, or whatever else takes moral priority. It is worth noting that this is not meant to be a criticism of a-practice; in fact, I take it to be a strength.

In light of the title of this chapter, does the defender of a-practice think that we should torture in ticking-time-bomb cases? For such a person, this question is just not interesting since it (allegedly) gains no traction with the world. What matters is not whether we should torture in ticking-time-bomb cases but rather that there are no such cases. Ethics is about action, and we can act only in the world, not in imagined hypotheticals. In §5.2 above, I defended ticking-time-bomb methodology against its critics, but the criticism I now mean to engage is not concerned with the methodology per se but rather tries to render that methodology impotent by appeal to empirical facts.

In response, there are several important points to develop; I shall start here and continue in the next chapter. First, a-practice is only as plau-sible as its empirical claim that torture will *never* promote our core moral values. It is very hard to show that such a thesis is true. For example, the ivory-billed woodpecker was thought to have been extinct since 1944, only to turn up in an Arkansas swamp in 2005. None of these woodpeckers was seen for over sixty years, and the received view was that they were gone forever. It turns out that the birds were still around and the naysayers were wrong. The point is that it takes only one case to falsify a negative ex-istential claim, whether it be a sighting of a believed-to-be-extinct bird or some constellation of improbable features leading to justifiable torture.

The defender of a-practice is, doubtless, going to say that this is all hopelessly confused. His claim is, not that justifiable torture is as elusive as the ivory-billed woodpecker, but rather that justifiable torture *cannot* exist (in the real world) because the benefits are too low and/or the costs too high. While it is *possible* for a rare bird to be spotted, it is not possible to justify an act of torture. But, as I read this response, it just denies my premise, namely, that the empirical possibility of justified torture cannot be ruled out. My position clearly has the dialectical advantage insofar as its only claim is that I allow that such and so *might* happen (in the real world) and that, if so, torture could be permissible. My opponent has to say that this is false, but such empirical omniscience is untenable from the philosophical armchair.

The better way to go is quasi-historically: to say that we have never seen a ticking-time-bomb case in the real world, have no reason to think that there ever will be one, and so on. Sure, it is *possible* that such a case will attain, though we have no good reason to think that it will and, indeed, many good reasons to think that it will not. On this sort of inductive ap-proach, we have a lot more confidence that we could find an ivory-billed woodpecker than that torture could be justified; there might have been some reason to hold out hope in the former case (e.g., ornithologists have sometimes made mistakes), but there is no such reason in the latter.

These are empirical claims rarely supported by actual empirical evi-dence. That said, it is probably more fair for the defender of torture to owe an actual ticking-time-bomb case than for the critic to have to show that there have not been any, and I will return to this in the next chapter. The point at present is merely that the empirical details matter. And, in fact, a-practice rarely takes this challenge very seriously. We hear plausible-sounding claims about institutional requirements, potential for abuse, the ineffectiveness of torture, and so on, but these are almost always of-fered without any serious empirical engagement. Disparaging remarks about torture in Argentina and Abu Ghraib are also common, yet these are about as far from ticking-time-bomb cases as one could get and still be talking about torture. Nevertheless, the empirical work is sometimes taken quite seriously, and Darius Rejali's painstaking and magisterial work is the best example.[58] As impressive as Rejali's book is, however, it makes hardly any reference to the relevant philosophical literature. This is not necessarily a criticism of his work, particularly insofar as he has different goals and comes from a different disciplinary orientation. Rather, the point is that, at the end of the day, the empirical and the philosophical need to be integrated.

Let me make a few final—or at least transitioning—remarks about a-practice. I certainly think that this is the best way to go in opposing torture; as §§6.1–6.3 indicated, it is just not very hard to justify torture in theory. Rather, the rub comes when the move is made to practice, and a-practice is unequivocal in that regard: no torture in practice, ever. This section has largely been preliminary given what is to come in the next chapter, but two central conclusions bear emphasis. First, there is strong antecedent pressure against the thesis that torture will *never* be justified for the simple reason that we do not know all the scenarios we will ultimately encounter. It seems to me that the more plausible route is to leave open the possibility of justifiable torture while being skeptical and protective about its application. A-practice is not content with this less ambitious approach, and, for me at least, therein lies one of its faults. Second, a-practice is highly committed to several empirical assumptions, whether about the nonexistence of ticking-time-bomb cases, the low benefits of torture, its high costs, or whatever. All these assumptions have to be examined and defended and in ways that are sufficiently attuned to the appropriate philosophical issues; suffice it to say that I have been dissatisfied how this has been carried out in various literatures. These two conclusions, however, are about the structure of a-practice, and substantive engagement with its empirical commitments is still due. That engagement will be the project of the next chapter.

PART III

TORTURE AND
THE REAL WORLD

7

Empirical
Objections to
Torture

This chapter begins the third part of the book wherein we transition from abstract and theoretical discussions about torture to empirical and pragmatic considerations thereof. To be sure, the treatment of these latter issues will be more abstract and theoretical than some would like, but it is, nevertheless, important for a book about torture—even one written by a philosopher—to make some serious engagement with the real world. The second part of the book was important in laying out various conceptual, methodological, and normative arguments, but those arguments have not yet extended beyond the philosophical realm. The last three chapters aim to make this extension by thinking seriously about how the previous philosophical work can bear on questions about the actual practice of torture. To that end, this chapter will be about empirical objections to torture. The next will be about the legislative and judicial pragmatics of torture—with an emphasis on torture warrants and the necessity defense—since, if torture is to be allowed, something should be said about how that works out practically. The final chapter is about the limits of torture; any defense of torture needs to be carefully circumscribed, and this last chapter is an important conclusion to that project.

In the present chapter, we shall return to empirical objections to torture; some of these were alluded to—and promptly dismissed—in earlier chapters. The project then was about ticking-time-bomb cases, so real-world considerations were just not relevant. But, for that discussion to get any grip on the actual world, ticking-time-bomb cases need not be philosophical fiction. Or, if they are, more needs to be said about how conclusions in those cases bear on the real world. My proposal in this chapter is to consider various stock objections to the actual use of torture. As I said at the end of the last chapter, these often tend to be deployed rather uncritically, though they nevertheless warrant discussion. In particular, something should be said about the efficacy and reliability of torture (§7.1), the institutional requirements for torture (§7.2), the nefarious spread of torture (§7.3), and whether there are better alternatives to torture (§7.4). In each of these discussions, let us frame them against the associated contentions made by critics regarding the nontransferability of ticking-time-bomb cases to the real world. The last two sections of the chapter consider whether the proponent of torture must come up with real-world ticking-time-bomb cases to defend the plausibility of his theory (§7.5) as well as what such cases might be (§7.6).

7.1 TORTURE DOESN'T WORK

One of the central assumptions of ticking-time-bomb methodology is that torture will be applied to a guilty terrorist who, once tortured, will readily divulge information that can be used to disarm a lethal threat in which he is complicit. Regarding the efficacy and reliability of torture, this assumption is collectively predicated on the following: that we have apprehended the responsible terrorist; that torture will produce valuable information; and, conversely, that torture will not produce confusing misinformation. In other words, there are various ways in which ticking-time-bomb assumptions can go wrong. First, we might have the wrong person, whether an innocent person altogether or else a person without actionable intelligence in the relevant regard (even if a terrorist overall); a related worry is that we would keep torturing someone once he has already given us all the information he had such that this torture was superfluous. Second, the terrorist, once tortured, might not reveal any valuable intelligence. Or worse, third, he might actually degrade the status of our countermeasures by giving us false intelligence, thus leading us to use our resources less well than we would have done had we not tortured at all.

Since critics have pressed all these issues, serious discussion is warranted; and I will turn to that shortly. But, first, it is important to clarify what the state of the dialectic is meant to be at this stage, particularly insofar as at least some critics have lost the thread. Granting that any of the three concerns raised in the previous paragraph are reasonable, what is supposed to follow? Or, to put it another way, when people say that "torture doesn't work," what is that supposed to mean? Assuming that the metric for whether torture works is whether it elicits valuable intelligence, an implausible position is that torture *never* works. I will return to this in §7.6, but it has to be the case that at least one person has, under torture, disclosed lifesaving information; whether the torture was necessary for that information is, for now, irrelevant. It also has to be the case that torture does not *always* work as there are surely cases where the victim of torture has failed to disclose valuable information. If the claim is that "torture never works," that can be rejected out of hand, but it is a straw man to saddle the defender of torture with the alternative claim that "torture always works" since nobody would say that anyway. Let us therefore agree that torture sometimes works, which seems the most reasonable empirical position.

What implications does that have for the permissibility of torture? In other words, if torture is not always efficacious, do we have less reason to endorse it? And the answer, of course, is yes: as the efficacy of torture goes down, the moral benefits thereof fall. Consider, for simplicity, a variant on the standard ticking-time-bomb case:

> *Red Sweatshirt.* Our intelligence reveals that a terrorist has just set up a bomb in a crowded building and has exited wearing a red sweatshirt. Law enforcement sets up a perimeter and starts to canvas the area; two men in red sweatshirts are apprehended, both of whom deny any knowledge of terroristic activity. Run the rest of the story as in standard ticking-time-bomb cases, the adjustment being that the bomb can be disarmed only if both men, one of whom is innocent, are tortured.

Is this torture permissible? Surely, it is worse to torture a guilty person and an innocent one than to torture only a guilty one, but I maintain that this torture could still be justified if there are enough people at risk in the building.

It is worth noting that the above hypothetical is synchronic rather than diachronic, but nothing changes—for me at least—if the considerations are diachronic. In other words, we were meant to imagine torturing two people at the same time in order to dispel some single threat (at that time). Change the case to one in which there are two threats (at different times) and we apprehend one suspect for each threat. Our intelligence is hardly infallible, and it is certain that one of these people is innocent; torture against the innocent one will not "work," and one of those threats will, therefore, be actualized. Should we torture in both cases if such torture ensures the elimination of only one threat? Again, I think that the answer is yes, so long as the other moral considerations are of sufficient magnitude. In either of these cases, it is worth recognizing that none of the arguments from the last chapter hangs on only the guilty person being tortured, even if that is the circumstance that ticking-time-bomb cases ask us to envision.

Regardless, my contention is that the fact that torture does not always elicit valuable information does not rule out the possibility of justified torture. So what is supposed to be going on when critics allege that torture does not work? As above, nobody said that it always worked: the contention can be only that torture could work often enough that the benefits still outweigh the costs. Ineffective torture increases the costs and moderates the benefits, but, if the benefits are high enough, those costs are still covered. At any rate, this discussion has been broadly methodological as it is not obvious what the (sometimes) inefficacy of torture really could mean for the moral debate. If the point is just meant to be that the moral calculus is more complicated than ticking-time-bomb cases suggest, then I welcome it. If it is somehow supposed to be that torture is, therefore, unjustified, this does not follow. In either case, let us now move on to some of the specifics.

Darius Rejali poses the key question as this: Can torture be precise, scientific, and professionally administered and yield accurate information in a timely manner? He then breaks out this question as comprising the following component questions: Can torture be scientific? Can one produce pain in a controlled manner? Does technology help torturers in this respect? Can pain be administered respectfully and professionally? Can interrogators separate deceptive from accurate information when it is given to them? How accurately do cooperative prisoners remember information after torture? Does this investigative method yield better results than others normally at an army's disposal? If not, does this investigative method yield better results under conditions of constrained time? In the following discussion, he contends that the answers to each question "give no comfort to advocates of torture, no matter how they qualify the questions. Apologists often assume that torture works, and all that is left is the moral justification. If torture does not work, then their apology is irrelevant. Deciding whether one *ought* or *ought not* to drive a car is a pointless debate if the car has no gas."[1]

I refer the interested reader to Rejali's ensuing discussion, all of which is carefully researched and quite compelling. My strategy is not to rebut any particular points that he makes but rather to deny that his conclusion follows from his premises. Before doing that, it will do some good to at least get a sense of some of the discussion on offer just so that we have a shared starting point. First, Rejali contends that pain is a highly complex phenomenon and implies that academic discussions of torture fail to understand these complexities.[2] For example, he denies that pain is a simple metric that can just be "increased" as the torturer needs: bodies are desensitized to pain; increases in pain stimulus portend no straightforward relationship to the pain actually experienced by the victim; humans differ unpredictably in their ability to endure extreme pain; there are various pain thresholds, all of which bear complicated relationships to each other (e.g., of sensation, of recognition as pain, of tolerance, of endurance); and so on. His ultimate conclusion is that

> the notion of a science of torture rests on simple folklore about pain. This folklore teaches that all people avoid pain and seek pleasure, more injury produces more pain, and so it is simply a matter of calibrating the quantity of pain for each individual. These views do not make any sense in torture. The people interrogators most want to question are also those most likely to embrace and resist pain. More injury often produces less pain, especially over the course of an interrogation. Pain is not an undifferentiated sensation that is amenable to a scale. If there turns out to be a science of torture one day, it will look nothing like common folklore imagines it.[3]

Again, let us grant everything that he has said. Torture is messy, and we cannot calculate ex ante how much pain will be needed to break some particular terrorist, much less how to deploy that quantum of pain. Surely, torture would be an easier affair with such knowledge, but it hardly follows that the lack thereof makes torture impermissible. Torture engenders pain, and—especially given time constraints—pain could be the most efficacious way to bring about the disclosure of lifesaving information. Rejali seems to think that a science of torture is necessary for its moral justification, but I simply disagree. All that matters is that some terrorist will not surrender the information absent the threat of torture coupled with the corollary that torture might lead to the release of that information; surely both these premises are straightforwardly true. As the associated probabilities fall (cf. "might"), then torture becomes less advisable. But, given the potential value of the intelligence, I submit that they do not even need to be that high in the first place.

Rejali's third and fourth questions are less central than the first two. His discussion of technology effectively just reiterates his point that torture is not scientific, which we have already discussed. If technology is just meant to offer new and creative ways to inflict pain (e.g., magnetos and stun guns), then it does not change the basic structure of the torture debate. Some technologies, however, really do have the potential to be transformational. Consider, for example, functional magnetic resonance imaging (fMRI); fMRI might be usable as a polygraph to determine whether those under torture are providing misinformation, either to mislead or else just for reprieve from interrogation. Whether the ordeal of torture compromises the efficacy of these diagnostics would hardly get research support from institutional review boards, but we can surely suspect that various government agencies are quite interested in the answer.

Can pain be administered professionally and respectfully? With many lives hanging in the balance, I am not sure that this question should be taking priority. Nevertheless, Rejali raises at least two important points that deserve mention: torture leads to brutality and deskilling.[4] The key here is *leads to*, which identifies a different focus in Rejali's book than mine. In particular, he is deeply concerned with pervasive, institutionalized torture and spends much of the book discussing problems thereof. By contrast, my focus is on exceptional cases rather than normalized ones. This bears notice, though I will talk about it more in §§7.2 and 7.5 and chapter 9. For me, torture does not "lead to" anything substantial because the cases are too infrequent. For example, Rejali worries that rivalries between interrogators will lead each of them to try to outdo the other or else that coercive interrogation undermines other professional skills (e.g., why do the fingerprinting and other processing when you have a bat?).[5] But imagine that torture is rare; for the sake of imagination, suppose that the U.S. government were to deploy it against ten suspected terrorists per year. If Rejali's worry that police forces will forget how to fingerprint because they just go ahead with torture is taken seriously—and I doubt that it could be—then it is a nonstarter because the (in)frequency of torture cannot get the worry off the ground. An analogous point could be made about brutality or any of the other systematic concerns he has in the associated discussion.

The fifth and sixth questions again get to the nuts and bolts about the efficacy of torture: Can interrogators spot the truth, and how well do tortured victims remember relevant information? For torture to be effective, we want the victims to give accurate information, and we also want the interrogators to be able to recognize misinformation. Rejali argues that interrogators barely do better than chance in identifying lies and, in some cases, do worse.[6] But what is supposed to follow from this? Imagine two cases, one in which a terrorist is not tortured and chooses not to disclose the truth and one in which the terrorist is tortured and reveals either good or bad intelligence, though we do not know which. The problem with Rejali's argument is the baseline: it is bad that we might get misinformation, but that does not tell the whole story. Rather, it is better that we *might* be getting actionable intelligence than that we surely get no intelligence at all. There could be costs of bad intelligence, such as when we move our security forces to the wrong place, thus wasting resources. But, even if we incorporate those risks into our intelligence calculus, the options are wasting some resources and having a chance at saving lives or else not having a chance at saving those lives at all; the former could easily come out as superior to the latter.[7]

The complementary worry to intelligence officers not recognizing the truth is those under torture being unable to offer it. For example, imagine that we are after the details of some attack, the coordinates of which happen to be 48.41° north latitude and 114.34° west longitude. That is a lot of numbers to remember, and there is no doubt that torture would make it harder to produce them; surely, torture is traumatic, degrades the recall powers of its victims, and so on. But, if the terrorist would have had access to that information in the first place, he surely would have known that the target was Whitefish, Montana, so the exact coordinates are really irrelevant, and the city's name is simple enough to remember. Would he be able to remember whether the bomb was at 123 Central Avenue, 213 Central Avenue, or 312 Central Avenue? Maybe not, and this would leave local law enforcement with some work to do. As it turns out, however, the 100 block is much more crowded than the 300 block, so they might reasonably suspect the ill-intentioned terrorist to have planted the bomb on the former rather than the latter. Nobody suggested that torture was infallible, just that it might, in some cases, be our best option. And, regardless, if the options are the choice between a tortured terrorist scrambling some of the details and letting people die, the former could well be the way to go. Finally, pace Rejali's worries about the science of torture, it is at least the case that some forms of torture will be more or less psychologically debilitating than others or else that reasonable recovery periods will allow for psychological reconstitution. Without presupposing some perfect system in this regard, it can, nevertheless, be recognized that we will torture somewhat better or worse in regard to this metric by recognizing the mental degradation of those under torture.

Finally, Rejali wonders whether torture is comparatively advisable given alternatives available to the intelligence community, whether in general or when time is a factor. More broadly, he thinks that public cooperation through the recruitment of informants is the most successful way to combat terrorist threats;[8] this is true in virtue of the low costs (e.g., no torture), higher reliability of information, and so on. This is fine as far as it goes, and I certainly agree that we should try to recruit informants as opposed to torturing rapaciously. That said, this line is silent about the cases wherein we do not have any informants and time is too short to find any. In response, Rejali argues that torture would not work under time constraints anyway since "real torture—not the stuff of television—takes days, if not weeks."[9] Stress and duress tactics, for example, take a while to elicit information, should they ultimately be effective at all. But, surely, there are myriad forms of torture that hardly take any time at all (e.g., electroshock, beating), so Rejali's comments are curious. Regardless, the point needs to be only that torture operates on a faster timetable than the alternatives and that we can reasonably suppose it to be more expedient than building up a network of informants. Torture does not need to be instantly effective for it to be better than the alternatives.

Whether we torture—as opposed to doing something else—depends on the nature of the threat. Focusing on the temporal element, let us say that torture either does or does not stand in the relevant time frame with regard to the threat. For example, following Rejali, suppose that torture (usually) takes days to generate actionable intelligence. If the bomb is going to go off in days (as opposed to hours), then should we torture? A few days could be enough time to give us at least some confidence that torture would work while giving us less confidence that its alternatives would (e.g., building informant networks). Therefore, torture could be the best option. Alternatively, suppose that the bomb will go off in hours rather than days and that torture is less effective on this timetable. Should we torture? Supposing that we lack meaningful alternatives, we are sadly back in the position of torturing such that we might save lives or else not torturing and ensuring that we do not. Assuming that there is some reasonable chance that the torture would work, then I prefer the first option. It is worth emphasizing that nothing anyone has said denies that this possibility is reasonable; Rejali's own writing just suggests the possibility to be far from certain. The probabilities obviously matter, but there is nothing disingenuous in supposing those probabilities to be nonnegligible such that torture could still be justified when there are enough lives in the balance.

There are various reasons to be skeptical about the certainty that torture will elicit actionable intelligence. In ticking-time-bomb cases, this certainty is stipulated, but, in the real world, things are much more complicated. Rejali offers an important contribution in articulating various reasons to doubt the efficacy and reliability of actual torture, but my contention is that nothing he says changes the fundamental moral calculus or shows torture to be categorically unjustified. Again, his target is principally that of pervasive, institutionalized torture, but that is simply not the sort of torture that I defend. Even in exceptional applications, I can allow that torture does not always work, but, first, nobody ever said it did, and, second, it does not need to *always* work in order for it to be morally justifiable in *some* cases. Having now discussed this extension of ticking-time-bomb thinking to the real world, let me now turn to institutionalization.

7.2 TORTURE REQUIRES INSTITUTIONS

A second class of criticisms against the real-world implementation of torture invokes the failure of ticking-time-bomb cases to recognize essential institutional infrastructure. Ticking-time-bomb cases have it that we just "go torture" the terrorist. But how? Where? Who inflicts the torture? Where did this person learn his craft? Is there oversight of the process? If so, by whom? And so on. The complaint is that torture does not just appear ex nihilo but rather requires the existence of various institutions. Once we recognize these institutional requirements, then the costs side of the torture ledger starts to look a lot more pronounced. No longer are we simply absorbing the one-off torture of a terrorist, but rather we must acknowledge that such torture is possible only if a wide range of other costs are borne, whether social, economic, or moral.

Central to these criticisms is the contention that the institutional costs exist even if torture is rare; should that not be the case, then the criticisms cannot indict the position that torture is licensed only in exceptional cases. For example, consider Jean Maria Arrigo, who makes this point explicit:

> The use of sophisticated torture techniques by a trained staff entails the problematic institutional arrangement I have laid out: physician assistance; cutting edge, secret biomedical research for torture techniques unknown to the terrorist organization and tailored to the individual captive for swift effect; well-trained torturers, quickly accessible at major locations; pre-arranged permissions from the courts because of the urgency; rejection of independent monitoring due to security issues; and so on. These institutional arrangements will have to be in place, with all their unintended and accumulating consequences, *however rarely* terrorist suspects are tortured.[10]

Let us set aside the issue of training for torturers until later; enough people are worried about these sorts of institutional requirements that dedicated discussion is warranted. In general, however, my response to the institutionalization objections is twofold: first, I deny that we need as much institutional apparatus as critics allege, and, second, even if we did, we can either accept the institutions as a necessary cost or else make do as well as we can without them should those costs be too high. This second response is more broadly theoretical, however, so let us start with Arrigo's arguments. In doing so, I propose to use a paper other than the one from which the quote given above derives; this other paper, coauthored with Vittorio Bufacchi, more neatly designates the institutions allegedly in play.[11] In particular, Arrigo and Bufacchi maintain that torture requires the complicity of the following establishments: medical, scientific, police and military, and legal.

There is little doubt that medical personnel have been used to develop more efficacious interrogation patterns. For example, psychologists at Guantánamo were organized into "behavioral science consultation teams" (BSCTs, or "biscuits") that advised on interrogations. Medical personnel have, presumably, also been used to resuscitate those suffering the ills of hostile interrogations, sometimes such that those interrogations can be thereafter resumed. I have written elsewhere on the moral status of these collaborations,[12] but the present discussion is, instead, simply about institutions rather than medical ethics. Are medical personnel *necessary* for torture? In a straightforward way, the answer is obviously no: the practice of torture does not require—either logically or pragmatically—the presence of medical personnel. The fact that medical personnel have been complicit in torture does not show that the medical establishment is essential for torture any more than the use of a book to prop a door open shows that the book was essential to keep the door from closing.

The relevant issue is not what is required for torture but rather what is required to torture "well." Even granting that medical personnel increase the efficacy of torture, it does not follow that torture would not be reasonably effective without them. Were some suspect to be rendered unconscious by an overzealous interrogator, actionable intelligence would be less likely to be ascertained in an expedient way. While this gives us reason to want some medical personnel on hand to revive the detainee—either for his health or for our ends—it hardly means that an entire medical *establishment* is needed to ensure the efficacy of torture. Imagine, for example, that we have somewhere on the order of ten torture sites set up around the world and that we want each of those sites to be staffed with a few medical personnel (physicians, psychologists, etc.). If we assign, say, three medical personnel to each site, then this amounts to only thirty medical personnel *worldwide*. Not much of an institution. Allowing these thirty to collaborate (e.g., through teleconference and/or videoconference) ensures that the medical bases can be adequately covered. Or, to the extent that they are not, more will be said below.

The second institution identified by Bufacchi and Arrigo is scientific: some group needs to develop the techniques that will be used for torture, particularly technological correlates thereof. In §7.1, for example, I suggested that fMRI might be used to ensure the honesty of the suspect under torture, but there are a range of problems with this proposal. For one, the duress of torture might compromise the integrity of fMRI results, though we would not know whether that is true until some scientist figures it out. And it could be even worse than that insofar as institutional oversight would have to license this research, thus further multiplying the resources that would, ultimately, be required to support torture.

There are a few things to say in response. First, much of the scientific research that ultimately contributes to torture need not originally be undertaken for that reason. Tasers, for example, were first developed for police as a nonlethal way to subdue aggressive suspects; now they provide one sort of off-the-shelf technology that can be used in torture.[13] In this case, it would be inappropriate to account for the associated researchers on torture's institutional ledger since their research had nothing (directly) to do with torture. It is not as if these people would have been off developing cures for malaria, cures that were, ultimately, held up for research into torture. That scenario would reasonably give us pause since limited institutional resources could have been used in some other (and potentially better) way, but the disanalogy with the Taser is straightforward insofar as Taser research was meant to serve as a legitimate aid in law enforcement. If that research was later deployed for use in torture, it was done so without any additional cost and, indeed, without any (direct) support from the scientific community.

The second and third responses are ones that will reverberate throughout this discussion. The former holds that the institutional costs could be justified, in which case the objection just has us adjust our balance sheets without changing our conclusions. So, while the Taser research might be freely appropriated for torture, it could be hard to determine whether fMRI results would break down given the duress of torture unless we specifically assigned researchers to study that (i.e., to directly involve scientists in torture research). If the advantages of this sort of research are high enough, then the associated costs could be justified. If the advantages are more moderate, then we might just have to forsake them given the costs. More on this below.

Next, Bufacchi and Arrigo point to police and military infrastructures, all of which would have to be reconfigured to support torture; there could also be further psychological effects on those demographics who directly participate in torture. Throughout their article, the authors conflate the notions of *exceptional torture* and *normalized torture*, though that conflation bears particular emphasis in this regard. For example, they write: "Police departments have struggled for decades with the overwhelming bad consequences of coercive interrogation."[14] But I am not proposing that police departments torture or even that the entire military establishment be involved. Surely there are high institutional costs on either of these proposals, which is why nobody has ever made them. Again, we are considering torture under rare and exceptional cases, not as some sort of quotidian practice in every precinct or on every military base.

Something should be said more in the way of specifics, however, and this would be a good time to offer some discussion in that regard. Remember that Arrigo's earlier work postulated the need for torturers to be "quickly accessible at major locations."[15] This sounds right; note that such a commitment is a far cry from having torture extend throughout all levels of law enforcement and military. As suggested above, we might countenance ten U.S. torture sites throughout the world. If three of these were domestic—one on each coast plus one around St. Louis—then no apprehended suspect would be more than two to three hours by plane from the nearest site. The other seven sites could be strategically placed around the world in ways sensitive to security needs (e.g., a couple in the Middle East, none in Oceania). If the local circumstances do not provide for such a site—which we both could and have run as black sites (e.g., secret prisons)—then arrangements could be made on carriers in international waters. Such sites would be fully secured, and the U.S. military would stand to defend them. All told, this hardly adds up to the extensive institutionalization that critics decry: there are a small number of sites with correspondingly limited personnel requirements.

Bufacchi and Arrigo go on to discuss legal institutions, but I will return to that topic in the next chapter and, therefore, defer it for now. However, before moving on to more general remarks regarding institutional requirements for torture, the issue of torturer training should be addressed; this is one of the most common institutional requirements lamented by critics of torture. For example, consider Jessica Wolfendale, who contends: "The scope and training to produce the torturer needed in the ticking bomb scenario raises serious questions about the legitimacy of these kinds of arguments for the use of torture. . . . [T]his training cannot be neatly contained within the parameters of the ticking bomb scenario because permitting torture in these cases requires *already* having a well-established training regime for torturers."[16] Similar is Henry Shue: "Torture is not for amateurs—successful torturers need to be real 'pros,' and no one becomes a 'pro' overnight. At a minimum, one must practice—perhaps do research, be mentored by the still more experienced. In short, torture needs a bureaucracy, with apprentices and experts, of the kind that torture has in fact always had. . . . Torture is an institution."[17]

It is most certainly false that torturers *have to be* "real 'pros'"; the history of torture is rife with examples of anything but. Torturers are often far from professional, particularly in any robust sense of the word: they do not have professional associations, promulgated codes of ethics, or any of the other hallmarks of professionalism. The only way that this claim could be plausible is if it were read to mean that the best, most idealized torturers were ones who had a lot of practice, training, and mentorship. But maybe we simply cannot have torturers of that sort. Given the rarity with which I would propose torture, a lot of these training opportunities will simply not be available, though there might be approximations thereof (e.g., recordings, simulations, etc.).

My real objection, however, has to do with this dichotomy between trained and untrained torturers, which I take to be spurious. Wolfendale, for example, writes: "It would not do to take an ordinary soldier and make him torture a terrorist suspect at the last minute. One has only to look at the incompetence of the guards at Abu Ghraib (they took *photos*) to see the danger of allowing mere amateurs to torture prisoners." But this saddles her opposition with the completely implausible position that ordinary soldiers or prison guards are all that the intelligence community has access to without creating a cadre of professional and dedicated torturers. Of course, we should not have privates or reservists (cf. Lynndie England) doing this sort of work, but nobody said that we should. Ironically, Wolfendale acknowledges this on the next page: "In the real world, most torturers are soldiers or military policemen who have been trained in elite units."[18] This certainly sounds more promising and is a far cry from Abu Ghraib guards. Torturers should, therefore, be drawn, not from the general enlisted population, but rather from special forces like Delta Force, Green Berets, or Navy SEALs. These special forces are trained in relevant ways, including interrogation and interrogation resistance; Navy SEALs are even subjected to simulated drowning (cf. waterboarding) as part of their training. In other words, these units know what a hostile interrogation looks like, so they would not be starting from scratch if imported into such settings.

None of this is to say that a wholly dedicated class of professional torturers would not be more effective than whatever other group we co-opted into that role. Rather, the point is that the distinction between "trained" and "untrained" torturers is a nonstarter insofar as our torturers would not be randomly selected from a nearby street corner; rather, they would be highly trained individuals who already possess an allied skill set, extreme mental fortitude, and a dedication to their craft and country. Psychological profiling could further identify the over- and underzealous, thus giving us a starting group. Couple its potential with on-the-job training and experienced personnel already in the field, and I am far from skeptical about the prospects for effective torturers. To return to the original objection, the point is simply that we do not need dedicated torturer training programs or even a significant number of torturers. Some of these critics seem to envision some sort of "torture college" with things like students, faculty, academic advisers, secretarial staff, administrative support, and so on, but something far more minimal would go a long way toward effective, if not optimal, torture.

More generally, I am skeptical as to how much training is actually required for torture. In some sense, the answer could pretty clearly be none. For example, we could just hand an interrogator a baseball bat and see what happens; the chance of getting actionable intelligence from someone who has it is surely greater than zero. The point is not that this is what we should do—to be clear, I do not propose it—but rather that the issue is how *effective* we want our torture to be. Institutions might make torture more effective, but none is essential for torture. And this is the central point missed by those who raise institutional objections against torture, whether in regard to the training of torturers or otherwise.

Consider how institutional investment in torture would improve outcomes (namely, the retrieval of actionable intelligence). Or, before doing that, consider how any sort of investment would lead to improved outcomes. Roughly, there is a diminishing return on each subsequent unit of investment: the first unit of investment will lead to a large improvement, and each unit of investment thereafter engenders smaller gains. And the aggregated investments do not portend infinite advance of the desired project but rather asymptotically approach some maximum. There are probably irregular processes that eschew this simple model, such as when our first hour on some task gets us nowhere and then we suddenly see the light during the second hour. Nevertheless, as a general rule of investment and results, something like this is approximately right.

I submit that something similar would go on with institutional investment in torture insofar as more investment leads to better outcomes, but with diminishing results. Consider the abstract metrics of institutional investment and the efficacy of torture such that higher numbers indicate greater investment and better outcomes (i.e., more actionable intelligence). If we plot that relationship on a generic (and non-percentage-

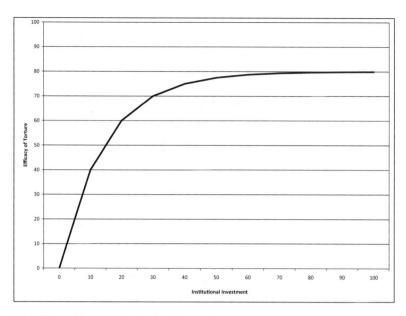

Fig. 6. Efficacy of Torture vs. Institutional Investment

based) scale, it would look something like figure 6. The critics considered so far in this section allege that torture requires institutions, but my response has continually been that, while (maximally) effective torture might, torture simpliciter certainly does not; this chart makes that point visually. Our solo torturer with the baseball bat would be on the left side, and the sorts of institutionalized torture envisioned by Bufacchi, Arrigo, Wolfendale, and Shue would be on the right side. There is no reason to move toward their sort of institutionalization if the outcomes fall off as this chart holds simply because such investments are paying such a poor return vis-à-vis outcomes.

Of course, the details matter, and I offer the figure to make a conceptual point rather than a practical one. For example, if the payoffs looked like this, I might not propose institutionalization past the "10" level since the institutional costs have to be reflected in the ledgers. If those costs are high enough, then we simply have to do without the associated institutions since our moral calculus cannot cover them. This is not to say that we will be diminished to interrogators with bats, but the torture college might well be off the table. What ultimately matters is that we not institutionalize torture beyond what our moral calculus supports; similarly, if torture becomes less effective in the process, then our moral calculus has to recognize that as well. The key conclusion, however, is that this less effective torture might still be preferable to overwhelming institutional costs being incurred. As I have argued throughout this section, however, I am more sanguine about institutionally minimal torture than others.

7.3 THE NEFARIOUS SPREAD OF TORTURE

Ticking-time-bomb cases ask us to consider torture in isolation; our consent to torture in those cases has no implications for the practice of torture in other cases. Critics complain that this sort of isolation does not exist in the real world and that the legitimization of torture establishes a dangerous precedent. Once we are willing to torture in some cases, we will be willing to torture in others.[19] Eventually, those cases might bear little resemblance to ticking-time-bomb cases, so we best never embark on this slippery slope. Parallel to this expansion of torture, there are worries about how torture brutalizes the torturer or otherwise affects the psychologies of those involved with torture. As these people gain exposure to torture, they might become desensitized toward it, which could lead to causing more, or less-discriminating, pain. Or maybe the normalization of torture will lead to the normalization of other immoral acts.[20] All of these concerns are effectively that the allowance of torture in isolated cases will have negative downstream consequences.

The most substantial worry is the one mentioned first, that torture in exceptional cases threatens its normalization. Shue makes this point eloquently:

> Rousseau says at one point that pure democracy is a system of government suitable only for angels—ordinary mortals cannot handle it. . . . As devilish as terroristic torture is, in a sense it too may be a technique only for angels; perhaps only angels could use it within the only constraints which would make it permissible and, then, lay it aside.[21]

So imagine that ticking-time-bomb cases show us that torture is permissible in cases that satisfy various conditions, $C_1, C_2, C_3, \ldots, C_n$. Further imagine that we meet a case wherein all but one of those conditions is satisfied (e.g., $\sim C_1, C_2, C_3, \ldots, C_n$). One worry is that we deem the latter case to be "close enough" to the former and go ahead and torture anyway. Another worry is that we simply cannot help ourselves, such are the pleasures of torture. In other words, the first worry portends a moral progression and the second a psychological one. Let us take these in order.

Regarding the moral progression, it obviously matters which conditions are (not) satisfied. As I argued in §5.2 above, ticking-time-bomb cases are not meant to put necessary conditions on the application of torture; rather, those conditions are meant to be sufficient. If torture is justified under conditions $C_1, C_2, C_3, \ldots, C_n$, then it does not follow that torture is not justified under $\sim C_1, C_2, C_3, \ldots, C_n$. Assuming for the sake of argument that torture is justified in ticking-time-bomb cases, the formal worry cannot be that such cases would lead to unjustified torture in the real world since it would still be an open question whether torture could be justified in cases sufficiently resembling—yet nevertheless different from—ticking-time-bomb cases.

What matters is simply that lesser harms can be effectuated through torture than through its absence. For this reason, there is nothing inherently wrong with the spread of torture, regardless of how many conditions are relaxed from ticking-time-bomb cases. Can torture be justified if the conditions of the case are not identical to those of ticking-time-bomb cases? Per the red sweatshirt case in §7.1, I think that the answer is yes, though I also suspect that the relations need to be reasonably close. To put it another way, nothing mostly or completely different from a ticking-time-bomb case has much going for it vis-à-vis the justification of torture.

Returning to the critic, what is wrong with the spread of torture? Most simply, nothing: the problem could be only with the spread of *unjustified* torture. If our allowance of justified torture leads to the spread of more (justified) torture, then this has to be a good thing. What we need to worry about is, not simply the spread of torture, but rather how the use of *justified* torture could lead to the spread of *unjustified* torture. Certainly, this is something that warrants discussion, but, from the outset, it is worth asking why anyone would practice unjustified torture. For example, imagine that we could torture ten people—nine of them innocent, but we know not which—in order to have a small chance of saving one other. Is this worth it? Filling in more details as we like, the answer can easily come out in the negative. Are we seriously worried that torture in ticking-time-bomb-like cases will lead to torture in a case like this one? Nobody would seriously propose such torture.

Getting clear on exactly what the objection amounts to is, therefore, an important part of the dialectic. From a social-political standpoint, I propose that the prolific spread of unjustified torture is not something that we need to worry about insofar as there is no advantage to pursuing such torture and, furthermore, that there are myriad disadvantages. This has to sound naïve given the fact that torture has become normalized under some regimes; see, for example, the discussion of Argentina and Chile in

§2.1 above. But these are *radically* different situations wherein dictators are trying to suppress their opposition. The sorts of torture that we are countenancing are, not those of political suppression, but rather those that interfere with terrorists' threats. Is the dialectic really supposed to be that the torture of a few (suspected) terrorists would lead to the widespread torture of a Pinochetesque thirty thousand? That is radically implausible.

We have yet to get the proper point on the objection that torture will spread. Just to be charitable, here is a scenario that we might reasonably countenance. Imagine that we license torture in a ticking-time-bomb case and that the use of torture saved many thousands of lives. Another case thereafter arises that is far less clear-cut: we round up a group of people, most of whom are likely to be innocent. Only one hundred people are threatened. Intelligence reveals that the threat is hyperimminent, such that torture may not be effective anyway (i.e., the bomb might go off before we would be able to disarm it). Should we torture? Maybe not. Would we? Maybe we are overly enthusiastic because of our recent success and want to move forward even if the moral calculus is compromised. What protections are in place to prevent the overextension of torture to inappropriate cases? Will we be able to restrain ourselves?

Contra Shue, I am more optimistic: we just owe an honest costs and benefits assessment. Why would that be so hard? Imagine that the military deployed a bomb against a terrorists' meeting, killing several terrorists and, therefore, accomplishing important strategic ends. It is possible that the next meeting takes place under the cover of a wedding and that the success of the first attack threatens judicious deliberation in the second. Does that mean that the first bomb should not have been dropped? Of course not. It means that the second bomb should not be dropped unless the collateral damage can be justified. During wartime, military officers have to make just these sorts of decisions; there is a lot of pressure on those officers to make the decisions well. Whoever authorizes torture— and at whatever level—will be under similar pressure and accountability.

Thus far, I have argued for various points. First, the spread of (justified) torture is not necessarily bad. Second, that the torture of terrorists could spread to anything close to the magnitude of torture as practiced by the worst dictators is dubious. Third, vigilance is required to prevent the spread of torture from justified to unjustified cases, though such vigilance is already required—and practiced—in various other settings wherein we might reasonably worry about slippery slopes. A fourth point, that there should be various legal safeguards in place to prevent abuses of torture, will be developed in the next chapter. The scandal at Abu Ghraib, for example, was just that, and those involved should be punished. Such punishments should be harsh, and they should be publicized. The spread of torture will be further curtailed by proper oversight and accountability; again, more on that in the next chapter.

This response paves the way for the next type of objection, which is not so much about the spread of torture across cases as about the worsening of detainee treatment within cases. In other words, we could worry that the admission of any torture threatens extension to unjustified cases, as discussed above. But another worry is that torture will be more malicious than it needs to be once torturers are desensitized toward its practice. Given studies like the Milgram experiment[22] or the Stanford prison experiment,[23] this is hardly a worry that can be easily dismissed. But the principal response is that overly zealous torture should not be tolerated and, furthermore, that it should be punished. Torturers need to exercise due restraint, and, insofar as they fail to, they should be removed from their positions and held accountable.

Important work has been done regarding the psychology of torturers,[24] and I can only imagine what psychological fortitude it must take to torture another human being. Furthermore, there is somewhat of a conundrum here insofar as the most effective torturers might be those who are sufficiently desensitized but, at the same time, those might be exactly the sort of people we do not want practicing torture for fear of abuse. I suspect that the best way to go would be to have torturers rotate out after tours of only a few years; this could promote a balance between desensitization and experience, both of which run at cross-purposes (i.e., we want one low and the other high, but they rise together). Again, however, I recommend that standards be put into place and that they be enforced. As will be argued in the next chapter, this can be done without compromising some of the institutional desiderata from §7.2.

7.4 ALTERNATIVES TO TORTURE

Everyone agrees that torture should not be practiced if we can accomplish the same outcomes—such as the retrieval of lifesaving information—in less morally costly ways. Do such alternatives exist, and, if so, what is their implication for the moral status of interrogational torture? There is the straightforward sense in which alternatives to torture exist insofar as we can simply choose not to torture, instead choosing to do something else (or nothing). It hardly follows from this, however, that there are meaningful alternatives to torture vis-à-vis successful intelligence gathering since nothing has yet been said about the efficacy of those alternatives. There are various ways that this dialectic could go, at least two of which are interesting: first, we could say that alternatives to torture are both more effective and less morally costly, thus making them superior; second, we could say that the alternatives are less effective and less morally costly but that these moral savings are worth recouping.[25] Regarding this second, the point is that we could allow the alternatives to be less effective while still preferring them insofar as they lack the associated moral hazards of torture. I have read most of the literature as endorsing this first proposal, though the second is certainly a live one as well. In what follows, I shall not maintain the distinction, but it bears acknowledgment.

So what are some of the alternatives to torture? In a recent book, Matthew Alexander tells the story of the search for Abu Musab al Zarqawi, the former leader of al-Qaeda in Iraq; Alexander was one of the interrogators responsible for the intelligence work that led to al Zarqawi's death.[26] Throughout the interrogations, Alexander favored nonhostile techniques, and the book is meant to be a celebration of the success of those techniques insofar as al Zarqawi was eventually killed through intelligence acquired without torture.[27] The techniques that Alexander advocates play off the psychological states of detainees (i.e., they are not physically threatening); these are drawn directly from the *Army Field Manual* (*AFM*).[28] While that list in the *AFM* is somewhat longer, the techniques that Alexander emphasizes include love of family, love of comrade, fear-down, futility, and rapport. The first two invite the detainee to countenance a life without his family or friends or else suggest that loved ones are at risk and can be protected only if the detainee cooperates. Fear-down mitigates some preexisting fear of the detainee (e.g., by promising safety from it). Futility is meant to show that the detainee's cause will be frustrated regardless and that he might as well draw favor by facilitating expedient countermeasures. Finally, rapport consists in building a positive, trusting relationship with the detainee. Alexander clearly favors rapport, though he concedes that more intransigent detainees might force another approach if rapport is clearly off the table.

Certainly, Alexander thinks that the aforementioned techniques should be preferred to torture, but he allows for other psychological interventions that are hardly benign. For example, he approvingly cites the following from the *AFM*: "Limitations on the use of [violence or intimidations, including physical or mental torture or exposure to inhumane treatment] should not be confused with psychological ploys, verbal trickery, or other nonviolent or noncoercive ruses used by the interrogator in the successful interrogation of hesitant or uncooperative sources."[29] In other words, even though torture and inhumane treatment are explicitly proscribed, there are various forms of deception that are legitimate interrogational tactics.

Of course, nonviolent or other noncoercive means could be preferable to torture, but two important disclaimers should be registered; unpacking them will make Alexander's case far less compelling. First, whatever these alternatives amount to, they must be less morally costly than torture. Once we start looking at how some of these cases unfold, the supremacy of nontorture will hardly be obvious. Second, these alternatives need to be effective, particularly given time constraints. If they are far less effective than torture—even in a small subset of cases—then a strong argument against torture has not been made (in those cases). Imagine that someone says, for example, that some action φ is less morally costly than ψ, but, as it turns out, φ is far less effective than ψ in realizing some end, E. Should we φ or ψ? As suggested at the beginning of this section, it depends on the relative moral costs, moral benefits, and degrees of efficacy.[30]

The first point is that alternatives to torture are hardly benign, at least insofar as they are likely to be effective. This contention trades on two different variables, so let me illustrate by example. One alternative to torture is just to extend gracious hospitality to our detained terrorist, hoping that he will reciprocate by helping us disarm his terrorist threat. Quite benign, but not very likely to be effective. From there, rapport is less benign—for example, it is disingenuous and, therefore, not wholly morally innocuous—and probably more effective. Very effective? I certainly doubt it—especially since the interrogating personnel quite probably represent those whom the terrorist is ideologically predisposed to despise—but there is no doubt that rapport can work. But for the present argument, however, all that matters is that rapport does not *always* work, which can hardly be controversial (cf. time constraints). For emphasis, let me make plain that rapport should be pursued when it is reasonably likely to work or else when it is at least as reasonably likely to work as torture.

Now that we have cut the logical space down to cases in which rapport will not work, let us look at the effects of Alexander's alternatives to torture. What bore notice to me in reading his book was that these were far from docile. For example, he approvingly notes that a fellow interrogator "set the air conditioner on the lowest setting" and that it was "chilly" during an interrogation. Elsewhere he admits that a detainee "looks tired. He's got bags under his eyes. His mouth is sagging. He doesn't seem as alert as he did yesterday." He once tells a detainee: "Put your mask back on. . . . His hands tremble so badly that I have to help him get it over his head." After a tumultuous interrogation of a man who turned out to be *innocent*, Alexander admits: "I psychologically savaged him."[31]

While I have immense gratitude for Alexander's service, I respectfully contend that the distinctions between these treatments and torture are far more tenuous than he contends. Philosophically—if not legally—does it really make a difference that he never beat a detainee? To my mind, not really; in fact, torture might have caused less overall suffering insofar as it could have been more expedient. The alternatives to torture that he advocates apparently allow for temperature manipulation, sleep deprivation, and hooding. As argued in §4.1 above, I think that these fall short of torture; nevertheless, they are clearly coercive and, therefore, morally contentious. Beyond the stress and duress tactics, Alexander is willing to subject his detainees to extreme psychological duress by reneging on false promises, threatening the safety of family members, and so on.

Either Alexander thinks that psychological torture is impossible, or else he thinks that these techniques fall short of it. Per §4.1, I am skeptical about whether psychological attacks can satisfy the specific intent requirement for torture (i.e., that the torturer specifically intends "prolonged mental harm,"[32] which is really orthogonal to his goals). That said, psychological attack clearly constitutes a moral harm, and there is no reason to think that such attacks are categorically less offensive than their physical complements. In other words, even if psychological techniques are not torture, it does not follow that they are necessarily better. On the other horn of the dilemma, Alexander could acknowledge the possibility of psychological torture but deny that the crippling effects rendered by his interrogations reached the relevant threshold. To that, I can only ask: What would? Threatening death?[33] Threatening the indefinite detention of a detainee's family members?[34] Since he does both of these, one can surmise only that Alexander finds them permissible.

The argument thus far portends a red herring: maybe not only is torture impermissible, but so are many of the practices in which Alexander engages (even if they fall short of torture). By arguing that his practices are not morally innocuous, the proper conclusion might be to reject them all rather than to endorse torture. What tools are then left for interrogators? Bufacchi and Arrigo return to rapport, endorsing the "social skills method" of Hans Scharff, a master interrogator of the German Luftwaffe (i.e., air force) during World War II;[35] the idea here is to solicit seemingly unimportant information through cordial treatment and then, ultimately, piece together some substantial revelation. As another example, they praise Islamic clerics who have been successful in "reformulating the religious commitments of some terrorists."[36] Or else maybe chronically ill or badly wounded detainees would become cooperative after being offered medical service. Rejali almost seems to pay a backhanded compliment to

Christian Masuy, a Belgian national who ended up working for the German Abwehr (i.e., military intelligence) during World War II. Masuy's preferred method of torture was to hold the victim's head under water in the bathtub, but with a curious twist. Following the torture,

> Masuy's "patient would be conscientiously dried in a bathrobe, warmed up, rubbed with eau de cologne, and consoled with Cognac." Masuy would then praise the victim for his courage, but remind him that it was useless, urge him to come clean, and if not, repeat the torture.[37]

Is Masuy's rapport-building method better than torture that lacks such amenities? Maybe, but this is hardly an *alternative* to torture—nor does Rejali suggest it is—but rather just a variant thereof.

What about the suggestions of Bufacchi and Arrigo? I cannot imagine that "reformulating the religious commitments of some terrorists" is even reasonably expedient, and it must be granted that such an approach would fail on at least some, if not many, terrorists. Medical treatment? Sure, this has some potential, but I suspect the more promising approach is to deny medical treatment—especially for painful afflictions—under promises of its dispensation after intelligence disclosures. Regardless, such considerations can be only a part of our intelligence apparatus insofar as some of our detainees will not be in immediate medical need. That still leaves torture on the table for the rest. So now we are down to Scharff's social skills as the principal alternative to torture in at least some cases. Any semblance of time constraints would severely compromise an interrogator's ability to string together some relevant intelligence finding from sundry information, as would a detainee's unwillingness to communicate at all. It does not hurt my position at all to allow that there are some cases in which these techniques—or the allied ones more directly involving rapport—are superior to torture. Let psychological profiling play an important determination in which way we go as well as assessments by the intelligence community regarding the imminence of attack. Regardless, torture will still be the only viable recourse when we are short on time and/or dealing with a recalcitrant detainee.

A final point brings us back to Alexander: this is an experienced military interrogator who has spent extensive time with important intelligence assets. In his book, he lauds rapport building but acknowledges its limits. Medical generosity never came into play with any of the interrogations detailed in his book, and, certainly, the reformulation of religious commitments was never considered within his operational time frame. Ultimately, I do not see a tremendous moral distinction between the practices advocated by Alexander and physical torture. The proposals made by Bufachi and Arrigo have lower moral costs than the practices employed by Alexander, yet he does not explicitly endorse them. Why? The obvious answer would be that they are not efficacious given time constraints. But herein lies the rub because neither are Alexander's. As he says of a particular psychological approach:

> This will take days, maybe weeks, to develop. And in the meantime, how many innocent Iraqis will die? How many American soldiers will be ambushed and killed? How many suicide bombers will turn marketplaces into bloody bedlam?[38]

We do not always have the days or weeks that Alexander requires. Yes, his techniques netted al Zarqawi, and this should be a regaled accomplishment. How long did it take? His assignment began sometime in March 2006, and al Zarqawi was killed June 7, 2006.[39] That is over two months and maybe even over three. How many more lives could have been saved were we to have accepted torture as a legitimate tool in our intelligence arsenal?

In closing this section, let me reiterate that torture is not a panacea (cf. §9.1 below) and that there will surely be cases when we should do things other than torture. In fact, those cases will constitute the overwhelming preponderance of our intelligence activity. Nevertheless, there are limited cases in which torture offers advantages to its alternatives, particularly given time constraints. I suspect that torture has greater efficacy as well; I will remain circumspect on this issue for now but will return to it in the next section. Even if torture effects greater moral harms than its alternatives, it can still be justified if its probability of success is sufficiently better than those alternatives. When time constraints eliminate those alternatives out of hand, even a low success rate for torture could be justified given the threat of a serious harm. Let us now turn to whether such cases ever exist, starting with whether the existence of such cases even matters.

7.5 THE FOLLY OF CASES

Critics of torture often propose a dialectic in which they call for a single real-world example of a ticking-time-bomb case and then deny—either rhetorically or substantively—that such a case exists.[40] Given the moral hazards of torture, this methodology is supposed to shift the burden of proof to the advocate of torture, which is not completely unreasonable. Certainly, it would be odd to think that this goes the other way: the critic of torture cannot be asked to prove that no ticking-time-bomb case has ever existed. That said, the cases card is often overplayed, and torture could be justified even in the absence of unequivocal, historically justified cases. There are at least two compelling reasons for this.

First, the contemporary advent of terrorism is much more dangerous than its predecessors. Many of the more noteworthy terroristic events caused the death of, say, one to four hundred people, yet 9/11 caused the death of almost three thousand.[41] Aside from 9/11-like risks, new forms of bioterrorism can also threaten thousands of lives (e.g., contamination of water supplies); the simple point is that terrorism can and has become more lethal than it was in the past. As terrorism threatens more lives, the moral imperative to stop it becomes greater. So, even if we cannot agree on cases in which torture was justified against lesser threats, it does not follow that we would not agree on cases in which torture will be justified against greater threats. The fact that we do not have these latter cases may simply be that the terroristic landscape has continued to evolve and that such cases have not yet presented themselves. In the absence of such cases, there is no harm in thinking of them hypothetically: if terrorism threatened some great moral harm (e.g., one on the order of thousands of lives lost), would torture be permissible? So, even though the relevant cases might not (yet) be on offer, we should not therefore assume that torture will never be justified.

Second, the critic is under a misapprehension if he thinks that successful cases of torture will be publicized. If ticking-time-bomb cases cannot be produced, then there are two conclusions we could draw. The first is that no ticking-time-bomb case has ever existed in the real world. The second is that either no such case has existed or else such a case did exist and we do not know about it. As a simple point of logic, the second conclusion is more likely to be true than is the first; a disjunction is more often true than either disjunct.[42] And, more substantively, there is good reason to believe that successful cases of torture (i.e., ones that lead to the retrieval of actionable intelligence) will not be widely advertised since there are obvious political costs to this sort of publicity.

By way of example, consider that stress and duress tactics have been widely deployed by the United States in its War on Terror and also that waterboarding has been used in more limited circumstances. Either these practices have yielded lifesaving intelligence, or they have not. Which scenario is more likely? To deny that these techniques have accomplished anything takes a very dim view of our government and military: the allegation would be that our intelligence community has, over a nontrivial period of time, continued practices that were not producing results. What possible reason could there be for this? By analogy, imagine that I went around hitting people with tire irons in the hopes of acquiring the contents of their wallets. Furthermore, imagine that this never worked; after numerous attempts, I had made no economic progress. Finally, imagine that those attempts took place over a protracted time period, over various demographics, with some experimental variations on a core theme, and so on. Given that they were not leading to the desired outcome, would I continue them? Only if I lacked any sort of instrumental rationality or else were masochistic.

Surely, some of its more vociferous critics would proffer precisely these criticisms against the Bush administration, but such criticisms are too often disingenuous and rhetorical. Vice President Cheney, for example, has been adamant that "enhanced interrogation techniques were absolutely essential in saving thousands of American lives and preventing further attacks against the United States."[43] Critics take this to be hubris, but I am not cynical enough to issue wholesale indictments against our political or military leadership: if enhanced interrogation techniques were continued over some number of years, it would defy credibility that such techniques never produced any positive outcomes.

Consider, for example, the immoderate waterboarding of Khalid Shiekh Mohammed—who was allegedly waterboarded 183 times[44]—which is meant to reveal the excesses of an overzealous Bush administration: if waterboarding were to work at all, it surely would not require this many iterations.[45] Maybe, but maybe not; there is no a priori reason that this should be true. And, if the waterboarding did lead to the stoppage of the "Second Wave" and, in particular, an attack on Los Angeles's Library Tower, then it would have been justified.[46] The details of this case are uncertain enough that we should not place too much stock in it,[47] but that is precisely the point: we do not always know—if we ever do—the details of the cases because those details are hidden behind public relations considerations, security clearances, and so on. If the details ever do come out, the sources (e.g., disgruntled and ex-insiders) do not always inspire confidence.

The argument thus far has simply been that we should not be too greedy in our demand for actual and clear-cut ticking-time-bomb cases. First, some skepticism is warranted insofar as to whether the present and future will resemble the past: the changing face of terrorism makes ticking-time-bomb-like scenarios more likely. It therefore follows that the lack of historical cases has limited implications for their ensuing prospects. Second, even if there has been historical precedent, there are all sorts of reasons to doubt that we would know about it. To wit, there are political and security factors that straightforwardly make it unlikely that actual cases would enter public consciousness. While some of us believe the Bush administration when it says that enhanced interrogation has saved lives, many will obviously be less charitable. Surely, however, it takes immense cynicism to allege that those enhanced techniques would be continued over several years if they were patently worthless.

I therefore submit to my interlocutors that it is a faulty dialectic in which we ask for real-world ticking-time-bomb cases and then try to draw any substantive conclusions when none is on offer. That said, the proponent of torture in exceptional cases does owe more than a circumstantial and impressionistic argument. While the considerations offered above go some way toward mitigating the burden-of-proof game, they hardly obviate it. Therefore, in the remainder of this chapter, let us consider some plausible ticking-time-bomb cases. The actual details of these cases are less important than the critics would have us believe for the simple reason that what matters is what *could* happen, not what *has* happened. Regardless, it will be illustrative to consider some actual cases that at least bear relevant isomorphisms to the philosophers' construct. Toward that end, I will offer three cases, one celebrated, one uncelebrated, and one fictional; the reasons for these choices, as well as the ill-formed juxtaposition between the actual and the fictional, will become clear as we proceed.

7.6 TICKING-TIME-BOMB CASES REDUX

For our first case, I start with one that Alan Dershowitz has championed: the torture of Abdul Hakim Murad by the Filipino police in 1995. Murad was arrested in a security sweep ahead of Pope John Paul II's visit to the Philippines and was subsequently tortured for sixty-seven days. The torture was effectuated through beating—which broke most of his ribs—forcing water into his mouth, forcing him to sit on ice, and burning his genitalia with cigarettes.[48] During his ordeal, Murad disclosed information that helped foil "plots to assassinate the pope and to crash eleven commercial airliners carrying approximately four thousand passengers into the Pacific Ocean, as well as a plan to fly a private Cessna into CIA headquarters."[49] Following his ultimate confessions, Murad was handed over to the U.S. authorities, along with the information that the Filipino police had gleaned.

While this looks like a model ticking-time-bomb case, there are some features that bear further discussion. Rejali, for example, has been critical of it for at least two reasons. First, the sweep also resulted in the acquisition of an encrypted computer and disks; once these files were decrypted, they revealed the same information—less the Cessna plot—that was disclosed under torture. Second, the torture lasted sixty-seven days and was, therefore, not used against an imminent threat (i.e., lest that threat would have been realized in the interim). Furthermore, Murad began to talk only once a new team of interrogators introduced themselves as Mossad agents and said that they were taking him to Israel.[50] Rejali thinks that this fact therefore means it was Murad's "imagination and personality [i.e., susceptibility to the faux Israeli threat], not actual torture, that got him talking."[51] Both these are fair objections, so let me take them in turn.

Regarding the computer and disks, they were not decrypted in time such as to make the torture redundant. Therefore, it is misleading to portray the torture as unnecessary given that the information gained through torture was also on the computer and disks since that information was unknown and inaccessible to the authorities.[52] Rejali approvingly evokes a discussion initiated by Jay Winik in which Winik wonders what would have happened if Murad had been handed over to the Americans earlier; Rejali thinks it is straightforward that the decryption would have been faster, presumably in such a time frame that torture would not have been needed. The idea is that, even if the Filipinos could not run the decryption, the Americans could have and that the computer and disks should, therefore, have been immediately handed over to the Americans. But, supposing that the Americans could have readily decrypted these materials or else could have done so much faster than the Filipinos—neither of which seems obvious to me—there was no reasonable basis for the Filipinos to know what would have been on them in the first place and, therefore, no motivation to seek American help.

A quick refrain might be "if you don't know what you have, hand it to the Americans"—or some other technologically sophisticated country—but there are all sorts of reasons to find this problematic. These range from considerations of national sovereignty, to national security (namely, that of the Philippines), to resources (e.g., the United States cannot provide integral support to everyone else's counterterrorism), to simple logistics. To put it another way, the costs—whether economic or moral—of torturing Murad seem to me far lower than whatever alternative Rejali means to suggest (i.e., he never makes a concrete proposal). Regardless, the Filipino authorities *did* contact the Americans:

Philippine investigators called in their American counterparts for help. This was standard operating procedure. According to US and Philippine officials interviewed . . . both the CIA Manila station chief and the resident FBI legal attaché were notified. A team of intelligence agents flew from in from Washington.[53]

Furthermore, the only mention of decryption is that the "data were encrypted and in Arabic, but Philippine technicians eventually deciphered the code and translated the texts."[54] Nothing in the news article says that the Filipino authorities were unable to decrypt the information in a reasonable time frame or that the Americans would have been able to do any better. For all these reasons, the existence of the computer and disks does not undermine the case for torture.

The second central issue in this case is the sixty-seven days of torture. If these written accounts are really meant to be believed, Murad gave up nothing until the very last day of interrogation, the day on which he was lied to about a pending transfer to the Israelis. For the sake of argument, let us grant that this is true. Does it undermine the case for torture? First, why would it? The reason is supposed to be that ticking-time-bomb cases require imminent threats; if the associated threat were more than two months distant, then there would be no cause for torture since other intelligence avenues could be pursued.

The facts of this case are revealing as to why this sort of response fails. We can rest assured that, while Murad was being tortured, other intelligence avenues were being pursued: it is certainly not the case that the entire intelligence community did nothing else in the interim other than torture Murad in the hope that such torture would pan out. Investigations continued, leads were followed, and so on. And, as it turns out, none of this revealed the nature of the threats: only his confession did. The electronic materials would have given similar information, but they were still encrypted, and there was no reasonable basis for suspecting that they contained relevant material.

This leads to a second point, which is more general: what matters is, not imminence, but necessity.[55] Ticking-time-bomb cases are often formulated in terms of imminence, but that is misleading insofar as imminence and necessity come together in those cases. In other words, a threat may be imminent, but it can also be true that no method but torture would lead to its abrogation; torture is necessary to prevent the threat. When these features are run together, we lose sight of which feature matters. Regardless, it is easy enough to pull them apart:

Imminence. A bomb will go off in the near future and kill thousands; the torture of a detainee will ensure the deactivation of the bomb and the preservation of all the lives. Aside from torture, there is some other act, φ, that will also ensure the preservation of all the lives. Unlike torture, φ has no moral hazards.

Necessity. A bomb will go off in two years and will kill thousands; the torture of a detainee will ensure the deactivation of the bomb and the preservation of all the lives. The detainee has acted alone and is the only one who knows the bomb's location. The bomb is undetectable and will not be found without his testimony. Unfortunately, the detainee is dying of an aggressive form of cancer; while he is still strong enough to undergo torture, he will assuredly die in the near future, thus severing any hope of deactivating the bomb.

I submit that torture is not justified in the imminence example, that the necessity example is the same in every morally relevant way as standard ticking-time-bomb cases, and that, if we think that torture is justified in those cases, then we should think that it is also justified in the necessity example. Imminence is often suggestive of necessity, and nonimminence also tends to run contrary to necessity; nevertheless, these are at best probabilistic relationships that bear exceptions. What we should look for when countenancing torture is necessity—not imminence—even if is true that necessity will often require imminence.

Returning to Murad's case, the prolonged length of his torture is morally adventitious. The question is not, how long it took to get the information from him, but whether torture was necessary to get it. And, furthermore, the fact that he ultimately relented under threat of interrogation from Israeli interrogators does not undermine the case for the antecedent torture: that torture may well have undermined his resolve and led to capitulation. Would he have caved had that threat been wielded earlier? Maybe, maybe not. One has to suspect that it *was wielded* in sixty-seven days as that is a long enough period of time that a lot must have been said; the ultimate appearance of officers dressed as Mossad agents just reified the threat. Even granting that there might have been some more expedient way to engender the confession, that shows, not that torture was not justified, but only that some other regimen could have been advisable. That said, the intelligence community should be afforded reasonable—and probably even extensive—latitude in this regard given the stakes, the vagaries of real-world interrogations, epistemic limitations, and so on.

This first case I chose for its celebrity as well as the opportunity to draw the aforementioned distinction between imminence and necessity. The second case—to be presented shortly—was chosen precisely because of its lack of celebrity: it appears nowhere in the torture literature, and I have never heard anyone discuss it. In fact, I just happened to come across it in the *New York Times* one morning, without any research or agenda. The point is that there are probably various cases like this one and that many of us are completely unaware of their existence; it is important for the defender of torture not to singularly cling to cases like Murad's. There are few enough cases of legitimate torture so as not to call into doubt the presupposition that such cases need to be fairly rare and be the exception rather than the rule, but we can reasonably expect there to be at least a few cases per year. Let us now turn to the details of this second case.

Since the United States deposed the old Iraqi regime, American and Iraqi security forces have worked together, both to increase the overall security and to train the Iraqi forces ahead of the prospective departure of American forces. As was reported in April 2007—with the date of the incident unspecified but presumably somewhat proximate—Iraqi soldiers were on patrol in Ghazaliya, a neighborhood in the northwest of Baghdad. These soldiers picked up Mustafa Subhi Jassam after Jassam was seen loitering around the patrol route twice in the same day; two other suspected insurgents were picked up separately. The Iraqis beat Jassam in front of the other two detainees, and the stripes on Jassam's back indicated that he was probably beaten with electrical cables. Jassam was then handed over to the Americans and took them to one of the houses in which al-Qaeda agents made bombs. In this house, those agents had been making fuses for improvised explosive devices (IEDs), and various other materials were found: large quantities of soap (for making explosives), coils of blasting wire, two large antiaircraft guns, three propane tanks, and an oxygen tank that had been modified to house a bomb. Large piles of homemade explosives were drying on the roof. According to the commanding officer, Captain Darren Fowler, the detainees also gave the names of al-Qaeda agents (including those of high rank), identified safe houses and weapons caches, and disclosed holding cells for kidnap victims, and other tactical information.[56]

This case has all the features of a ticking-time-bomb case, or at least as many as any empirical finding would reasonably be able to identify. Did the Iraqis know that Jassam was a terrorist? They did not, but they apprehended him because of suspicious activity in a conspicuous place. If we were even minimally charitable, we would grant that the Iraqis had some cause to start the beating, such as guilty or erratic behavior after Jassam's apprehension. Might Jassam have been innocent? Sure, but the number of lives hanging in the balance invites at least some risk. And, regardless, Jassam was not innocent insofar as he was complicit in terroristic activity and had firsthand knowledge of plans that threatened many.

Was torture necessary to force Jassam to talk? Let us assume that the Iraqis asked Jassam for whatever he knew before they grabbed the electrical cables; this is only the most minimal extension of charity. Or, to put it another way, Jassam could have confessed when the prospective beating was imminent but before it had commenced, yet he chose not to. Would there have been another way to find all the information that he surrendered? As suggested earlier, the intelligence community does not sit around waiting for torture to produce information: intelligence officers are constantly—if not always for the overwhelming majority of them—pursuing other recourses. As it turns out, none of those had yet worked. Would something else have panned out before these weapons were deployed? While we will never know for sure, there are reasons to suggest a negative answer. First, it is virtually impossible that the Iraqis were building weapons they never planned to use. Second, if they had no plans to use them in the (at least somewhat) near future, why build them prematurely? Having weapons on hand increases the chances that they would be confiscated, that the insurgents would be captured, and so on. It is, therefore, only logical that these weapons would have been used at least reasonably soon after Jassam led the Americans to them. We cannot rule out the possibility that there would have been another way to eliminate the threat, but we also have no reason to think that there was.

This case identifies the straightforward torture of a terrorist such that life-threatening weapons were captured; other potentially lifesaving personnel and tactical evidence were also gained. Furthermore, there was good reason to think that Jassam was up to something: his repeated presence along the patrol route suggests that he was doing reconnaissance either for future attacks or else to learn the vulnerabilities of that route (e.g., in order to move weapons). The readiness of the weapons suggests imminence, and the lack of other intelligence measures to have discovered this very active facility at least makes necessity (for near-term recovery) a plausible claim. In point of fact, the torture did work, and it hardly required any sort of elaborate institutional configuration, just a few Iraqis and some electrical cables. And there are probably a handful or two of cases like this that have developed since the American incursion in Iraq; I strongly doubt that this one is completely unique in any morally relevant ways. Regardless, I certainly think that it represents a case of justified torture.

As a final case, consider the following:

Height of the [Australian] summer, Mercury at the century-mark; the noon-day sun softened the [asphalt] beneath the [tires] of her little Hyundai sedan to the consistency of putty. Her three year old son, quiet at last, snuffled in his sleep on the back seat. He had a summer cold and wailed like a banshee in the supermarket, forcing her to cut short her shopping. Her car needed [gas]. Her tot was asleep on the back seat. She poured twenty [liters] into the tank; thumbing notes from her purse, harried and distracted, her keys dangled from the ignition.

[While] she was in the service station a man drove off in her car. Police wound back the [service station's close-captioned television], saw a heavy set Pacific Islander with a blonde-streaked Afro entering her car. "Don't panic," a Constable advised the mother, "as soon as he sees your little boy in the back he will abandon the car." He did; police arrived at the railway station before the car thief did and arrested him after a struggle when he vaulted over the station barrier.

In the [patrol car] on the way to the police station: "Where did you leave the [car]?" Denial instead of dissimulation: "It wasn't me." It was—property stolen from the car was found in his pockets. In the detectives' office: "[It's] been twenty minutes since you took the car—little tin box like that car—It will heat up like an oven under this sun. Another twenty minutes and the child's dead or brain damaged. Where did you dump the car?" Again: "It wasn't me."

Appeals to decency, to reason, to self-interest: "It's not too late; tell us where you left the car and you will only be charged with Take-and-Use. That's just a six month extension of your recognizance." Threats: "If the child dies I will charge you with Manslaughter!" Sneering, defiant and belligerent; he made no secret of his contempt for the police. Part-way through his umpteenth, "It wasn't me," a questioner clipped him across the ear as if he were a child, an insult calculated to bring the Islander to his feet to fight, there a body-punch elicited a roar of pain, but he fought back until he lapsed into semi-consciousness under a rain of blows. He [had gotten into fights from time to time], but now, kneeling on hands and knees in his own urine, in pain he had never known, he finally [realized] the beating would go on until he told the police where he had abandoned the child and the car.

. . . When found, the stolen child was dehydrated, too weak to cry; there were ice packs and dehydration in the casualty ward but no long-time prognosis on brain damage.[57]

There are various reasons that I have chose to use this case, so some commentary is warranted. First, this is obviously a case, not of terrorism, but rather of kidnapping. At the beginning of chapter 4, I mentioned that torture need not always be practiced against terrorists and that kidnapping cases might serve as other appropriate contexts. What ultimately matters is simply that the benefits of torture outweigh the costs of abstinence, and cases like the above make such a supposition plausible. Unlike with earlier sections of this chapter, I shall not go through myriad long-term effects of the criminal justice system as might be effected vis-à-vis torture, but suffice it to say that analogous arguments could be developed.[58] Note that, in this case, we know that the detainee is guilty: he is caught on tape and has stolen property from the car in his possession. Note also that this case postulates saving, not the lives of thousands, but the life of a single small child. While cases become more dramatic—and, to my mind, easier to reconcile—as greater numbers are at risk, I do not think that such numbers are always required. And, as with the previous case, note that no grand institutional structure is required for this torture, at least not any more than is already in place (e.g., a police force). Finally, we really do have straightforward necessity in this case: the outdoor heat and the unknown—and, in the relevant time scale, unknowable—location of the car force a decision between the child's death and the beating of the detainee.

As it turns out, this case is fictional; it was written by a former police officer, perhaps as a teaching tool for cadets. So why use it? Nothing in the case strains credulity: there are no wild stipulations, and the case could easily enough be seen on the evening news, if rarely. Ticking-time-bomb cases are criticized as being overextensions of our empirical circumstances,[59] but nothing in this case sounds even remotely foreign. To be sure, I am not proposing that cases like this are often realized; the point is simply that they are absolutely empirically possible. As suggested in §7.4, actual cases are obviously going to go underreported, so the critic should not overplay their apparent dearth. But, whether we have a catalog of such cases or not, the point of using a fictional case is to drive home the point that such cases are less fantastic than commonly alleged. Regardless of whether the cases are actual or not, we can still ask what should be done in them, and it is reasonable to assume that something like the above will happen, somewhere or sometime, in human experience. So the point of this case—aside from illustrating a nonterroristic context of torture—is to make plain that the actual and the fictional need not be that far apart.

As I said at the end of the last section, I think that these three examples provide an illustrative basis for what actual cases do or could look like. Critics might allege that more cases are needed, but, to my mind, even one would be enough. Regardless—and to repeat an ongoing point—more cases have to exist than we know about. For present purposes, these will suffice, especially given space constraints. Dershowitz talks about others, as, less sympathetically, does Rejali.[60] The objective has been, not to be comprehensive, but rather to give some sort of concrete context to the previously abstract treatment of ticking-time-bomb cases; these examples and the associated discussion make good on that.

This chapter—the longest in the book by a considerable margin—has meant to take seriously real-world objections to torture. Defenders of torture have had curiously little to say about these challenges, so the responses deserve adequate space. Surely, more empirical criticisms will or have come in, yet I cannot stem them all at present; this chapter represents part of a broader (and more philosophical) project against which adjudications must be made for space. My principal hope is to rebut claims of empirical obliviousness, whether through direct empirical engagement or else through further elucidation of the theoretical project. On the former, many empirical claims have been made in this chapter, and they are either true or false; discussion of them is certainly invited. On the latter, I have continued to articulate the position espoused most directly in the previous chapter: the central point is just that the vagaries of actual experience (e.g., the loss of epistemic certainties) complicate rather than derail ticking-time-bomb thinking. Now resting on empirical objections to torture, let us consider legislative and judicial pragmatics.

8

Ex Ante and Ex Post Justifications

Having now made the theoretical case for torture (part II) as well as dealt with some empirical objections (chapter 7), I now turn to the legislative and judicial pragmatics of torture. In particular, if torture can be justified in exceptional cases, how should we procedurally authorize it? In the literature—and conceptually—there are three basic approaches to authorizing torture. The first is not to authorize it at all, which is to say that torture—even if justified—requires some sort of punishable civil disobedience (§8.1). Another approach is to authorize torture ex ante, such as through torture warrants. On this approach, torture remains prohibited except when a judge grants permission for its application. Torture warrants have been recently defended by Alan Dershowitz, and I will consider his proposal (§8.2). Finally, torture can be handled ex post, which is to say that it remains illegal but can, nevertheless, be (legally) justified or excused; my discussion will focus on the justifications of self-defense (§8.3) and necessity (§8.4).

For the sake of this argument, let us agree that torture is currently illegal, both in domestic and in international law. As discussed in §4.1, the principal domestic law is U.S.C. §§2340–2340A; the United States passed this under its obligation to the international Convention against Torture and Other Cruel, Inhuman or Degrading Treatment or Punishment (CAT; 1975/1987).[1] Furthermore, torture is decried in §§3.1a, 17, 87, and 110 of the Third Geneva Convention (1949). Alongside these legal proscriptions are hortatory ones, including §5 of the Universal Declaration of Human Rights (1948) and the Declaration of Tokyo (1975). Given this corpus, critics of torture often seem dumbfounded that anyone could seriously defend it.[2] There are a couple of simple responses, however; in fact, they are so simple that the dumbfoundedness is curious.

First, there are completely separate questions as to whether torture is or should be illegal. There have been all sorts of bad laws: those that legalized slavery, those that denied women the right to vote, and those that denied equal rights on the basis of sexual orientation, among others. Ultimately, the interesting question is, not what the laws are, but rather what they should be. And no matter how many laws oppose torture—or whether those laws are international or domestic—we can always ask whether they get it right, whether they are appropriate for our times, whether they are adequate to protect us, and so on. So, to be clear, let us grant that torture is illegal—whether under domestic or international law—and instead wonder whether it should be. If the arguments of the preceding chapters have been compelling, there are or could be cases of justifiable torture. Whether the existence of exceptional cases means that we should revisit our laws is a separate issue altogether—Oliver Wendell Holmes famously argued that hard cases make bad law[3]—but the moral justifiability of torture would give us at least a prima facie reason to think that it should be legally accommodated (in those cases).

Second, even if torture should be illegal, it hardly follows that there are not cases in which people should torture. Rather, there might be reasons against having some sort of torture policy—for example, fear of abuse—while, at the same time, an acknowledgment that torture could be justified in individual cases. Those cases might be rare enough that we need not explicitly build them into our policies but could rather allow for a post hoc recognition of the appropriate circumstances as well as providing for the associated legal exoneration. In §§8.3–8.4, I will discuss self-defense and necessity in greater detail, but suffice it to say that they work the same way insofar as those defense are just that: defenses against violations of the law. Whether torture can avail itself of either is a critical issue,[4] though the present contention is simply that (at least some) social policies are subject to exceptions.

The point of these previous two paragraphs is not to defend any substantive position but rather to locate the issues within the proper dialectical space. And, to reiterate, the illegality of torture is really neither here nor there with regard to our investigation. Rather, what we care about is figuring out how to accommodate justified torture, and there are two possibilities: rework our legal frameworks, or else countenance torture within them. What ultimately matters is that we have torture when it is justified and that we do not have it when it is not. If the legal status of torture prevents a justifiable act of torture from taking place, then something has gone wrong. Maybe that wrong is tolerable given broader policy considerations, but maybe not. Alternatively, paving the way for unjustified torture is no better—and is potentially worse—than not having justified torture. Such are the Scylla and Charybdis of torture policy: getting the justified torture, but only the justified torture.

8.1 CIVIL DISOBEDIENCE

While I think that the primary focus in this debate should be on torture warrants and the necessity defense, something should first be said about the possibility of civil disobedience. The idea here would be that we leave torture illegal and that we also fail to provide legal exoneration for (justified) torture.[5] What could be said in favor of such a position? The central thrust has to be that cases of justified torture are extremely rare and that any sort of judicial apparatus that licenses that torture—whether ex ante or ex post—threatens a proliferation of unjustified torture.[6] The risks of unjustified torture portend more harm than the harms we (might not) avert in exceptional cases, so we are better off shutting it all down. And, not only do we risk unjustified torture, but we also add a cumbersome judicial function—for example, adjudicating justified from unjustified torture—and compromise judicial integrity by threatening judicial complicity in torture.[7] These negative prospects for our judiciaries further attenuate the case for torture, which is already supposed to be quite tenuous indeed.

Granting all this, what should happen when a case of justifiable torture presents itself? If torture were illegal, and if no legal defenses were available to the would-be torturer, then he would torture at his own peril: his act of torture would be legally liable, and legal sanctions could follow conviction. 118 U.S.C. §2340A, for example, allows up to twenty years of incarceration for nondomestic torture—whether actual or attempted—and for execution or life imprisonment if torture leads to the death of its victim. Imagine now that torture could be used to save many lives and that an individual had the option of either performing that torture (and saving the lives) or else allowing those lives to be lost. What should he do?

Our absolutist friends force the would-be torturer into a precipitous decision between his own freedom and the lives of others: torture and save the lives if you like, but then get ready for jail (or execution). There are at least two problems with this offer, one practical and one theoretical. Starting with the practical, it obviously—and on purpose—provides a disincentive to torture. Someone who might otherwise be willing to torture in order to save lives could now be either unwilling or unable, ultimately allowing those lives to be lost. Maybe there are practical gains insofar as unjustified torture would not be as readily administered, but this invocation presupposes that there are not ways to license the justified torture while preventing the unjustified torture. Such a supposition is hardly obvious to me and, in fact, seems false; I shall return to this in §8.4.

Second, however, is the theoretical worry: someone is being punished for doing something that is, ex hypothesi, morally justified. In other words, someone does something that he has the moral license to do, and then he gets sent to prison. To me, this is a very strange proposition. The response is that we punish this person so that other people do not perpetuate unjustified torture, but why not just punish *those people* if and when such unjustified torture occurs? Consider Seumas Miller, who writes:

> [The] law in particular, and social institutions more generally, are blunt instruments. They are designed to deal with recurring situations confronted by numerous institutional actors over relatively long periods of time. Laws abstract away from differences between situations across space and time, and differences between institutional actors across space and time. The law, therefore, consists of a set of generalizations to which the particular situation must be made to fit. . . . By contrast with the law, morality is a sharp instrument. Morality can be, and typically ought to be, made to apply to a given situation in all its particularity. . . . Accordingly, what might be, all things considered, the morally best action for an agent to perform in some one-off, i.e., non-recurring, situation might not be an action that should be made lawful.

Miller's point is that our institutional and moral commitments can come apart insofar as there are negative consequences of institutionalized torture, but it could still be the case that torture is morally justified in particular cases. And then what? Miller thinks that whoever commits torture should be "tried, convicted, and, if found guilty, sentenced for committing the crime of torture."[8]

To this, I still have to ask: *Why?* We would be sentencing someone for a justifiable act such that other people are less inclined to commit unjustified acts. This brings us back to an argument offered by Robert Nozick—and considered in §6.2 above—wherein he objected to rights-based utilitarianism on the grounds that it allows certain people to bear harms such that others reap benefits. For example, a rights-based utilitarian would be seemingly indifferent to whom we torture to avert some act of terrorism—whether a guilty terrorist or his innocent daughter—so long as the rights calculus came out the same in the end.[9] While the context here is somewhat different, the ultimate problem is the same insofar as someone who has not done anything wrong would be punished such that some other group of people is disincentivized. As a general approach to punishment and responsibility, there is something deeply flawed going on here: we should punish and hold responsible the people who do something wrong rather than the people who do not. For example, take the stock objection to utilitarianism in which we convict and execute an innocent man to appease the mob. The entire reason that this example is supposed to be compelling is because it so radically misallocates the locus of punishment and responsibility. And, in fact, it does no better a job in that regard than a proposal that would send the justified torturer to prison.

Surely, the critic will now object that I am trying to have it both ways: as a utilitarian, I cannot appeal to objections against utilitarianism to attack other positions. Or, to put it another way, isn't a proposal like Miller's exactly what the utilitarian would propose? The entire point of proposals like that is that they lead to better consequences than the alternatives. If this were true, then I would be sympathetic; I simply deny that it is true. Rather, as mentioned above, I think that the focus should be on identifying and punishing the *unjustified* cases of torture rather than on resigning the justified torturers to an identical fate. Miller thinks that the law is more blunt than morality, and this could well be right. However, it hardly follows that the law does not have the wherewithal to be able to distinguish between justified and unjustified torture. For example, it clearly has the wherewithal to distinguish between justified and unjustified killing; self-defense and the necessity defense are offered in exactly this regard.

Ultimately, Miller agrees: he acknowledges that necessity might be an appropriate defense for the torturer and also allows that, even if such a defense were inappropriate, "the sentence should be commuted to, say, one day in prison." He goes on to say that the torturer "should resign or be dismissed from [his] position; public institutions cannot suffer among their ranks those who commit serious crimes."[10] As we will see in §8.4, I do think that necessity is an appropriate defense, but, even if it were not, the token—as opposed to substantive—punishment sounds right. That said, I disagree with Miller that resignation should be required for the justified torturer. First, this person simply has not done anything wrong. Second, and as mentioned above, such a disincentive could preclude life-saving torture from taking place. Third, these sorts of torture do not even strike me as crimes, at least not any more than someone killing in self-defense; the entire point is that the actions are justified. At the end of it, I think that the justified torturer should be celebrated for an act of courage or fortitude, in much the same way that we would celebrate a war hero.

Politically, this sort of proposal has to be a nonstarter, but, morally, I just cannot embrace any other conclusion.

Civil disobedience has a long history, dating at least to Crito's failed exhortations to Socrates to flee his trial and ultimate execution.[11] And it has noble precedents, such as Rosa Parks's refusal to obey the bus driver James Blake's order to surrender her seat to a white man. The reason that these invocations miss the mark in the torture context has to do with a straightforward conflation between the descriptive and the normative: our question is how the justified torturer *should* be accommodated, rather than how he *is* (not) accommodated under present law. Whether Socrates should have left his cell and whether Ms. Parks should have retained her seat are meaningful issues only insofar as their present circumstances pitted morality against law. Our question is not what the justified torturer should do given the current laws but rather what sort of legal or judicial framework should be enacted given the possibility or reality of justified torture. For these reasons, I reject the position that the justified torturer should be convicted and punished since he is, ex hypothesi, justified in his actions. Let us now consider other possibilities, starting with torture warrants.

8.2 TORTURE WARRANTS

The central idea behind torture warrants is that some judiciary authorizes torture *before* it happens; the torturer tortures with such authorization and is, therefore, not subject to prosecution, at least insofar as the applied torture was reasonably in line with what was authorized (e.g., it was not excessive). Torture warrants have been most recently championed by Alan Dershowitz, however, as we saw in §4.2 above, they have an older history. To wit, approximately eighty-one torture warrants were issued in England between the years 1540 and 1640, for which suspicion of sedition or treason was the most common invocation.[12] Judicially sanctioned torture was much more common throughout continental Europe, but the goal in Europe was predominantly to elicit confessions rather than actionable intelligence; this is a critical difference from the sorts of warrants we will consider in this section.

History notwithstanding, the present discourse certainly centers on Dershowitz's proposal. In addition to espousing his ideas in academic works, he has also made them well-known on television and in the op-ed pages, thus catapulting the idea into public consciousness. The core idea is quite simple:

It seems logical that a formal, visible, accountable, and centralized system is somewhat easier to control than an *ad hoc*, off-the-books, and under-the-radar-screen nonsystem. I believe, though I certainly cannot prove, that a formal requirement of a judicial warrant as a prerequisite to nonlethal torture would decrease the amount of physical violence directed against suspects. At the most obvious level, a double check is always more protective than a single check. In every instance in which a warrant is requested, a field officer has already decided that torture is justified and, in the absence of a warrant requirement, would simply proceed with the torture. Requiring that decision to be approved by a judicial officer will result in fewer instances of torture even if the judge rarely turns down a request. Moreover, I believe that most judges would require compelling evidence before they would authorize so extraordinary a departure from our constitutional norms, and law enforcement officials would be reluctant to seek a warrant unless they had compelling evidence that the suspect had information needed to prevent an imminent terrorist attack.[13]

And we can make the idea simpler yet: torture warrants offer the promise of less overall torture as well as a transparency that secretive torture betrays. Through this sort of judicial authorization, we introduce a check on unjustified torture while, at the same time—and contra ideas considered in §8.1—still having access to justified torture. So what are the problems with Dershowitz's proposal?

From the outset, let me say that I am far more sanguine about its prospects than the negative reception conferred in the literature. This comparative optimism notwithstanding, I will consider the necessity defense in §8.4; to my mind, this is the better way to go insofar as it can provide for justified torture without any of the hazards Dershowitz's proposal engenders. In other words, whatever Dershowitz's torture warrants have going for them, we can realize the advantages in some other way and more economically, whether morally, judicially, or legislatively. Still, some direct engagement with his proposal is owed.

To me, the most important issue is whether warrants would actually lower the overall incidence of (unjustified) torture.[14] Dershowitz's argument is, ultimately, a logical one insofar as he thinks that the second check (i.e., the judicial one) will necessarily be more restrictive than a single check (i.e., the field officer's judgment). By comparison, consider that a hypothetical Linda is less likely to be a feminist bank teller than she is to be a bank teller simply because her being a bank teller satisfies the latter but she has to be a feminist *as well* in order to satisfy the former.[15] But herein lies the problem for Dershowitz: while Linda *cannot*—on pain of logic—be more likely to be a feminist bank teller than a bank teller, the second judicial check *could* increase the incidence of (unjustified) torture. In other words, his argument is not a logical one at all but rather an empirical one; furthermore, I suspect that it would founder empirically.

Why? Recall Dershowitz's claim: "In every instance in which a warrant is requested, a field officer has already decided that torture is justified and, in the absence of a warrant requirement, would simply proceed with the torture.... Law enforcement officials would be reluctant to seek a warrant unless they had compelling evidence." But this is almost surely false. If the field officer faced jail time (cf. §8.1 and §§8.3–8.4), then he would not proceed without some sort of certainty regarding the moral status of torture. Under Dershowitz's proposal, however, the field officer bears *no liability* because the judiciary explicitly abrogates that liability in authorizing the torture.

Imagine a field officer who suspects that torture is permissible in some case but really is not so sure. Under the necessity defense, the field officer tortures at his own peril, but, on Dershowitz's proposal, why not request the torture warrant? There is no disincentive to do so because the decision is transferred to the judiciary. Were torture warrants a possibility, field officers could reason that they might as well put in for the warrant because they have nothing to lose. Of course, Dershowitz could tack on some penalties for frivolous applications, but now those have to be adjudicated as well. Regardless, borderline and not so borderline (yet short of frivolous) applications will still be submitted; the only way to really fix this is to say that the field officer will be punished if his warrant is not granted. But that is not really any different than allowing for the necessity defense, which effectively says the same thing, though probably with differing punishments.

Additionally, there are epistemic problems insofar as judiciaries are not trained to evaluate circumstances of life-threatening catastrophe. So what happens is that a field officer—who is trained in such appraisals—asks for a warrant. The judiciary can either trust his judgment or not. If it trusts his judgment, then it renders itself superfluous. On the other hand, it may choose not to trust his judgment, in which case the judgments are ultimately being made by the judiciary rather than by the field officer. Either horn of this dilemma is unpalatable.

To my thinking, these are sufficient reasons to reject torture warrants. Some others have been given, however, and they deserve discussion. Since I do not defend torture warrants, the other ways that they can go wrong are not of primary interest; I can, therefore, keep the ensuing discussion short. Broadly speaking, these other objections can be broken into the following categories:[16]

1. torture warrants will lead to more torture (or other moral harms);[17]
2. they are pragmatically intractable;[18]
3. they compromise judicial integrity;[19] and
4. they undermine the values of a liberal democracy.[20]

One problem with this list is that its components are often articulated in ways that do not have anything to do with torture warrants in particular but rather with torture more generally. The first category of objections could have to do specifically with torture warrants, but the arguments used in its service tend to be much broader. That said—and as indicated above—I do think that torture warrants could lead to more torture, or at least it is not obvious to me that they would not. So, if these arguments are framed narrowly enough to attach only to torture warrants, then I am sympathetic.

I have never seen the fourth category of objections developed only against torture warrants; it certainly is not in the references indicated above. And, if the concern has nothing intrinsically to do with torture warrants—but is rather with legitimized torture—then I am obviously dubious. This discussion has already been carried out in §§7.2–7.3 above, and I will not rehearse it here. Suffice it to say that the values of a liberal democracy mandate security and protection of its citizenry, particularly against nefarious attacks. Surely, there are limits to how far such security and protection can extend, but the arguments of chapter 6 establish the moral basis of my position.

The second category of objections could indict torture warrants, depending on how they are developed. In some sense, these objections resonate with the contention that we do not need torture warrants since we already have the necessity defense. My accusation is not as strong as pragmatic intractability; rather, it is the comparatively moderate "more trouble that it is worth." Law and policy are far from my areas of expertise, but I see no principled reason why we could not just legislate in ways that provide for torture warrants. However, this is where the philosopher's "in principle" runs against the empirical "in practice," and I will beg off that engagement. The simple point is that we do not need torture warrants; I do not see what we ultimately gain by having them, and it would take some work to get them going in the first place. Again, this is weaker than the claim that torture warrants are pragmatically intractable, but it is in a similarly pragmatic vein.

This notion of judicial integrity, however, is making inroads in the literature, so let me say something about it before moving on to the next section. The basic idea has nothing to do with torture in particular but rather with the more general "role of the judiciary in leading by example and in invalidating or rectifying certain kinds of offensive official action."[21] To put it another way, the judiciary occupies—in addition to its functional role—a symbolic role that is essential to maintaining a lawful society; this role commits it to opposing "pernicious doctrine" in which the ends justify the means.[22] I do not have any complaint about judicial integrity as an abstract concept, but I also do not think that it is terribly useful: what will really matter is how we understand certain policies in regard to the desiderata that judicial integrity portends.

Turning to torture in particular, Chanterelle Sung writes:

> From the outset, judicially sanctioned torture undermines the integrity of the criminal justice system. The problem with judicially sanctioned torture is not only that the torture itself violates the human dignity of the individual suspects, but that the act of judicially sanctioning the torture taints the "purity of [the] courts." Because torture violates human dignity, having judges issue torture warrants entangles the judiciary in an abuse of human dignity.[23]

This is a bad argument because it runs together all sorts of different issues. First, the sorts of torture that we are considering are, ex hypothesi, morally justified. The entire dialectic is meant to query how to pragmatically accommodate justified torture; nobody deigns to accommodate unjustified torture. As Sung makes clear in the rest of her essay, she thinks that torture cannot be justified, which means that she and I have different starting points. Her contention that judiciaries should not be complicit in unjustified torture is one that we can agree on, but nobody would have ever defended this in the first place.

Second, *terrorism* is an abuse of human dignity: the terrorist violates the dignity of those he attacks. It is just a straightforward oversimplification of the issue to say that torture violates human dignity and is, therefore, off the table, whether morally or for judiciaries. In §6.4 above, I argued that invocations of dignity to ground absolutism in principle were implausible: if we care about dignity, then we should care about maximally preserving it. If (justifiable) torture could be used to save many lives, then the judiciary is put in a situation wherein it must decide whether to sanction the torture of a guilty terrorist or else fail to prevent many deaths.

It is obvious to me what judicial integrity requires in such cases, but, regardless, the issue cannot be that the judiciary would be participating in an immoral act; adjust the details as you like, but, as above, the presupposition is that the torture is justified. Even someone who denies that justified cases of torture have existed can remain silent on the issue of whether torture could be justified were such cases to present themselves. Rather, the issue then would be whether we should acknowledge the existence of such cases; as I argued in §7.6 above, I think that we can. But then the question is a substantive one and not one that judicial integrity has anything to do with: we all agree that judiciaries should not authorize unjustified torture, and, furthermore, the notion of judicial integrity is a nonstarter if it impugns judiciaries from authorizing justified acts.

For these reasons, judicial integrity is not the right way to argue against torture warrants. Rather—and as argued in more detail above—we should just say that torture warrants are more trouble than they are worth insofar as they carry costs and they do not offer benefits that cannot be realized in other ways. If there were no other way to realize those benefits, then maybe the costs would be worth it; as it stands, this is not the case. In §8.4, I will propose the necessity defense as an attractive alternative, but let us first consider self-defense.

8.3 SELF-DEFENSE

In §5.2 above, I introduced the distinction between a justification and an excuse; this is a distinction well entrenched in our approach to criminal law. The difference between the two can be expressed as follows: "A justification claim . . . seeks to show that the act was *not wrongful*, [whereas] an excuse . . . tries to show that the actor is not morally culpable for his wrongful conduct."[24] Or else consider Michael Moore: "A justification shows that *prima facie* wrongful and unlawful conduct is *not wrongful or unlawful at all*. . . . [B]y contrast, an excuse does not take away our prima facie judgment that an act is wrongful and unlawful; rather, it shows that the actor was not culpable in his doing of an admittedly wrongful and unlawful act."[25]

As I said in that earlier section, one of the principal differences between justification and excuse is that, if someone is justified, then he did not do anything wrong; if he is (merely) excused, then he did something wrong, but it is not his fault. Self-defense and necessity are justifications insofar as, when these are adequately established, we acknowledge that the accused did not act wrongly. Excuse, however, goes to incapacity, such as would be manifest through duress or insanity. If the accused kills a family but can establish insanity, then we do not hold him (morally or criminally) liable since it was not his fault. But, in excusing him from legal punishment, we do not say that the killings were justified. Self-defense and necessity are justifications insofar as we invoke them for legal exoneration of justified acts; compare them, for example, to the insanity defense, which does not maintain that the act was justified, only that its perpetrator lacked the relevant mental capacities.

Let us start with self-defense since I propose that we hereafter set it aside. The doctrine of self-defense is most basically that "the use of force on or toward another person is justifiable when the actor [correctly] believes that such force is immediately necessary for the purpose or protecting himself against the use of unlawful force by such other person on the present occasion."[26] So, if someone is being attacked and he kills the attacker before the attacker can kill him, the killing is justified by self-defense. This sort of archetypal case has two obvious features: the person who is killed in self-defense is the one who threatens the unlawful killing, and the person who does the killing is the one who is being attacked (cf. *self*-defense). While self-defense is a perfectly reasonable legal justification, it is hard to see how it could have anything to do with torture since neither of these basic features is satisfied. Imagine that we are trying to justify the torture of a detainee such that myriad lives are saved. The torturer is not threatened, so it cannot be a case of *self*-defense. Second, the detainee is not a threat at all in the most straightforward sense of *threat*. He may be complicit in some threat, he may have contributed to the threat, and so on, but *he* is not a threat; the threat is a bomb waiting to go off somewhere else altogether.

Nevertheless, John Yoo's infamous memo posits self-defense as a potential justification for torture. The language offered in defense of this position, however, is quite noteworthy, particularly insofar as it speaks more to necessity than to self-defense. To be sure, self-defense and necessity are closely related—I think of self-defense as a limiting case of necessity—but Yoo actually means to offer self-defense as a sui generis option. Or at least it looks like it. Curiously, he seems to give it all back midway through his discussion:

> To be sure, this situation is different from the usual self-defense justification, and, indeed, it overlaps with elements of the necessity defense. Self-defense as usually discussed involves using force against an individual who is about to conduct the attack. In the current circumstance, however, an enemy combatant in detention does not himself present a threat of

harm. He is not actually carrying out the attack; rather he has participated in the planning and preparation for the attack, or merely has knowledge of the attack through his membership in the terrorist organization.[27]

Despite this, Yoo still thinks that self-defense could be an appropriate defense to violations of 118 U.S.C. §2340A because, quoting Michael Moore, the enemy combatant "has culpably caused the situation where someone might get hurt. If hurting him is the only means to prevent the death or injury of others put at risk by his actions, such torture should be permissible, and on the same basis that self-defense is permissible."[28] I agree with Moore that such torture would be permissible but simply deny that it would be on the same basis that self-defense is permissible: this case lacks the two characteristic features delineated above. That said, the torture could still be justified through the necessity defense, which I will consider in the next section.

Yoo concludes his discussion by offering a novel argument in which the *nation*, rather than the torturer, is what is under attack; the torturer is defending the nation, of which he is a part. While this sounds like a stretch, there is actually some relevant case law. *In re Neagle* (1890) exonerated U.S. Marshal David Neagle for shooting and killing the assailant of Supreme Court justice Stephen Field on the grounds that Neagle was asserting the executive branch's constitutional authority to protect the U.S. government (i.e., since Field was an agent of that government). Yoo goes on to cite various other cases, as well as the U.S. Constitution, in support of the thesis that the government can act to protect itself.

While I appreciate the creativity of the argument, there are at least three issues with it. First, it is far from clear how a terrorist is attacking the *nation*: it seems rather that he is attacking various individuals. Revealing is the disanalogy between the terrorism context and *Neagle* insofar as the reasoning in the latter was rendered precisely because Field was a Supreme Court justice; this is different from an attack on normal noncombatants. Even if some of the terrorist's targets were federal agents, I am not swayed. For example, do we really think that an attack against an FBI agent is an attack against the United States? I do not have that intuition, and, even if I did, it would be further attenuated if the FBI agent were under cover or his presence was incidental to the attack. And, again, there is no inherent reason to think that any federal agent would even be present at the site of a terrorist's attack. Second, the single case to which Yoo appeals for his argument is from 1890: there is no reason to think that this case is selectively chosen, but the evidence is certainly sparse and dated. Third, and most importantly, there is just no reason to turn to this self-defense argument if necessity can provide the appropriate justification; this is especially true if the argument from necessity is more straightforward and less attenuated. So maybe this argument could work, and maybe it cannot, but, regardless, we do not need it. Let us therefore now move on to consider necessity directly; even some critics of torture acknowledge that this approach bears the most promise.[29]

8.4 **THE NECESSITY DEFENSE**

The *Model Penal Code* offers a concise statement on the basis for the necessity defense that, illustratively, comes under the heading of "Justification Generally: Choice of Evils":

> 1. Conduct which the actor believes to be necessary to avoid a harm or evil to himself or to another is justifiable, provided that:
>   a. The harm or evil sought to be avoided by such conduct is greater than that sought to be prevented by the law defining the offense charged; and
>   b. Neither the Code nor other law defining the offense provides exceptions or defenses dealing with the specific situation involved; and
>   c. A legislative purpose to exclude the justification claimed does not otherwise plainly appear.[30]

Before turning to objections, let us go through these conditions individually see whether we can make plausible the idea that torture can be defended via necessity. Condition 1a bears particular emphasis from the outset: the harm or evil that some act is meant to prevent must be greater than whatever harm or evil the law proscribing that act is meant to avoid. In the case of ticking-time-bomb cases, this condition is certainly satisfied. To wit, there is the torture of a single individual such that many lives are saved, and the moral value of those lives (dramatically) exceeds the moral harm of the torture that is necessary to preserve them.[31] In this sense, the application of the necessity defense is as straightforward as other paradigmatic cases, such as when Jones shoots and kills a gangster before that gangster can execute five innocents. While the killing might otherwise be met with disapprobation, the circumstances justify it insofar as Jones chooses the lesser evil.[32]

The point of condition 1b is that we should not turn to the necessity defense when a statute already has exceptions explicitly built into it. If, for example, some statute said that φ was illegal unless A, then, given A, φ is not illegal; there is no reason to appeal to the necessity defense since the statute is not even violated. To see whether 1b is satisfied, we need to look at the actual statute, which, regarding the criminalization of torture, is 118 U.S.C. §2340A. This statute clearly does not provide any exceptions for emergency situations (or any other situations), so 1b is satisfied.

Condition 1c should give us the most pause. First, it bears emphasis that the official commentary of the *Model Penal Code* is quite clear that even serious crimes, such as homicide, are not meant to be excluded under the necessity defense.[33] That said, some jurisdictions have explicitly blocked (e.g., Kentucky and Missouri) or limited (e.g., Wisconsin) this defense in the case of homicide;[34] there is case law precedent for this limitation as well.[35] And, returning to torture, remember from §4.1 above that §2.2 of CAT specifically rules out torture in exceptional cases: "No exceptional circumstances whatsoever, whether a state of war or a threat of war, internal political instability or any other public emergency, may be invoked as a justification of torture." Regardless, the exact language of CAT does not bind the United States insofar as the United States was free to interpret CAT and to issue reservations, understandings, and declarations as it deemed necessary, which it did. What ultimately matters in terms of the U.S. obligations under CAT is what the United States legislated in accord with that treaty, namely, 118 U.S.C. §§2340–2340A. Or, to put it another way, CAT is not U.S. law, 118 U.S.C. §§2340–2340A are, and these sections do not plainly exclude appeals to necessity.[36]

As argued above, conditions 1a–1c are all plausibly satisfied for torture in emergency cases. Regardless, the literature has posed various arguments as to why necessity should, nevertheless, be unavailable for defense against torture; these arguments merit consideration. While I regret not being able to spend more time on this discussion, I do want to at least respond to some of the more obvious objections. The most pressing of these is probably that the necessity defense may be off the table completely in federal cases; there is no federal statute providing for necessity, and federal courts have remained agnostic as to whether the successful invocation of necessity in nonfederal cases establishes the legitimacy of appeals to necessity in federal cases.[37] Since the statute that proscribes torture is a federal one, the status of necessity vis-à-vis that statute is, therefore, unclear.

In *United States v. Oakland Cannabis Buyers' Cooperative* (2001), the Supreme Court specifically said that the status of necessity in federal courts is an "open question"; the Court found that there was no medical necessity exception to the Controlled Substance Act of 1970 (CSA) insofar as Congress found that marijuana had "no currently accepted medical use." In other words, even if the distribution of medical marijuana prevented a worse evil (namely, patient suffering) than it committed (namely, the violation of the CSA), necessity was unavailable because of the value judgment that Congress made in its legislation. It bears notice that 118 U.S.C. §2340A makes no analogous value judgment in regard to torture; this statute says nothing about whether torture might be advisable in some situations. At any rate, this case reiterated the Supreme Court's position that necessity is not a well-founded defense in federal cases, regardless of the specific statute against which such a defense would be deployed.

Some other cases deserve discussion as well. Going backward in time, *United States v. Bailey* (1980) considered a necessity defense for inmates who escaped from a federal detention facility, therefore violating a federal law. At the trial, they argued that the prison was unsafe owing to fires, beating by guards, and inadequate medical attention.[38] The court ruled out the necessity defense because, principally, "[the defendant] must proffer evidence of a bona fide effort to surrender or return to custody as soon as the claimed duress or necessity had lost its coercive force."[39] In other words, following the escape, the three escapees remained on the lam for anywhere between one and two and a half months before being recaptured: the Supreme Court interpreted this as a continuing crime that was unnecessary to avoid the risks the escapees sought to avert. The ruling left open the possibility that they could have escaped and thereafter surrendered to a safer situation, but this is not what the defendants in fact did. A key point, however, is that the Supreme Court did not rule out the necessity defense in general but rather said that it was unavailable in this particular case.

There are more cases worth mentioning,[40] but let us just consider one, *Baender v. Barnett* (1921). In this ruling, "the [Supreme] Court suggested that criminal statutes would be construed with the aid of the common law canons developed to prevent unjust punishments."[41] Surprisingly, the Supreme Court has considered necessity in just three cases since then, *Bailey*, *Oakland Cannabis Buyers' Cooperative*, and *Dixon v. United States*.[42] In each of those cases, it refused the necessity defense given the specifics of the case but, at the same time, remained silent as to whether it would be available in other cases. I think that there is little reason to think that it would not be available under the right circumstances, for at least the following three reasons.

First, *Baender v. Barnett* explicitly allows for common law canons to prevent unjust punishments; the invocation of necessity to forestall a conviction of lifesaving torture is, to me at least, a straightforward application of this edict. Second, there is no reason to think that either *Bailey* or *Oakland Cannabis Buyers' Cooperative* portends any skepticism regarding the admissibility of the necessity defense in federal court. As the Supreme Court pointed out in *Bailey*, the conditions for necessity were simply not satisfied since the defendants did not turn themselves in after the escape. To be sure, it is perfectly consistent to say that they considered that case on the merits of necessity and found it lacking, though they would not have allowed necessity even if the conditions were met. If that were true, however, why assess the merits? Why not just say that necessity is disallowed in federal courts? The fact that they considered the case on its merits is at least some evidence that they would be disposed to accept the defense. Similarly, *Oakland Cannabis Buyers' Cooperative* failed to successfully invoke necessity, but for a different reason: the relevant congressional legislation preempted the exception through the legislative language (cf. "no currently accepted medical use"). The torture statute has no such language in it, so there is no reason to think that the legislation would be immune to the necessity defense. Third, there really is no general reason to think that necessity would be inadmissible in federal court. In other words, the fact that the Supreme Court has yet to exonerate on those grounds in any particular case says nothing about its willingness to do so if the circumstances are appropriate: the right case just has not yet come forward. If some ticking-time-bomb torturer did invoke necessity, I would expect the federal courts to honor the defense; were it necessary to commit a lesser evil in order to prevent a greater one, it simply does not make sense to convict. And this is hardly my intuition alone, insofar as it is the entire reason that the necessity defense has been codified into our common law.

These preceding paragraphs have considered what I take to be the most interesting issue vis-à-vis necessity, namely, whether it is admissible as a defense. However, there are some other interesting arguments in the literature, so let me offer quick discussion of them as well. First, Jordan Paust has argued that the necessity defense will fail, though for a different reason than the one presented above; it is worth presenting his argument so that we can see why it does not apply to ticking-time-bomb cases. In particular, Paust quotes from *Bailey* that "if there was a reasonable, legal alternative to violating the law . . . the defense will fail." And, furthermore, the defendant must show that, "given the imminence of a threat, violation of . . . [a law] was his only reasonable alternative."[43] Paust is particularly concerned with the ongoing treatment of detainees at Guantánamo Bay; in particular, he is deeply skeptical that any enhanced interrogations are even necessary given that there exist alternate legal avenues that could be pursued. Whether he is right or wrong in this regard is irrelevant when we consider ticking-time-bomb cases: those cases are precisely those in which, ex hypothesi, torture is the only available option to prevent a greater evil. Therefore, I can remain agnostic on the treatments at Guantánamo Bay without relenting on the applicability of necessity in emergency cases.

A similar argument is developed by Paola Gaeta, who argues that torture "does not necessarily and ineluctably avert the imminent danger to life and limb, because the suspected terrorist may not have the information, or may not have the right information, or may remain silent."[44] To put it another way, the torturer does not know that his torture will save lives—because of various epistemic uncertainties discussed in §5.3 above—so Gaeta therefore thinks that necessity is inappropriate. My response here is simply that she misunderstands the burdens incumbent on the necessity defense. To see why, consider the following language from the *Model Penal Code*: "Conduct which the actor *believes to be necessary* to avoid a harm or evil to himself or to another is justifiable, provided that . . ." The relative epistemic standard is clearly not knowledge but rather (reasonable) belief. And there is good reason for this insofar as we can easily imagine cases wherein the less stringent requirement is appropriate.

For example, suppose that a terrorist has announced that he will detonate himself in a large public square, killing hundreds. He is strapped with explosives, has a verified motive (e.g., seeking revenge after a dishonorable discharge from the military), has a history of violence, and so on. A sniper can take him out and does. Afterward, forensics determines that the explosives were improperly wired and would not have detonated. The sniper did not *know* that the terrorist would detonate the explosives for the simple reason that such a detonation was impossible (i.e., he could not know a false proposition). Nevertheless, it was reasonable to believe that the terrorist could have killed hundreds—in fact, he was trying to—but we still do not hold the sniper morally culpable; knowledge is simply too high of an epistemic standard. In response to Gaeta, I therefore submit—both on intuition and on the text of the *Modern Penal Code*—that reasonable belief is the appropriate epistemic standard. And, furthermore, I contend that this can be reasonably met in ticking-time-bomb cases (cf. §7.6 above).

In addition to the arguments considered above, there are others. In particular, I considered the necessity defense vis-à-vis Supreme Court rulings, but there are relevant circuit court rulings as well.[45] Also, the engagement between U.S. domestic law and international law is important; even if U.S. law could allow the necessity defense in torture, there is relevant international law that might purport to limit such a defense.[46] A response here takes us too far afield, but let me offer two quick comments. First, as I said above, 118 U.S.C. §2240 reflects our understanding of CAT, and the United States did not codify the language preventing exceptions. Our ratification can be understood only in light of our ensuing legislation since that legislation reflects our understanding of the treaty. As a matter of law, I agree that "both treaty-based and customary international law . . . will trump inconsistent common law whether or not there might be such a common law defense to ordinary crime when international law has not been violated."[47] However, I deny that our common law is inconsistent on this issue: it consistently recognizes necessity as a legitimate defense. There have not been successful invocations of necessity regarding torture—or anything else—at the Supreme Court level, but this does not mean that the common law foundation for that defense is not well founded.

Second, my principal concern is with what the laws should be rather than what they are; I already made this point in the introductory paragraphs of this chapter. If international law were to inveigh against the necessity defense—or even if the Supreme Court were to wholesale disallow it—then we could still meaningfully ask whether there were differences between how the necessity defense *is* treated and how it *ought* to be treated with regard to torture. The fundamental kernel of wisdom underlying the necessity defense is simply that lesser evils are preferable to greater ones; how could anyone possibly argue against such a self-evident proposition? I doubt anyone would, which is why the necessity defense is so firmly entrenched in our criminal law. Rather, where it gets interesting is whether torture could ever be the lesser evil, particularly given worries about its efficacy (§7.1), institutional requirements (§7.2), nefarious spread (§7.3), and so on (§7.4). These issues were treated in the last chapter, so I will not have more to say about them here. That said, I certainly think that torture could be the lesser evil in some particular cases and, therefore, think that the necessity defense would be appropriate in those cases.

Before moving on to the concluding chapter, let me return to torture warrants and indicate why the necessity defense is preferable. Remember that one of my arguments against torture warrants was that they could lead to frivolous applications insofar as intelligence officers would have nothing to lose by applying for such a warrant and, once such a warrant were issued, they would have reasonably wide latitude in their applications of torture. This is not to deny that there could be penalties for frivolous applications or that the conditions and modes of torture could not be highly circumscribed; rather, the point is that these are some of the pragmatic obstacles assailing torture warrants. Necessity, on the other hand, has neither of these problems. To wit, anyone who tortures stands to be convicted unless he can clearly establish that he chose the lesser of two evils. If the lesser evil argument cannot be clearly established, then the torturer is criminally liable for torture and stands to go to jail or even to be executed if the torture victim expires under torture. Given the risks, would-be torturers will have to choose between caution and potential conviction, and I expect caution to come out on top.

Interestingly, the lesser evil argument does not seem to require the least possible evil; nothing in the text of the *Model Penal Code*, for example, says anything about being required to choose E_1 over E_2 when either will avert E_3 and the magnitudes of those evils are such that $E_3 > E_2 > E_1$. If a greater torture averts a terrible evil wherein a lesser torture would have done the same job—and assuming that the torturer would have reasonably believed the lesser torture to be sufficient—we at least find him morally liable. If we look to cases like *Bailey*, the necessity defense has been interpreted in line with this moral intuition: escaping and not surrendering was worse than the possible option of escaping and surrendering, so necessity was not established. The upshot in regard to torture is that excessive torture might not be protected by necessity, as it should not be.

Therefore necessity offers two straightforward advantages over torture warrants. First, it puts the onus on the torturer with regard to the merits of torture, rather than facilitating an ex ante pass from the judiciary. Second, it limits the zeal with which the would-be torturer would pursue torture insofar as overzealous torture would still be criminally liable.[48] While I take these to be appropriate safeguards on the practice of torture, note that they may result in justifiable torture not being deployed insofar as the justified torturer could be unwilling to risk criminal prosecution. It would be regrettable if self-interest trumped moral responsibility, but it is probably preferable to have some personal disincentive to torture rather than the ex ante authorization that torture warrants offer. Maybe justifiable torture would be occasionally forgone, but unjustified torture would be substantially more limited; this is a safeguard that even I would be willing to accept.

9

The Limits of
Torture

This last chapter comprises some concluding remarks regarding the themes explored in the book; in this sense, it is closer to an afterword than a substantive chapter. As I said in the preface, the central theme of this book has been that lesser harms are always preferable to greater harms and that torture, while bad, could, nevertheless, be the lesser harm in exceptional cases. In chapter 6, this *could* was presented as one of philosophical thought experiment, but chapter 7 tried to give it some traction in the real world. An important part of the project was to situate the debate about torture within the broader context of terrorism (part I) and then to make the associated philosophical discussion (part II) empirically engaged (part III). I can foresee objections coming from every angle, but I have tried to forestall them in the associated discussions. The purpose of these concluding remarks, then, is not to further the defense or to recapitulate key claims but rather to end the book by reflecting on two themes that have received insufficient attention so far. And, as the title of this chapter indicates, to acknowledge the limits of torture.

9.1 TORTURE IS NOT A PANACEA

In chapter 6, I argued that virtually any plausible moral theory could defend the permissibility of torture in exceptional cases; the key feature of these cases was simply that torture minimized overall harms. It is important to emphasize that I really do take these cases to be exceptional or, to say it another way, very uncommon. As was made clear in chapter 4, torture is bad and for various reasons. Torture causes suffering, and suffering is bad. Interrogational torture also forces the tortured into a position of self-betrayal, and that is also bad. So, at the end of the book, I want to emphasize that my defense of torture acknowledges the wrongs of torture; I do not unapologetically or unreservedly champion torture. Rather, I lament that we live in a world in which terrorism threatens lives and that torture might sometimes be our most prudent recourse against those threats.

If torture really would be so exceptional, why write an entire book about what might bear on only a handful of cases? I never have understood the point of this question insofar as, handful of cases or not, we still have to decide what to do in them. One time I went to a colloquium given by a speaker whose research area was the ethics of infectious disease; he almost seemed stupefied that applied ethicists would work on any other topic given how many annual deaths are attributable to HIV/AIDS, tuberculosis, and malaria (i.e., several million). If we think about the harms effected by diseases or other societal ills—such as poverty or global warming—why spend so much intellectual energy worrying about how to deal with some small number of ticking-time-bomb-like cases? For what it is worth, this is not just me: the literature on the moral status of interrogational torture is quite large and growing. Why is it that we find ourselves so captivated by these questions and so untaken with others? There are many answers here, but, for better or worse, torture is such a compelling and visceral topic to many of us. While much of disease afflicts those far away, 9/11 was an attack on us and our country; it left many of us feeling personally violated and instantly catapulted terrorism into our national consciousness. Even though there is no reason to think that torture could have readily prevented 9/11, that horrible day nevertheless catalyzed the ensuing discussion about how far we may go in order to protect ourselves.

Regardless, it should be recognized that there are only a small number of marginal cases in which torture is a live moral topic; the rest of the cases are as morally uncontroversial as those decried in §4.2 above. To some extent, however, the focus on marginal cases is similar to many other debates in applied ethics. In 2009, for example, there were fewer than fifty executions in the United States, though capital punishment remains a lightning rod for moral debate. Human reproductive cloning is hotly contested—and the associated discourse enjoys a wide public forum—even though there has never been a successful application thereof. This is not to deny that some debates in applied ethics pertain to more ubiquitous practices, such as abortion, pornography, and the treatment of nonhuman animals. Rather, the point is simply that torture does not stand alone in being contentious if infrequently justified. And, sadly, torture itself is hardly infrequent at all, even if the justified cases might be.

Still, people often ask why I wanted to write this book. A large part of it was simply that my views were not reflected anywhere else in the philosophical literature; there are few conservative voices in a very liberal profession. But it goes beyond that insofar as this is simply a fascinating moral question, regardless of how many ticking-time-bomb cases there actually are. For most of the quotidian issues we face, the ethical answers are more or less straightforward. When we get to the margins—to those rare cases in which various values are pitted against each other in nonstandard ways—is when ethics gets interesting. In other words, it is usually obvious what we should do, and we just need to have the character and resolve to do it. In the case of torturing a suspected terrorist, however, it is hardly obvious what to do, and reasonable people disagree vociferously on this issue.

That said, let me again emphasize that we are arguing over a small handful of cases. I do not believe in widespread, institutionalized torture, nor does anyone else seriously defend it. A defense of torture is not meant to extend beyond highly circumscribed cases, and, in fact, part of a defense owes an accounting for how such spillage can be foreclosed (cf. §7.3 above). Torture should not be deployed cavalierly, and our intelligence community must be vigilant against inappropriate uses. While torture that fails to yield actionable intelligence might be justified given our epistemic limitations, the number of lives that hang in the balance, and so on (cf. §7.1), it nevertheless must be minimized. And, furthermore, even if torture were to be successful in saving lives, it could be justified only if it were reasonably thought to be necessary or at least prudent.[1]

While the preceding paragraphs have meant to emphasize the scope of the project, there is another way in which torture is not a panacea: it does nothing to address the underlying causes of terrorism that recommend it in the first place. The premise of the book has been that we find ourselves in a situation wherein torture might disarm a terrorist threat. But how did we find ourselves in this situation in the first place? Why is there terrorism at all? Much less against us? These are immensely complicated questions and ones that have to do with far more than philosophy; geopolitics, economics, religion, and culture all play important contributory roles in explaining the root causes of terrorism. Torture is, at best, a temporary solution to a deeper problem. And, at worst, it makes that problem even worse by exacerbating the ill will borne against us.

In approaching this discussion, it is useful to consider terms from the health care debate, particularly the distinction between curative and preventative medicine. Our health care system—reform notwithstanding—is too heavily invested in fixing people after they get sick rather than preventing them from getting sick in the first place.[2] Faced with a public that would rather overeat, underexercise, and spend billions on Lipitor and other cholesterol-lowering drugs, it is no surprise that American health finds itself in such dire straits. There are surely endogenous avenues that the health care industry must pursue, but many of its obstacles are exogenous. In other words, if people did not get sick—especially from easily preventable afflictions—then there would be far less to debate vis-à-vis health care. And, furthermore, the health care debate would benefit from shifting the focus from what to do with sick people to how to prevent people from getting sick.

The discourse about torture is isomorphic to that about health care in so many ways. Instead of fostering the circumstances that give rise to terrorism, we should figure out how to mitigate or dispell them. If we can make progress in this regard, then we will not find ourselves—or at least find ourselves less often—forced to countenance torture. It is far beyond my expertise to offer any substantive commentary on how this should proceed, but the suggestion is hardly novel regardless; everyone wants to lower the incidence of terrorism, presumably including the terrorists themselves.[3] An exclusive focus on torture is, therefore, myopic insofar as, to continue the analogy with medicine, it fixates on a symptom rather than on the underlying disease.

To be clear, I am not proposing a singular focus on torture: of course we should, and do, care about the root causes of terrorism. The discourse about torture is often insufficiently attentive to this broader context, but that shortcoming is neither here nor there when considering what to actually do in exceptional cases. In other words, supposing that we actually find ourselves the victim of a terrorist threat, it is not helpful to wonder how to prevent future threats. Rather, we must respond to the ones currently at hand, and, after we disarm them, we can think about how we got there in the first place and how to prevent recurrences. This book is about what to do when faced with serious threats; my hope is, surely, that such threats do not present themselves, but it begs off a serious intellectual task to ignore the unfortunate potentiality or, more probably, eventuality.

9.2 HOW FAR SHOULD WE GO?

A second theme worth considering in these closing remarks is that the previously offered defense of torture could authorize some completely heinous acts, including highly brutalized torture and/or the torture of innocents. To wit, consider the claim that torture is justified if and only if it portends a lesser harm than we might reasonably expect to otherwise absorb. Such a claim puts no upward bound on how bad the torture could be; insofar as the terrorist threat gets worse, we are allowed to consider more egregious torture in order to prevent that threat. This does not deny that all torture is bad—of course it is—but only allows that it can be either bad or worse. If Khalid Sheikh Mohammed was waterboarded 183 times, that is a lot of suffering; it would have been less morally bad, for example, were he to have been waterboarded some fewer number of times insofar as fewer instances would have led to less suffering.[4]

In §5.1 above, we saw Jeremy Bentham's utilitarian basis for torture, and one of his precepts was that we should torture no more than is necessary to elicit our goal. While there are obvious epistemological and other empirical challenges to this moral edict (cf. §7.1), the moral principle is straightforward. Torturers should be held accountable for the torture that they inflict, and overly zealous torture—that is, torture that goes beyond what anyone might reasonably expect to be warranted—should be punished. This is not to deny that extreme torture can be justified, but it can be only when such torture could reasonably be expected to be the lesser harm. For example, if intelligence reveals a terrorist threat against many lives, then greater latitude should be extended vis-à-vis torture than when fewer lives were threatened. Even were that torture to ultimately be unsuccessful, it would at least have been deployed against a greater threat; the calculus of expected outcomes could, therefore, support it.

Nevertheless, there are limits on the sorts of torture that reasonable people could, ultimately, contemplate. Imagine that intelligence officers were to reach the conclusion that some detainee had no intelligence value or that they at least had no reason to think otherwise. They could either stop the battery of interrogations or else press forward with more aggressive techniques. While it *could* be the case that brutalizing the detainee prevents the next 9/11, there is simply no basis for believing that it *would*. In other words, even if the magnitude of the terrorist threat they sought to prevent was immensely grave, the likelihood that this particular detainee could diffuse the threat could be so remote as to not license his torture.

Of course, we never know exactly what the likelihoods are; if we found ourselves in perfect epistemic situations, we could talk about certainties rather than likelihoods. Rather, we do the best we can with whatever information we have, and we hold those accountable who make decisions that are unsupported by that information. If some intelligence officer were to brutally torture some detainee, we could ask him why he did it.

Maybe he has a good reason, in which case the torture could (but not necessarily would) be justified.[5] Or else he does not, in which case he should be punished.

But still, the critic might press, given the potential for some catastrophic threat, the torture calculus could come out positive even if the likelihood of torture being efficacious were extremely low. Agreed. That said, there should still need to be some nonnegligible reason to think that torture would work at all. If rounding up some random person on the street and torturing him might prevent a grave threat, should we countenance his torture? In such a case, we have no reason to think that the likelihood of torture is anything other than (marginally above) zero, so we should not torture; I cannot fathom any reasonable person saying otherwise. Furthermore, if we are just talking about some nonspecific terrorist threat (e.g., there may be such a threat, but we have no reason to think that there is), then whatever rational basis there could have even been for torture (e.g., against a specific threat) is further reduced.

Tweak the case somewhat such that we apprehend someone who is a former neighbor of a known terrorist; our captive steadfastly denies knowledge of any terrorist plot. In reality, this sort of case probably comes up pretty often, so what should we do? Of course, the details are going to matter, but, if the case really were this simple, there would be little reason to think that torture would be effective: just because our detainee lived next to a terrorist, we should not expect that the former would have details of the latter's machinations, both because the relationship is attenuated and because the operational details of the plot would not be casually shared. And, while some sort of stern interrogation might be justified, there is simply no cause for optimism that a course of protracted torture would be useful. Maybe it would have been, or maybe some released terrorist would have capitulated under one more application of waterboarding; we never know. The best that we can do is think critically about the expected outcomes, even as messy and ill informed as those can get on the ground. The more confident we are that our detainee is involved in some terrorist attack, or the more confident we are that said attack is against a greater number of people, the more latitude we have in trying to preempt it. Ultimately, however, the point is that we simply cannot torture without some reasoned basis. We can disagree as to what constitutes those bases, but arbitrary, capricious, or gratuitous torture plays no role in my account.

But what about the (reasoned) torture of the innocent? In §5.3 above, we considered ticking-time-bomb case variants, one of which involved the torture of a terrorist's innocent daughter such that the terrorist would relinquish information about his pending attack. Not surprisingly, support for torture in these cases was lower than when the terrorist himself was to be tortured. The critic could press that nothing in my account precludes the torture of the innocent daughter, and this could presumably be held up as a defect of the account. So, first, let me acknowledge that my account allows for the torture of innocents when such torture could reasonably be thought the least morally offensive way to prevent a greater harm. And, second, let me explore what such a commitment might amount to in practice.

Starting with the torture of an innocent daughter, this is at least doubly improbable as a standard ticking-time-bomb case. To wit, such a case asks us to imagine, not only that we find ourselves in a standard ticking-time-bomb case, but also that we have apprehended a terrorist's innocent daughter, and, furthermore, that, while impervious to torture himself, the terrorist would crack were his daughter to be tortured. If one thinks that ticking-time-bomb cases are rare, then one could reasonably expect the cases involving the daughter to virtually impossible. In other words, the conjoined probability of two exceedingly unlikely scenarios is vanishingly small, far smaller than the already unlikely probability of either scenario obtaining by itself. Terrorists simply do not travel around with their young daughters, and, even were there some independent way to apprehend the daughter, we might expect a dedicated terrorist to remain true to his cause despite her torture. Now it just seems that I am evading the question, all the worse since that was the same allegation I hurled at opponents of ticking-time-bomb methodology back in §5.2. But, as I already said above, I think that such torture could be justified, but I just deny that it ever would be.

The question of torturing innocents also arose in §7.1, where I presented the following case:

> Red Sweatshirt. Our intelligence reveals that the terrorist has just set up a bomb in a crowded building and has exited wearing a red sweatshirt. Law enforcement sets up a perimeter and starts to canvas the area; two men in red sweatshirts are apprehended, both of whom deny any knowledge of terroristic activity. Run the rest of the story as in standard ticking-time-bomb cases, the adjustment being that the bomb can be disarmed only if both men, one of whom is innocent, are tortured.

Empirically, this sort of case is far more likely than the daughter case, so I see it as more of a worry. That said, my strategy is still the same: to deny that it is very likely to happen or else to say that, if it does, then torture is justified. As I suggested in that earlier discussion, one way to look at the torture of innocents is as a sort of collateral damage, just as we think of the killing of noncombatants during war. Maybe torture is worse than killing, or maybe not; regardless, the point is that some sort of moral costs are allowable in the pursuit of a greater moral good. This does not deny that we must be vigilant against minimizing those costs, that some costs are not worth bearing, and so on. My view on torture is that it constitutes a moral wrong (cf. §4.2 above) but that that wrong is commensurable with all sorts of other moral values. To put it another way, torture still has to compete against other values in our moral calculus; if we should not torture, it is because our moral calculus recommends against it and not because there is anything about torture that sets it aside from that calculus altogether. Kantians undoubtedly see it differently, but their vision is not mine.

As a final point of discussion in this vein, consider what we might call *preventative torture*. Roughly, I have in mind a distinction—sometimes promulgated under the aegis of the *Bush doctrine*—between the use of force against actual aggressors and the use of force against (potential) future aggressors. While the just war tradition acknowledges the right of self-defense, that right is usually articulated in terms of defense against actual, as opposed to potential, aggression. So, if some state is attacking ours, we can defend ourselves. If that other state is gathering on the border and attack appears imminent, then we can attack before we are attacked. This second scheme often goes under *preemptive war* but can still be well grounded in classical just war theory, particularly if we understand the amassing of troops as an act of aggression, whether or not those troops have yet to attack.

As the temporal links become more attenuated, however, we shift the nomenclature from preemptive war toward preventative war: instead of preempting some particular attack, preventative action aims to prevent that attack from ever being either imminent or actual. If we bomb terrorist training grounds in Afghanistan, for example, that might reasonably be understood as preventative insofar as, let us suppose, attacks emanating thereof would be neither imminent nor actual. What about preventative torture? Just to have a concrete case for discussion, consider the following:

> *Media Officer.* The intelligence community is on the trail of a terrorist organization's chief media officer; this officer is solely responsible for the dissemination of propaganda used to recruit future terrorists. He is very effective at his job and produces anti-American flyers and DVDs that have

been very successful for recruitment. If he is not apprehended in the near future, his imminent marketing campaign will ensure the recruitment of many new terrorists as well as the associated calamities they would eventually perpetuate; if he were captured, distribution of the marketing campaign will be forestalled, and no new terrorists would be recruited. While the intelligence community has no other direct leads on this media officer, it has in custody several of his known, yet recalcitrant, associates. If torture of the media officer's associates is judged to be the only way to learn his location—and, therefore, secure his detention—before the marketing campaign was disseminated, would it be justified?[6]

Were this case to gain any empirical purchase, I would be deeply conflicted. The problem with preventative action is that it might ultimately prove unnecessary; given the time lag between the preventative action itself and whatever action it aims to prevent, any number of things could change. Maybe the political landscape changes in the interim such that the would-be terrorists are no longer compelled toward terrorism. Or maybe other terrorists are able to effect the sort of policy changes that would forestall other terrorist acts. Regardless, the simple point is that a number of things could happen, any of which would render the preventative attack an unnecessary cost.

On the other hand, preventative action might minimize overall harm, such as when we destroy weeds before they take over the rest of our garden; were we to wait, the intervention would be far more costly. I suspect that many would take exception to the details of the case presented above, questioning whether a media officer really has an effect on the recruiting of terrorists or whether he might be easily replaced by another (or even more effective) media officer such that the torture became superfluous. As it turns out, these possibilities are ruled out by the facts of the case, but we can always remain suspicious about how empirically plausible such cases are.

One thing that matters is how far removed the preventative action is from the action that it prevents; the greater the discrepancy, the more could change in the meantime. If we are countenancing the bombing of a training camp for very young children, then there is cause for skepticism about the necessity of the attack. Let us suppose that those children would not participate in terrorist attacks for some number of years, so political or diplomatic inroads would be plausible or even simple intervention from regular law enforcement. If the training is, instead, geared toward more proximate attacks, then the case for prevention is stronger.

Were there to be a case exactly like the one posited above, I think that torture could be justified. Regardless, I think that such a case is exceedingly unlikely, precisely because we will rarely have good reason to believe that the media officer is that effective, that irreplaceable, that there would not be other political or diplomatic ways to address the training camps, or that normal military action would not be appropriate for dismantling them. So, as with the daughter case, my theoretical commitments are straightforward; such commitments do not have any obvious application to real-world decisions. Rather, I suspect that torture would ever be justified only in cases reasonably close to ticking-time-bomb cases and that the torture of innocents and preventative torture are not likely to recommend themselves.

9.3 FINAL REMARKS

Before concluding, let me again emphasize that torture comprises various moral harms. One of myriad questions put to us by terrorism, however, is whether torture could be less morally harmful than the alternative. Terrorist threats portend grave moral harms as well, and we are surely able to defend ourselves against such harms. There will not be a great multitude of cases in which torture is the most prudent reply to terrorist threats, but nor are such cases ruled out, whether philosophically or empirically. To be sure, we must be extremely careful in choosing whether to utilize torture, paying close attention to our epistemic situations and our ability to constrain the use of torture to appropriate cases. These challenges are serious, but not insurmountable. It is to be hoped that we may eventually find ourselves in a world where we need not countenance torture as a response to terrorism, especially were that world bereft of terrorism altogether; unfortunately, such a world is not yet ours.

As I said in the preface, my own views on torture and terrorism are indelibly connected to the horrendous terrorist attacks of 9/11. While these attacks were among the most extreme imaginable, far lesser ones should still be vociferously opposed. The lives of innocents—particularly lives under nefarious attack—deserve our most ambitious protection. Let us not forswear any countermeasures in that defense.

Notes

PREFACE

1. Alexander and Bruning, *How to Break a Terrorist*; Bagaric and Clarke, *Torture*; Brecher, *Torture and the Ticking Bomb*; Levinson, ed., *Torture*; and Rejali, *Torture and Democracy*. The fact that Alexander and Bruning's and Brecher's books carry the same principal image further evidences this formulaic approach.
2. Allhoff, "Terrorism and Torture."

CHAPTER ONE

1. For a detailed history, see Fife, *The Terror*.
2. For more on the Committee of Public Safety, see Palmer, *Twelve Who Ruled*.
3. Coady, "Defining Terrorism."
4. Rodin, "Terrorism without Intention," 753–755.
5. Coady, "The Morality of Terrorism," 52.
6. Primoratz, "What Is Terrorism?" 24.
7. McPherson, "Is Terrorism Distinctively Wrong?" 525.
8. Rodin, "Terrorism without Intention," 755.
9. As we will see below, I deny that a threat of terrorism can be terroristic. McPherson and Rodin do not explicitly deny this, but, unlike Coady and Primoratz, they do not make positive room in their account for it either.
10. While attacks on property are not specifically included in Primoratz's definition of *terrorism*, he nevertheless seems sympathetic to counting such attacks so long as they threaten lives (e.g., the destruction of crops). See Primoratz, "What Is Terrorism?" 21. I will return to this below.
11. Coady, "The Morality of Terrorism," 52.
12. I will use *violence* in the following discussion so as not to change the terms used by other authors; the argument applies, mutatis mutandis, to *force*.
13. Again, the same point applies to *force*; I continue to follow Coady's and Primoratz's locution in response to their arguments.

14. At a workshop on this manuscript, the following objection was collectively developed against my denial that threats can be terroristic: Imagine that the Irish Republican Army previously detonated a bomb and threatens to do it again, thus causing fear. Can such a threat be terroristic (e.g., if it satisfies the other elements of the definition)? While many of the participants seemed to think so, I disagree: as the preceding text indicates, this allowance would, at least in some cases, make *threatening terrorism* redundant, and there is no reason to impoverish our concepts in such a way. As the workshop discussion indicated, one of the principal reasons for declaring these cases terroristic is to be able to assign moral blame, but there are obviously grounds for disapprobation besides ascriptions of *terrorism*; the causing of fear can be morally liable whether it is an instance of terrorism or not. In other words, by denying the ascription, we lose nothing of normative import, while, at the same time, we are able to preserve an intuitive conceptual account.

15. Wellman, "On Terrorism Itself," 251, 251–52.

16. Rodin, "Terrorism without Intention."

17. Kamm, "The Doctrine of Triple Effect," 23, quoted in Rodin, "Terrorism without Intention," 762.

18. Aquinas, *Summa theologica* 2.2.64.7. The contemporary literature is quite substantial, but see, e.g., Foot, "The Problem of Abortion"; Quinn, "Actions, Intentions, and Consequences"; and Kagan, *The Limits of Morality*, 128–82. For direct application to just war theory, see Walzer, *Just and Unjust Wars*, 151–59. For an extended critique—especially as pertains to just war theory—see Kamm, "Failures of Just War Theory."

19. Thomson, "Self-Defense," 293, referenced in Rodin, "Terrorism without Intention," 763.

20. Rodin, "Terrorism without Intention," 764.

21. See also McPherson, "Is Terrorism Distinctively Wrong," 535.

22. Rodin, "Terrorism without Intention," 770.

23. Jeff McMahan notes, "The English term 'innocent' derives from the Latin *nocentes*, which means 'those who injure or are harmful.'" McMahan, "The Ethics of Killing in War," 695. This concords with an observation by Thomas Nagel that "'innocent' means 'currently harmless,' and is opposed not to 'guilty' but to 'doing harm.'" Nagel, "War and Massacre," 69, quoted in McMahan, "The Ethics of Killing in War," 69. McMahan and Nagel could (perhaps rightly) hold that my worry owes to a misapprehension, but the prevalence of the misapprehension is sufficient to ground the worry.

24. Graves, *Goodbye to All That*, 132, quoted in Walzer, *Just and Unjust Wars*, 140.

25. Walzer, *Just and Unjust Wars*, 138.

26. In the movie *Saving Private Ryan*, this point is made real wherein the protagonist does not kill an unarmed adversary who fails to be as considerate when they next meet.

27. For more discussion—if in a somewhat different context—see Statman, "Supreme Emergencies Revisited."

28. Coady, "Defining Terrorism," 5.

29. Teichman, *Pacifism and the Just War*, 92, quoted in Primoratz, "What Is Terrorism?" 21.

30. Rodin, "Terrorism without Intention," 761.

31. Or maybe even the long term, though we tend to have short memories and the fear created by particular attacks is unlikely to persist for, say, decades to come. Interesting cases might be older generations who had lived through terrible situations, such as the aforementioned Reign of Terror or else something like the Bolshevik's Red Terror. Survivors of these regimes could carry fear for the rest of their lives, even if the regimes themselves had been dismantled.

32. Teichman, "How to Define Terrorism," 511, quoted in Rodin, "Terrorism without Intention," 760.

33. Coady, "Defining Terrorism," 6.

34. Or could it? If nobody felt fear, then my account precludes the attack from being terroristic. If most feel fear, then it probably still is, but what if that most is reduced to many, some, or few? Is there a threshold for how many people must be afraid for an act to have succeeded as one of terrorism? I am not sure.

35. Of course, there could be interesting cases. Imagine that terrorists try to instill fear in city A and fail while, at the same time, instill fear in city B. Is the fact that A was targeted and B affected relevant for ascriptions of terrorism? It seems to me that the terror caused must have been that which the terrorists reasonably expected to achieve. In other words, it cannot be the case that they intended to cause fear, any fear, and did; rather, they need to cause fear in roughly the place that they intend for theirs to be an act of terrorism.

36. More could be said about what *political* and *ideological* mean, though I shall not pursue that here; the usages that follow are meant to be generic enough that nothing of any importance hangs on the precise details. Roughly—and similarly to the *Oxford English Dictionary*—I take *political* to be concerned with the administration of a state and its relations with other states. *Ideological* covers the realm of ideas more broadly, of which political ideas are a proper subset.

37. Rodin, "Terrorism without Intention," 757. Rodin thereafter goes on to give various examples, though some of them seem political to me: he cites, among others, national separatists (e.g., the IRA) and antifederalists (e.g., Timothy McVeigh). Don't these groups want political change? I would rather not try to figure out the difference between political and extrapolitical aims, but I doubt that these are the best examples.

38. For example, if we took religious terrorism to be nonpolitical, then the idea might be that some religious facility or practitioners were targeted such that some other facility or practitioners did something else (e.g., stopped practicing).

39. Primoratz, "What Is Terrorism?" 24.

40. Bruce Edwards Ivins, a researcher at the U.S. Army Medical Research Institute of Infectious Diseases, was identified as the offender but committed suicide before formal charges were filed.

41. For more discussion, see Primoratz, "State Terrorism."

42. The number of deaths in the Dresden bombings has been a significant controversy, at least in part for obvious political reasons; while some claims have been well in excess of 100,000, contemporary estimates places the toll closer to 25,000. See Taylor, "How Many Died in the Bombing of Dresden?" For more details of the terror campaign against Germany, see Garrett, "Terror Bombings of German Cities."

CHAPTER TWO

1. Walzer, *Just and Unjust Wars*, 21.
2. For example, the discussion offered below of supreme emergency challenges this independence; ironically, Walzer introduces this idea. Consider whether, as the justice of the war (*jus ad bellum*) becomes more pressing (e.g., against a greater evil), the strictures of *jus in bello* diminish in status. Walzer thinks so, at least in extreme cases, per his discussion of both "sliding scales" and supreme emergencies. See ibid., 228–32, 251–68. On such a conception, however, *jus ad bellum* and *jus in bello* are not logically independent. This is not to challenge Walzer's claim that it is possible for a just war to be fought unjustly and for an unjust war to be fought justly but only to deny that a logical independence between the two therefore follows. Walzer's account is hardly uncontroversial; the point here is not to defend it but only to note a tension between the independence claim made earlier in his book and other discussions that come later. For various other reasons to doubt this independence, see McMahan, "The Ethics of Killing in War," esp. §5.
3. Frances Kamm offers an analogy between war and boxing as it pertains to noncombatant immunity: people in the audience are not liable to being punched. See Kamm, "Failures of Just War Theory," 675.
4. In most characterizations of the moral status of terrorism, the targeting of noncombatants figures centrally. For other relevant features—as well as more discussion on this one—see Pogge, "Making War on Terrorists," esp. §§3–6.
5. Coady, "Terrorism, Morality, and Supreme Emergency," 77. See also Walzer, *Just and Unjust Wars*, esp. chap. 16.
6. Rawls, "Fifty Years after Hiroshima," referenced in Coady, "Terrorism, Morality, and Supreme Emergency," 77.
7. Walzer, *Just and Unjust Wars*, 252. See also Statman, "Supreme Emergencies Revisited," esp. §1.
8. Coady, "Terrorism, Morality, and Supreme Emergency," 781–82.
9. For more details, see Melgunov, *The Red Terror in Russia*. See also Leggett, *The Cheka*.
10. Trotsky, *Terrorism and Communism*, esp. chap. 4. That chapter was reprinted in a slightly abridged form as "A Defense of the 'Red Terror.'"
11. Primoratz, ed., *Terrorism*, xiv. See also Kautsky, *Terrorism and Communism*.
12. The worry here is the one that Robert Nozick has expressed about rights-based utilitarianism: violating the rights of A such that B and C fail to

have their rights violated raises important questions about fairness and distributive justice (namely, toward A). I shall return to this issue in §6.2 below.

13. See, e.g., Fotion, "The Burdens of Terrorism."
14. Coady, "Terrorism, Morality, and Supreme Emergency," 782.
15. Walzer, *Just and Unjust Wars*, 254, quoted in Coady, "Terrorism, Morality, and Supreme Emergency," 783.
16. Walzer, "Terrorism," 238, quoted in Coady, "Terrorism, Morality, and Supreme Emergency," 784.
17. Walzer, *Just and Unjust Wars*, 254, quoted in Coady, "Terrorism, Morality, and Supreme Emergency," 784.
18. Coady, "Terrorism, Morality, and Supreme Emergency," 787.
19. See Machiavelli, *The Prince*; Weber, "Politics as Vocation"; and Walzer, "Political Action."
20. Similarly, I deny the existence of what virtue ethicists often refer to as "tragic dilemmas" wherein there is inescapable wrongdoing. See, e.g., Hursthouse, *On Virtue Ethics*, esp. chap. 3.
21. This example presupposes that the theft is justifiable, which it might not always be. In one case, imagine that, absent his car, the owner misses an important consultancy meeting, suffers mental anguish, and so on: the compensation would be for the lost wages, something toward the anguish, and so on. In the other case, maybe compensation is impossible, however, such as were he to be meeting his love under some ultimatum that he either turn up or she return to some distant land, never to be heard from again. Whether compensation here is possible at all is an open question as maybe there is not enough money to leave him indifferent to her departure. In this case, perhaps the theft was not justified in the first place, and my wife should have had to give birth without the benefits of a hospital.
22. Nagel, "War and Massacre," 62, quoted in Coady, "Terrorism, Morality, and Supreme Emergency," 779.
23. Coady, "Terrorism, Morality, and Supreme Emergency," 787.
24. This answer is actually different from Walzer's: for Walzer, the preservation of the political community constitutes a preeminent value, and utilitarian calculations in the service of lesser values (e.g., saving a greater number of lives) are inappropriate. See, e.g., Walzer, *Just and Unjust Wars*, 268. In this regard, he could mean either that the value of the political community is lexically prior to any other values or else that the value of the political community outweighs other values (i.e., the difference is whether these two sets of values are commensurable). The former is the more natural reading of Walzer, though the less plausible. While I shall not develop that criticism here, suffice it to say that I find it implausible to always prefer the deaths of however many noncombatants—e.g., millions, billions, etc.—to the death of a political community. The other reading, however, is not expressly antiutilitarian; it just gives a lot of moral weight to preserving the political community (i.e., such a weight as could, in principle, be accommodated under a utilitarian framework). Walzer is avowedly antiutilitarian,

but the utilitarian could, nevertheless, accommodate a similar position, albeit one that is contingent rather than necessary.

25. Coady, "Terrorism, Morality, and Supreme Emergency," 789.

26. Looney, "Economic Costs to the United States." See also Kunreuther, Michel-Kerjan, and Porter, "Assessing, Managing, and Financing Extreme Events." This second work puts the "inflicted damage" at $80 billion (p. 4), though it does not make clear where this figure comes from or which damages are meant to be included; I suspect that it does not include many of the long-term costs that Looney identifies, which is why the estimate that I develop is significantly higher.

   The global economic impact of "transnational terrorism"—as well as the cost-effectiveness of our responses to it—is assessed in Sandler, Arce, and Enders, "Transnational Terrorism." For a response, see Blomberg, "The Copenhagen Consensus." See also Enders and Sandler, *The Political Economy of Terrorism.*

27. Looney, "Economic Costs to the United States."

28. Blimes and Stiglitz, "The Iraq War Will Cost Us $3 Trillion."

29. Belasco, *The Cost of Iraq*, 2.

30. Looney, "Economic Costs to the United States."

31. Its strategic plan says that the department "was created to secure our country against those who seek to disrupt the American way of life," though it makes the further provision that "our charter also includes preparation for and response to all hazards and disasters." Elsewhere, it continues: "We will prevent and deter terrorist attacks and protect against and respond to threats and hazards to the Nation. We will secure our national borders while welcoming lawful immigrants, visitors, and trade." Department of Homeland Security, *Strategic Plan*, 2–3.

32. See Hobijn and Sager, "What Has Homeland Security Cost?"

33. Ibid., 1–2.

34. Again, for a more rigorous economic analysis of the worldwide costs of terrorism, see Sandler, Arce, and Enders, "Transnational Terrorism"; and Blomberg, "The Copenhagen Consensus."

35. Wolfendale, "Terrorism, Security, and the Threat of Counterterrorism," 75. The Bush and Powell quotes originally appeared in Jackson, *Writing the War on Terror*, 99.

36. Sandler, Arce, and Enders, "Transnational Terrorism," 516.

37. Jackson, *Writing the War on Terror*, 92–93, quoted in Wolfendale, "Terrorism, Security, and the Threat of Counterterrorism," 77.

38. Pogge, "Making War on Terrorists," 1–2. For Pogge's figures, see Global Fund to Fight AIDS, Tuberculosis and Malaria, "Current Grant Commitments and Disbursements." See also Belasco, *The Cost of Iraq*. Note that Belasco's sum does not include all the costs of 9/11 but only money that Congress has approved "for military operations, base security, reconstruction, foreign aid, embassy costs, and veterans' health care for the three operations initiated since the 9/11 attacks: Operation Enduring Freedom (OEF) Afghanistan and other counter terror operations; Operation Noble Eagle (ONE), providing enhanced security at military bases; and Operation

Iraqi Freedom (OIF)." Belasco, *The Cost of Iraq*, 2. In other words, hers is only a partial accounting of our counterterrorism spending.

Note also that Pogge's reference and calculation are based on spending levels through 2006, whereas—at the time of writing—the current report includes congressional approvals through June 30, 2008. This new total is $864 billion, significantly higher than the $438 billion Pogge cites; were we to keep the number of U.S. fatalities the same, this adjustment would take the amount spent from $146 to $288 million per fatality.

39. And Wolfendale agrees. See Wolfendale, "Terrorism, Security, and the Threat of Counterterrorism," 80–82.

40. For example, consider the following table, which identifies some of the most significant transnational terror attacks ever perpetrated:

Date	Event	Perpetrator	Deaths
July 22, 1946	Bombing of local British military headquarters at King David Hotel, Jerusalem	Irgun Zai Leumi	91
August 2, 1980	Bombing of Bologna railway station	Armed Revolutionary Nuclei	84
October 23, 1983	Suicide truck bombing of U.S. marine barracks, Beirut	Hezbollah	241
June 23, 1985	Downing of Air India 182, en route from Montreal to London	Sikh extremists	329
December 21, 1988	Downing of Pan Am 103, en route from London to New York	Libyan intelligence agent	270
September 19, 1989	Downing of Union des Transports 772, en route from Brazzaville (Republic of the Congo) to Paris	Hezbollah	171

(Continued on next page)

Date	Event	Perpetrator	Deaths
March 12, 1993	Thirteen bombings in Bombay	Pakistani agents	317
August 7, 1998	Simultaneous bombings of U.S. embassies in Nairobi, Kenya, and Dar es Salaam, Tanzania	Al-Qaeda	223
September 11, 2001	Four suicide hijackings that crashed into the World Trade Center, the Pentagon, and a field in Pennsylvania	Al-Qaeda	2,974 (plus 19 hijackers)
October 12, 2002	Two bombs outside Bali nightclubs	Jemaah Islamiyah	202
March 11, 2004	Bombing of Madrid commuter trains and stations during morning rush hour	Al-Qaeda	190
September 1, 2004	Barricade hostage seizure of schoolchildren and parents in Belan, North Ossetia-Alania (Russia)	Chechen rebels	344

Note: Adapted from Sandler, Arce, and Enders, "Transnational Terrorism." See also Quillen, "A Historical Analysis of Mass Casualty Bombers," and Quillen, "Mass Casualty Bombings Chronology."

Note that the bombings in Jerusalem (1946) and Beirut (1983) were against military installations, so it is not obvious that my account of terrorism and its emphasis on noncombatant targets would categorize these bombings as terroristic (cf. §1.3 above). The American soldiers in Beirut were mostly marines, ostensibly there on a peacekeeping mission; some Lebanese Muslims instead saw them as a faction in the ongoing civil war. Whether peacekeeping or humanitarian forces are properly understood as noncombatant lies outside the scope of this project, but an argument in the affirmative can certainly be made. The bombing of Jerusalem's King

David Hotel was carried out by the Irgun, an underground Zionist organization that was responding to British action under Operation Agatha (or "Black Saturday"); the British coordinated searches and arrests in various Jewish cities and settlements as well at the Jewish Agency (i.e., the prestate Jewish government). While the British forces were headquartered in the hotel, so were various other administrative and government contingents. At least some of the casualties were, therefore, noncombatants, though some were clearly military command. In either case, determinations as to whether the bombings were terroristic does not matter for present purposes, but provocative issues are raised in both.

41. Though, for a sophisticated attempt, see Sandler, Arce, and Enders, "Transnational Terrorism."

42. See the discussion in n. 40 above.

43. It is worth acknowledging that, while these four attacks were primarily against Americans, three of them took place abroad. How effective would our counterterrorism campaign—especially under the auspices of *homeland* security—been in preventing them? I think that some optimism is warranted here, at least for the national focus placed on terrorism and some of the relevant infrastructures now provided. For example, despite the continuation of anti-American sentiment, not a single one of these attacks has occurred since 9/11.

44. As mentioned in the preface, the Fort Hood shootings are one potential exception. However, I doubt that the shooter, Dr. Nidal Malik Hasan, was acting on any ideological grounds and was, instead, just disturbed about his pending deployment to Afghanistan. Absent ideological aims, I would not classify this act as terroristic (cf. §1.5 above).

45. A particular concern in this regard is the loss of innocent life effected by counterterrorist operations. See, e.g., Meyer, "The Predator War."

CHAPTER THREE

1. See, e.g., Crawford, "Just War Theory and the US Counterterror War."

2. See, e.g., Walzer, *Just and Unjust Wars*. See also the classic treatment of just war theory in Aquinas, *Summa theologica*, question 40, esp. art. 1. See also Orend, "War."

3. See, e.g., Shanahan, ed., *Philosophy 9/11*. For skepticism regarding the distinctiveness of terrorism, see McPherson, "Is Terrorism Distinctively Wrong?"

4. For more discussion, see Meisels, "Combatants."

5. Michael Gross has also discussed blackmail as such a practice, though I will not consider it here. See Gross, *Moral Dilemmas of Modern War*, esp. chap. 7. The development of chemical and biological weapons might also be visited in this context. See Cooper, "Pre-Empting Emergence." Cooper is especially interested in germ warfare and the U.S. military's growing interest in biodefense research. See also Allhoff, ed., *Physicians at War*, esp. pt. 3.

6. The opposition to torture has been codified in various declarations and treaties, including §5 of the Universal Declaration of Human Rights (1948), §§3.1a, 17, 87, and 130 of the Third Geneva Convention, the Declaration of

Tokyo (1975), and the Convention against Torture and Other Cruel, Inhuman or Degrading Treatment or Punishment (CAT; 1984). For more discussion of CAT, see §4.1 below.

7. See, e.g., Wolfendale, "The Myth of 'Torture Lite.'"

8. Henceforth, I shall just use *torture*, though I mean it to include most sorts of coercive interrogations. This locution is not meant to morally load those practices; rather, it is undertaken for facility and concordance with common usage. For more discussion, see §4.1 above.

9. Associated Press, "Poll Finds Broad Approval." I suspect that public sentiment against torture has been rising in the past couple of years, though that is just a hypothesis; I could not find more recent data. Regardless, polls are fickle, so we should not take them too seriously.

10. Just to be clear, I am not proposing that existing norms are necessarily revised in light of terrorism; my proposal is far more modest and simply suggests that the norms are subject to review. Certainly, this review might, ultimately, reaffirm those norms, even if they are liable to revision.

11. In the literature, we see the term *assassination* alongside the closely related *targeted killing*, though this distinction is never made clear. According to Michael Gross (personal communication, May 5, 2008), *assassination* is linked to "perfidious killing in war," while *targeted killing* lacks this connotation; it is, therefore, less morally loaded. However, some interpret *targeted killing* as being a sort of extrajudicial execution and, therefore, more appropriate to law enforcement than to armed conflict. I shall use *assassination* for my discussion, though take it that discussion would apply equally to targeted killing.

 Regarding *assassination* itself, Franklin Ford defines it as "the intentional killing of a specified victim or group of victims perpetrated for reasons related to his (her, their) public prominence and undertaken with a political purpose in view." Ford, *Political Murder*, 2. For some other conceptual work on assassination, see Zellner, ed., *Assassination*. Especially helpful is Rachels, "Political Assassination."

12. A good historical account of assassinations is Ford, *Political Murder*.

13. Tzu, *The Art of War*, esp. chap. 13; Machiavelli, *The Prince*, esp. chap. 19; More, *Utopia*, 65, referenced in Altman and Wellman, "From Humanitarian Intervention to Assassination," 251–52.

14. Carter, "Executive Order 12036"; Reagan, "Executive Order 12333."

15. Woodward, "CIA Told to Do 'Whatever Necessary.'"

16. Ward, "The New Age of Assassination." See also Gross, *Moral Dilemmas of Modern War*, esp. chap. 5.

17. For discussion of this question, see, e.g., Altman and Wellman, "From Humanitarian Intervention to Assassination"; David, "Israel's Policy of Targeted Killing"; Gross, "Assassination and Targeted Killing"; Kasher and Yadlin, "Military Ethics of Fighting Terror"; Kershnar, "Assassination and the Immunity Theory"; Meisels, "Targeting Terror"; and Statman, "Targeted Killing."

18. *Ex Parte Quirin*, 317 U.S. 1, 30–31 (1942). The case upheld the jurisdiction of a U.S. military tribunal over a group of German saboteurs that had been apprehended in the United States, two of whom were American citizens.

19. See, e.g., Murphy, ed., "Ability of Detainees in Cuba." For critical discussion, see Gill and van Sliedregt, "Guantánamo Bay." I thank Don Scheid (personal communication, December 16, 2009) and Jonathan Marks (personal communication, December 18, 2009) for helpful discussions on enemy combatancy status. As Professor Marks pointed out, enemy combatancy status is recognized neither in international law nor in the Third Geneva Convention (which postdated *Quirin*).

20. See *Hamdan v. Rumsfeld*. See also *Boumediene v. Bush*. President Bush signed the Military Commissions Act of 2006 (MCA) into law following an unfavorable ruling in *Hamdan*; *Boumediene* found §7 of the MCA—which denied habeas corpus to unlawful enemy combatants—unconstitutional. See also n. 38 below.

21. Gonzales, "Memorandum for the President," cited in Marks, "9/11 + 3/11 + 7/7 = ?" 118.

22. *Gitmo*, 22:58–23:21.

23. Following his service at Guantánamo, General Miller was sent to Abu Ghraib, where, it is widely believed, he transformed the interrogation program to include some of the more aggressive techniques practiced at Guantánamo. For more discussion of these techniques, see Wolfendale, "The Myth of 'Torture Lite.'"

24. See, e.g., Brough, "Legitimate Combatancy." See also n. 20 above.

25. For a contrary position, see Fiala, "A Critique of Exceptions." Fiala is worried that exceptions can, ultimately, normalize immoral behavior. This seems a misplaced worry to me insofar as the exceptions that are of interest to us are the ones that are morally justifiable; there is no reason to consider morally unjustifiable exceptions. Therefore, what we are normalizing is not immoral behavior but rather behavior that, in other contexts, was not necessary. If the worry is that the normalized behavior would persist if and when the present context reverted to the earlier one, then this becomes more interesting legislatively than philosophically. Philosophically, there would be no longer any justification for the exception, so the unexcepted norm should be restored. Exceptions in war are also considered in Rodin, "The Ethics of War."

26. There is a growing literature on moral particularism, though much of it is orthogonal to the present project. In its more extreme forms, moral particularism denies that there are moral principles. More conservatively, it admits of moral principles but denies the preeminence of these principles. See, e.g., Hooker and Little, eds., *Moral Particularism*; and Dancy, *Ethics without Principles*. See also Dancy, "Moral Particularism." Some of this literature mentions exceptions. See, e.g., Dancy, "Defending Particularism"; and Goldman, *Practical Rules*.

27. Note, however, that exceptionalism can be construed even more generally than moral and legal norms. Consider, e.g., Mendel's Second Law (the Law of Independent Assortment), which holds that the inheritance pattern of one trait will not affect the inheritance pattern of another trait. However, this is not quite right: this "law" is true except when genes are linked to each other (as might happen with genes proximally situated on the same chromosome such that they might segregate together during meiosis), in

which case it is not. Again, the exception is to some stricture (namely, that independent assortment is required), and what is being excepted is some phenomena (namely, transmission of linked genes). My analysis can similarly accommodate these examples as well, though the emphasis will be on exceptions to moral and legal norms.

28. For example, consider: "All X's must φ, except Y's." This norm does not imply that there are Y's; rather, it implies only that, if there were any Y's, they would not have to φ. This is still a well-formed excepted norm, even if there might not be any Y's at present.

29. These examples will motivate distinctions similar to those suggested in Marks, "9/11 + 3/11 + 7/7 = ?" esp. 119–20. We both derive spatial and temporal exceptionalisms, and his collective exceptionalism is similar to my group-based exceptionalism. Further discussion of his account will appear below.

Marks's taxonomy also includes "*interpretive exceptionalism*, in which norms are reinterpreted in order to narrow the scope of the protection conferred or of the conduct that is prohibited" (121). His example of this includes (re)interpretation of torture as that which requires pain "equivalent in intensity to the pain accompanying serious physical injury, such as organ failure, the permanent impairment of a significant bodily function, or even death." Bybee, "Memorandum for Alberto R. Gonzales," 1, cited in Marks, "9/11 + 3/11 + 7/7 = ?" 121.

Another example that Marks uses is the view once expressed by Department of Defense officials that medically trained personnel assigned to develop interrogation strategies at Guantánamo and Abu Ghraib were not acting as physicians and, therefore, not subject to the strictures of medical ethics. See Bloche and Marks, "When Doctors Go to War."

There are a few different reasons why I do not bring Marks's interpretive exceptionalism into my account. First, interpretive exceptionalism seems necessarily post hoc and, therefore, not very philosophically interesting: of course people should not change their conceptions of something merely because it is convenient or expedient. What is interesting, in both the torture and the physician cases, is to *acknowledge* that we have torture or physicians and then to talk about whether these things are acceptable; mere semantic recourse to move the bar somewhere else just seems disingenuous rather than philosophically suggestive. Second, the interesting facets of the interpretive approach—if there are any—can be subsumed under another form of exceptionalism, most likely group-based exceptionalism. In the torture case, e.g., there would be a certain group of people, namely, the interrogatees, who are excepted from protections against some practices. In the physicians case, there would be a certain group of people, namely, medically trained interrogators, who are excepted from medical duties. Marks's interpretive exceptionalism can, therefore, be subsumed under my group-based exceptionalism (see §3.3 below).

30. For wine shipping laws, see Wine Institute, "State Shipping Laws." For discussion, see Massey, "Shipping across State Lines."

31. Abruzzese, "Maryland Parents Told to Have Children Immunized." See also Chaddock, "One Maryland County Takes Tough Tack on Vaccinations."

32. Marks, "9/11 + 3/11 + 7/7 = ?" 119. See also Fleck, ed., *Handbook of Humanitarian Law*, 13; and Baker, "A Theory of International Bioethics," 201, 211; both are cited in Marks, "9/11 + 3/11 + 7/7 = ?" 119.

33. For a list of these provisions, see Doyle, "Patriot Act: Sunset Provisions." They include §§201 (wiretapping in terrorism cases), 202 (wiretapping in computer fraud and abuse felony cases), 203(b) (sharing wiretap information), 203(d) (sharing foreign intelligence information), 204 (Foreign Intelligence Surveillance Act [FISA]) pen register/trap and trace exceptions), 206 (roving FISA wiretaps), 207 (duration of FISA surveillance of non-U.S. persons who are agents of a foreign power), 209 (seizure of voice-mail messages pursuant to warrants), 212 (emergency disclosure of electronic surveillance), 214 (FISA pen register/trap and trace authority), 215 (FISA access to tangible items), 217 (interception of computer trespasser communications), 218 (purpose for FISA orders), 220 (nationwide service of search warrants for electronic evidence), 223 (civil liability and discipline for privacy violations), and 225 (provider immunity for FISA wiretap assistance). Cited in Marks, "9/11 + 3/11 + 7/7 = ?" 121.

34. The PATRIOT Act was renewed and amended through two subsequent pieces of legislation. The first was the USA PATRIOT Improvement and Reauthorization Act of 2005, the second the USA PATRIOT Act Additional Reauthorizing Amendments Act of 2006. For analysis, see Doyle, "USA PATRIOT Act Reauthorization in Brief."

35. For a more comprehensive discussion of sunset provisions than can be offered here, see Davis, "Review Procedures and Public Accountability." For a recent proposal to apply a sunset provision model to judicial decisions, see Katya, "Sunsetting Judicial Opinions."

36. See U.S. Congress, Alien and Sedition Acts.

37. For discussion, see Massey, "Shipping across State Lines."

38. Marks, "9/11 + 3/11 + 7/7 = ?" 120. Marks also mentions CIA interrogation centers in Eastern Europe that "were established in order to circumvent the ban on cruel, inhuman, and degrading treatment, pursuant to the administration's view that the ban did not apply to aliens held outside the United States" (ibid.). I will not discuss this example in particular, though my forthcoming discussion applies, mutatis mutandis, to it.

Note that, while the Bush administration is routinely criticized for denying habeas corpus to detainees, Bush's is certainly not the first presidency to restrict or undermine this protection. (It further bears notice that, according to the U.S. Constitution, the protection is hardly unalienable. According to Article I, section 9, clause 2: "The Privilege of the Writ of Habeas Corpus shall not be suspended, unless when in Cases of Rebellion or Invasion the public Safety may require it." This clause, of course, does not grant the *president* the right to suspend it, of which more shortly.)

During the Civil War, President Lincoln suspended habeas corpus several times. The first suspension took place after the attack on Fort Sumter in April 1861 and applied to the military line between Philadelphia and Washington, DC. This action was challenged and overturned in *Ex Parte Merryman*, in which Supreme Court chief justice Roger Taney held that only Congress, not the president, could suspend the writ. Lincoln went on to ignore Taney's order to restore it. For more details, see *Ex Parte Merryman*. The suspension ended in February 1862, though it was reissued—this time over the entire North—that September. Congress then passed the Habeas Corpus Act in 1863, which was meant to indemnify the president against judicial challenges as had arisen in *Merryman*. President Johnson then restored the writ state by state between December 1865 and August 1866. In the early 1870s, President Grant suspended it in nine South Carolina counties as part of action against the Ku Klux Klan. See Johnson, "Habeas Corpus."

In 1987, President Reagan refused to ratify Protocol I, an amendment to the Geneva conventions that the United States had signed in 1977. At stake primarily was article 44, paragraphs 3–5; Regan interpreted these paragraphs as extending protections to terrorists. By not ratifying the protocol, the United States would not owe those fighters the judicial provisions made in article 3(1)(d) of the Third Geneva Convention, thus, effectively, denying them habeas corpus. Despite the protocol having been ratified by over 160 countries, the United States has still not ratified it, whether under Reagan or any subsequent administration. (Iraq, Iran, and Israel are other notable exceptions.) See Reagan, "Message to the Senate Transmitting a Protocol to the 1949 Geneva Conventions."

President Clinton signed into law the Antiterrorism and Effective Death Penalty Act of 1996, in which §101 set a statute of limitations for the request of habeas corpus and further limited the power of federal judges to grant relief.

There have also been various Supreme Court cases that have upheld the limitation of habeas corpus. *Ex Parte Quirin* (1942)—discussed in §3.1 above—held that enemy combatants could be denied habeas corpus. *Johnson v. Eisentrager* denied habeas corpus to nonresident aliens captured and imprisoned abroad. However, some important decisions have asserted habeas corpus protection, including *Hamdan* and *Boumediene*; see n. 20 above. See also *Hamdi et al. v. Rumsfeld*.

39. It is worth noting that constitutional provisions have already been explored in this regard as pertains especially to terrorist attacks. See Ackerman, "The Emergency Constitution." For a less technical discussion, see Ackerman, *Before the Next Attack*.

40. See, e.g., Wynia, "Ethics and Public Health Emergencies." See also Selgelid, "Ethics and Infectious Disease."

41. Rationing can take place in different contexts, but consider food rationing in the United States during World War II. See, e.g., Bentley, *Eating for Victory*. See also Zweiniger-Bargielowska, *Austerity in Britain*. There is also a literature about rationing in medicine. A classic is Rescher, "The Allocation of Exotic Medical Lifesaving Therapy."

42. For discussion of such rights in the time before World War II, see Swisher, "Civil Liberties in War Time." For a recent opinion against the suspension of such rights for the greater good, see Cassel, *The War on Civil Liberties*. For a general overview on such issues, see Duncan and Machan, *Libertarianism*.

43. For discussion, see Henderson, "The Patriot Act's Impact."

44. See Massey, "Shipping across State Lines."

45. As a counterexample to this claim, we might postulate some norm that could bear no exceptions, such as: "None may be subjected to genocide, except . . ." I still think that, logically, it matters what the group is that is being excepted and, even if no exceptions are justified, that the analysis must include the groups. For example, imagine a case in which the world will be destroyed unless some group is subjected to genocide. I further think that it is an open question whether genocide is justified in such a case, and we would want to think about the group to be excepted. Maybe it turns out to be the case that no exception is justified, but we would have to consider the groups who were candidate exceptions. The other alternative, then, is that there *are* exceptions to every norm, whether actually or possibly, and this is the view that I would be more inclined to endorse. If this is true, then, ex hypothesi, the groups matter.

46. Note that the group subject to torture is probably a subset of those classified as enemy combatants; it is probably unreasonable to think that most enemy combatants are tortured, though this presumably depends on the definitions that we employ.

47. See, e.g., Baldor, "More Than Half of Guantánamo Detainees Not Accused of Hostile Acts." See also Rejali, *Torture and Democracy*, 510.

48. This discussion typically starts with the doctrine of double effect. See Foot, "The Problem of Abortion." For discussion pertaining to the war and terrorism context in particular, see Brown, "Proportionality and Just War"; Haydar, "The Ethics of Fighting Terror"; and Kamm, "Terror and Collateral Damage." See also chapter 1, n. 18, above.

49. A conspicuous beginning to this discussion was in Thomson, "A Defense of Abortion." More recently, see Pettit, "Responsibility Incorporated," esp. §1. For discussion in the context of war, see Ingierd and Syse, "Responsibility and Culpability in War."

50. See, e.g., Wallace, *Responsibility and the Moral Sentiments*. See also Sher, *In Praise of Blame*. For a discussion relating responsibility to politics and law, see Matravers, *Responsibility and Justice*.

CHAPTER FOUR

1. On the other hand, we might find ourselves better off epistemically in kidnapping cases than in terrorism cases; for related discussion, see §§5.1 and 7.6 below. As will become clearer in chapter 6, my view is that the number of lives at risk matters significantly, and, so long as that number is high enough, we might still reasonably countenance torture in comparatively weak epistemic situations. However, this does not deny that the situations matter or that lack of knowledge makes the case for torture weaker; of course it does.

2. See also chapter 3, n. 6, above.

3. Part of the delay owes to the fact that CAT was not opened for signature until February 4, 1985. This still leaves the curious fact that countries

could not sign it until over nine years after the UN General Assembly adopted it.

4. United Nations Treaty Collection, IV.9.

5. All quotations of U.S. reservations are taken from United Nations Treaty Collection, IV.9.

6. For discussion of the War on Terror and its effects on Eighth Amendment protections, see Dayan, *The Story of Cruel and Unusual*.

7. For more discussion, see Yoo, "Memorandum for William J. Hynes II," 36–38.

   Another, and perhaps more, commonly referenced memo is Bybee, "Memorandum for Alberto R. Gonzales." This earlier memo is widely acknowledged to have been written by Yoo, despite the fact that it bears Bybee's signature. The later memo, however, is nearly twice as long and addresses additional legal questions; therefore, I take it to reflect Yoo's fullest thinking on the issues. Also, insofar as the ideas are attributed to Yoo, I prefer to use the memo on which his signature actually appears.

8. As Yoo acknowledges in the memo, this might not be as straightforward in legal practice as it is in theory; juries may infer specific intent given the facts of the case. Imagine that our guards *did* specifically intend to cause severe physical or mental pain or suffering by allowing rats into the detainee's cell. Merely saying that they did not would be bad faith and insufficient to nullify specific intent. Rather, general intent would require that the rat infestation was foreseeable but could reasonably have been expected not to happen. In this case, the infestation would not have been (specifically) intended since it quite possibly could have not happened and the guards did not otherwise do anything to bring it about. If the infestation was reasonably certain—i.e., it would have been unreasonable to think that it would not happen—then specific intent is more readily established.

9. For extended critique, see Luban, "The Torture Lawyers of Washington." See also Waldron, "Torture and Positive Law," esp. §1.D.

10. Yoo, "Memorandum for William J. Hynes II," 38.

11. *FDIC v. Meyer*, 510 U.S. 471, 476 (1994), quoted in Yoo, "Memorandum for William J. Hynes II," 38.

12. See, e.g., 8 U.S.C. §1369, and 42 U.S.C. §§1395w, 1395dd, 1396b, 1396u-2, referenced in Yoo, "Memorandum for William J. Hynes II," 38.

13. Yoo, "Memorandum for William J. Hynes II," 38–39.

14. See, e.g., Luban, "The Torture Lawyers of Washington."

15. Yoo, "Memorandum for William J. Hynes II," 38.

16. For more discussion, see Rejali, *Torture and Democracy*, chaps. 12, 16.

17. Yoo, "Memorandum for William J. Hynes II," 39.

18. Ibid., 38.

19. European Commission on Human Rights, "*Ireland v. United Kingdom*," esp. 512–16, 784. See also Rodley, *The Treatment of Prisoners under International Law*, 90–95.

20. *Ireland v. United Kingdom*, Eur. Ct. H.R. (ser. A, no. 25) (1978). Note that the European Court of Human Rights overturned a finding made by the now-defunct European Commission on Human Rights. That commission unanimously held that the combined use of the five techniques was tantamount

to torture on the grounds that their "systematic application . . . for the purpose of inducing a person to give information shows a clear resemblance to those methods of systematic torture which have been known over the ages." European Commission on Human Rights, "*Ireland v. United Kingdom*" 794. The court disagreed and found that these techniques were inhuman and degrading yet not torture. Many people no doubt find the commission's ruling more plausible, but it is the court's that stands.

21. By *drowning*, I mean actual drowning and not waterboarding; the latter is meant to simulate drowning. I am less sure that waterboarding falls short of torture, but actual drowning is certainly worse.

22. See Conroy, *Unspeakable Acts, Ordinary People*, 6. See also Priebe and Bauer, "Inclusion of Psychological Torture in PTSD Criterion A." Both are referenced in Wolfendale, "The Myth of 'Torture Lite.'"

23. Priest, "CIA Avoids Scrutiny of Detainee Treatment," referenced in Wolfendale, "The Myth of 'Torture Lite,'" 47.

24. Wolfendale "The Myth of 'Torture Lite,'" 51 (emphasis added).

25. I actually am inclined to think that it is reasonably exhaustive pragmatically, if not conceptually. Imagine that someone tortures someone else such that some third person will give the torturer some piece of property in exchange. Does this mean that we need to establish some sui generis category of *bargaining torture*? Or imagine that one person tortures another in the ill-guided aspiration to better intuit tomorrow's weather; do we need *weather torture* as well? Despite being conceptually coherent, these just do not seem categories that we really need to create (or else to acknowledge). So perhaps the thing to say is that, while there might be a multiplicity of purposes under which people *could* torture, there is, nevertheless, a fairly small subset of those under which they *do* (or have).

26. See, e.g., Dworkin, *Taking Rights Seriously*, ix.

27. See Mill, *Utilitarianism*, chap. 5.

28. For present purposes, the distinction between act utilitarianism and rule utilitarianism is irrelevant. Rather, all that matters is that the utilitarian jettisons rights so long as they bear the wrong relationship to utility.

29. And others, such as purity (and the associated extent): the sadist could quite well go on to cause more pain after his first act of torture.

30. See chapter 5, n. 5, below.

31. Note that John Langbein uses *judicial torture* to represent "the use of physical coercion by officers of the state in order to gather evidence for judicial proceedings"; on such a definition, the confusion with punitive torture is ruled out. Nevertheless, I shall use *confessional torture* and *punitive torture* as I find them to offer a useful disambiguation. Langbein, *Torture and the Law of Proof*, 3.

32. Interestingly, torture never became widespread in England. In the years 1540–1640, there are records of eighty-one torture warrants being issued in the country, and there is good evidence that these records are at least reasonably complete. Furthermore, almost half of these were issued against those suspected of sedition (twenty-eight) or treason (nine)—perhaps slightly more given that the reasons of issuance were not always well recorded. Ibid., 81–128. This is notable because torture was probably as

likely to ascertain conspirators as it was to elicit confessions; this century therefore establishes a historical precedent for judicially licensed interrogational torture. I will return to torture warrants in §8.2.

33. Ibid., 4.
34. For illustrations, see ibid., 18–26. Strappado lifts the suspect by his bound wrists from behind his back and may thereafter apply weights to his feet in order to increase the strain.
35. Ibid., 4–5.
36. Ibid., 8–9.
37. See Beccaria, *Of Crimes and Punishments*, 31–37; and Voltaire, "Commentaire sur le livre Des délits et des peines," and "Prix de la justice et de l'humanité." See also Maestro, *Voltaire and Beccaria as Reformers of Criminal Law*. Citations adapted from Langbein, *Torture and the Law of Proof*, 148.
38. Langbein, *Torture and the Law of Proof*, 9.
39. Ibid., 29–38.
40. Alternatively, the confessional torture might be a deterrent for other would-be criminals; I will return to this idea in the following discussion of punitive torture.
41. As disturbing as the fact that this still takes place are some of the infractions for which the punishment can be invoked under Sharia (i.e., Islamic law); these include drinking alcohol, theft, and premarital and extramarital sex.
42. For a more pessimistic view, see Dayan, *The Story of Cruel and Unusual*.
43. Or at least he could not commit a crime outside his detention facility; there are fewer opportunities within facilities to commit crimes than there are outside them, so detention improves outcomes overall. This is not to deny that brutal crimes can occur in detention facilities—or that the propensity for crime can, in some cases, be exacerbated by detention—but simply to say that we might reasonably expect detention to lower the overall incidence of crime.
44. See, e.g., Bedau, *The Death Penalty in America*.
45. For more detail, see Feitlowitz, *A Lexicon of Terror*. See also Lewis, *Guerillas and Generals*.
46. Berryman, trans., *Report of the Chilean National Commission on Truth and Reconciliation*.
47. *Informe de la Comisión Nacional Sobre Política y Tortura*. The report is more often referenced by its unofficial name, *The Valech Report*. This name owes to Bishop Sergio Valech, who led the commission that issued the report.
48. Ibid. See also Payne, *Unsettling Accounts*, 162.
49. For a magisterial cataloging of these, see Rejali, *Torture and Democracy*.
50. My own view is that extrinsic harms can be mitigated in practice as well, but a defense of this more ambitious claim is unnecessary for present purposes. For more discussion, see chapter 7 below.
51. For a comprehensive discussion, see ibid.
52. Sussman, "What's Wrong with Torture?" 4.
53. Ibid., 3, 4.
54. Ibid., 6.

55. If he is complicit in an ongoing terrorist threat, then it is not clear to me that he really is a noncombatant, and even Sussman acknowledges that the terrorist's silence "might well be considered a part of his attack, understood as temporally extended in action." Ibid., 16. However, this is unimportant for my ultimate position: as argued in §2.2 above, I think that noncombatant immunity is derogable in supreme emergencies. Whether a terrorist remains a combatant or else deserves noncombatancy status, I still think that the assault could—at least in principle—be justified.

56. Shue, "Torture," 131, 135–36.

57. Sussman, "What's Wrong with Torture?" 8.

58. Ibid., 13, 14.

59. Ibid., 22, 22–23 (internal footnotes omitted).

60. Ibid., 15.

61. Ibid., 4.

62. Davis, "Torture and the Inhumane." See also Davis, "The Moral Justifiability of Torture."

63. Davis, "Torture and the Inhumane," 36, 35.

64. Ibid., 36.

65. Ibid., 37.

66. Ibid.

CHAPTER FIVE

1. Shue, "Torture," 141.

2. Levin, "The Case for Torture," 7. Levin is a philosopher, albeit one of the few to be published in *Newsweek*.

3. Quinton, "Views." I thank Bob Brecher for directing me to this source and Ryan Pflum for being able to track it down.

4. For discussion, see Rejali, *Torture and Democracy*, 535, 545–48, 775 n. 51.

5. Bentham discussed torture in several manuscript fragments. The two most important constitute Jeremy Bentham, "Of Torture" (ca. 1776–80), box 46, fols. 56–62 and 63–70, Bentham MSS, University College London Library, and have been reprinted in W. L. Twining and P. E. Twining, "Bentham on Torture," *Northern Ireland Legal Quarterly* 24 (1973): 305–56, 308–37. The Twinings suggest that the second fragment was actually written first and is more usefully read first; this is the order in which they present the material. For other fragments in which Bentham discusses torture, see Jeremy Bentham, "Of Torture" (ca. 1778–79), box 99, fol. 173, and "Of Torture" (1804), box 74.b, fols. 405–6, 414, and 426–429, both Bentham MSS. (The Twinings do not reproduce these other fragments, but reference parts thereof in their commentary.) Unless otherwise specified, quotations are from the box 46 manuscript.

   Bentham's published work barely mentions torture, aside from a few casual references: Bentham, *Works*, 1:231, 393, 414, 424–44; 4:211; 7:454–55, 522–23, 525. For discussion, see Twining and Twining, "Bentham on Torture," 307.

6. "Torture, as I understand it, is where a person is made to suffer any violent pain of body in order to compel him to do something or to desist from doing something which done or desisted from the penal application is immediately made to cease" (Twining and Twining, "Bentham on Torture," 309).

7. Ibid., 347 n. 3 (the box 74.b manuscript).

8. Ibid., 312–13.

9. See also ibid., 348–50.

10. Some critics allege that this distinction is untenable and that exceptional torture would inevitably result in normalized torture. I will return to this issue in §§7.2–7.3.

11. As I read them, rule 3 is curiously at odds with the forthcoming rule 5. First, consider rule 3, which says that torture "ought not to be employed but in cases which admit of no delay." And now rule 5: "Even on occasions which admit not of delay, [torture] ought not be employed but in Cases where the benefit produced by doing of the thing required is such as can warrant the employing of so extreme a remedy." Twining and Twining, "Bentham on Torture," 313. The straightforward part of rule 5 is that torture should not be practiced when the costs outweigh the benefits. But, even if the benefits outweigh the costs, it does not follow that torture should be practiced since there might be some other way to achieve a better net outcome. In cases that admit of delay, one might as well wait before torturing since this alternative might present itself; it is only when the cases do not admit of delay that such alternatives can be ruled out. It seems to me that Bentham had it right with rule 3 and should not have thereafter gone on to contradict—or at least weaken—it in rule 5.

12. Ibid., 312–15.

13. Bentham, *An Introduction to the Principles of Morals and Legislation*, esp. chap. 4.

14. Note that Levin goes the other way and even assumes that the terrorist need be subjected to the "most excruciating possible pain." Levin, "The Case for Torture."

15. See, e.g., Shue, "Torture in Dreamland."

16. Davis, "The Moral Justifiability of Torture."

17. Wolfendale, "Training Torturers."

18. Luban, "Liberalism, Torture, and the Ticking Bomb." See also Bufacchi and Arrigo, "Torture, Terrorism and the State."

19. Arrigo, "A Utilitarian Argument against Torture." See also Wynia, "Consequentialism and Harsh Interrogations."

20. Fiala, "A Critique of Exceptions." See also Kleinig, "Ticking Bombs and Torture Warrants."

21. For a thorough discussion on many of these issues, see Brecher, *Torture and the Ticking Bomb*, esp. chaps. 2–3.

22. Note that there are some analogies with the critics' responses here and those elicited through Jonathan Haidt's work: even when some morally salient features are ruled out ex ante, subjects nevertheless try to rationalize their preferred conclusion ex post by searching for a plausible justification.

    In one of Haidt's cases, subjects are asked to consider a brother and sister who have had sex and then to explain whether and why they find the act wrong. The details of the case are such as to preclude any of the answers given: the siblings were careful about contraception; they keep it a secret; they enjoy it and it makes them closer; and so on. Nevertheless, subjects continue to express disapprobation and, after having it pointed out that none of their reasons is applicable, often revert to something like, "Still, it's just wrong." See Haidt, "The Emotional Dog and Its Rational Tail."

23. Kleinig, "Ticking Bombs and Torture Warrants," 614.

24. For example, consider that someone has to be at least thirty-five years old to be eligible to be president of the United States. But satisfying this condition is insufficient for eligibility since there are two additional requirements: being a natural-born citizen and having lived in the United States for fourteen years. Therefore, we cannot infer anything about anyone's eligibility merely on the grounds that he has satisfied the age requirement. Analogously, if ticking-time-bomb conditions were necessary for the permissibility of torture, we still would not know whether torture was permissible since there could be other conditions required for (joint) sufficiency, as in the case of those for presidential eligibility.

25. Compare, e.g., Bufacchi and Arrigo, "Torture, Terrorism and the State."

26. I have in mind something like John Rawls's reflective equilibrium, though the particular details—whether Rawlsian or otherwise—are not important for present purposes. See Rawls, *A Theory of Justice*, 18–19, 42–45.

27. Luban, "Liberalism, Torture, and the Ticking Bomb," 1427.

28. Davis, "The Moral Justifiability of Torture," 161, 171.

29. Or at least I take this to be self-evident. For a controversial dissent, see Taurek, "Should the Numbers Count?"

30. Thomson, "A Defense of Abortion," 48–49.

31. Singer, "Famine, Affluence, and Morality," 231.

32. Thomson, "The Trolley Problem," 1395. See also Thomson, "Killing, Letting Die, and the Trolley Problem." Thomson even acknowledges that "most of [her] examples are just long-winded expansion's of [Foot's]." Ibid., 217 n. 2. While the trolley problem is attributed to Foot, her presentation is actually somewhat different: imagine "the driver of a runaway tram which he can only steer from one narrow track on to another; five men are working on one track and one man on the other; anyone on the track he enters is bound to be killed." Foot, "The Problem of Abortion," 23. Note that, in Foot's case, the driver has to choose which track to steer the trolley onto whereas, in Thomson's retelling, the trolley is already going toward the five and the question is whether to redirect toward the one. None of these details matters for present purposes.

33. Of course, I acknowledge that more could be said about the role of thought experiments in moral methodology, though that takes us too far afield from the current project. This is an area that has historically received less discussion than would be expected, though the newfound interest in experimental philosophy—with its strong reliance on thought experiments—presages a corrective. For a more general discussion of thought experiments in moral philosophy, see Dancy, "The Role of Imaginary Cases in Ethics." For a discussion of the role of thought experiments in philosophy more generally, see Sorenson, *Thought Experiments*.

34. Davis, "The Moral Justifiability of Torture," 161.
35. Shue, "Torture," 143, cited in Davis, "The Moral Justifiability of Torture," 172.
36. Davis, "The Moral Justifiability of Torture," 172.
37. For more discussion, see Baron, "Justifications and Excuses." See also Husak, "On the Supposed Priority of Justification." I thank Hans Allhoff and Matt Hanser for helpful discussion on differences between justification and excuse.
38. Dressler, *Understanding Criminal Law*, 558, quoted in Husak, "On the Supposed Priority of Justification," 558.
39. Byrd, "Wrongdoing and Attribution," 1289–90, quoted in Husak, "On the Supposed Priority of Justification," 558–559.
40. Moore, *Placing Blame*, 674, quoted in Husak, "On the Supposed Priority of Justification," 559.
41. While I take this to be uncontroversial, see Cohen, "The Development of the Modern Law of Necessity." (Cohen argues that the German conception of necessity is importantly different from that indoctrinated in Anglo-American law.)
42. Milhizer, "Justification and Excuse," 726.
43. American Law and Legal Information, "Justification and Excuse."
44. See, e.g., Milhizer, "Justification and Excuse." See also Baron, "Justifications and Excuses."
45. O'Neill, "Ethical Reasoning and Ideological Pluralism," 705, 711–12, referenced in Shue, "Torture in Dreamland," 231.
46. Shue, "Torture in Dreamland," 231.
47. Ibid., 233.
48. Ibid., 235.
49. I thank Joshua Knobe for helpful discussions about the design of the cases.
50. When this research was presented, some objected to the use of *daughter* rather than the more gender-neutral *child*. I am not sure why this matters. If the sense is that torturing daughters is worse than torturing children (who may be sons), then presumably there is a reason why. For example, if daughters are thought to be especially innocent (and, therefore, especially undeserving of torture), then this is precisely the most appropriate wording given the features that I want to test. However, maybe the objection is supposed to be that there is some irrelevant emotional feature that attaches to daughters, thus distorting the results.

    Regardless, given that the objection came up multiple times, I reran the experiments with a change in wording: the responses with *daughter* were compared to responses with *child*. The analysis was done using a post hoc linear contrast: $F(2,445) = 0.40$, $p = 0.52$. Qualitatively, this means that there was no statistical difference between moral judgments in cases using *daughter* and those using *child*.
51. The one sort of uncertainty that this methodology cannot accommodate is uncertainty about whether we have actually apprehended a terrorist. As will become clearer shortly, I need four different cases for my aims: guilt/certainty, guilty/uncertainty, innocence/certainty, and innocence/uncer-

tainty. Using *suspected terrorist* rather than *terrorist* accommodates further uncertainty, but it also rules out this second case since the suspected terrorist is not necessarily guilty.

The point of these thought experiments is, therefore, not to remove *all* the idealizations from ticking-time-bomb cases. For example, they also do not test the rare, isolated case idealization that Shue postulates (though which I think is less empirically suspect than some of the other alleged idealizations). Rather, the goal is to remove as much idealization as is straightforwardly possible and then to make some observations about the results, including as to how they might extend.

52. Some critics have objected to varying the number of lives on the grounds that doing so would affect the results despite the associated percentages. Having already given the reasons for the adopted strategy, I allow that this is possible, even if there is no reason to think that it is true; more data in this regard are certainly invited. (There are various ways in which such a result would make no difference to my ultimate conclusions, though I shall not pursue that discussion here.)

53. In other words, the idea was to not have reactions to one case influence reactions to another case; had the research subjects seen multiple cases, it is possible/probable that their responses would have been biased as against subjects who only received a single case.

54. For more discussion of Likert scales, see Likert, "A Technique for the Measurement of Attitudes."

55. They were also asked to report the number of philosophy classes that they had taken, including ones in which they were currently enrolled. Statistical analysis showed that this made no difference to the results, so this feature will be dropped from forthcoming discussion.

56. I thank Daniel Beaudoin, Joshua Knobe, and Jennifer Cole Wright for help with the statistical analyses. The results will be explained qualitatively after presentation of the data; no background in statistics is presupposed in that discussion.

57. Someone might argue that the consequences *could* be different as if, for example, word got out that we were torturing innocents; this might have negative societal effects. As the cases are constructed, however, such negative effects are not in play, and the wording of these cases was otherwise kept simple for obvious reasons.

58. See, e.g., Arrigo, "A Utilitarian Argument against Torture"; Bufacchi and Arrigo, "Torture, Terrorism and the State"; Luban, "Liberalism, Torture, and the Ticking Bomb"; Shue, "Torture in Dreamland"; Wolfendale, "Training Torturers"; and Wynia, "Consequentialism and Harsh Interrogations." It should be noted that not all these authors consider *only* the consequences of torture and, furthermore, that, insofar as they do, this is surely a dialectical maneuver (i.e., to beat the proponents' arguments on their own terms), rather than an endorsement of consequentialism.

59. Again, see Davis, "The Moral Justifiability of Torture." See also Davis, "Torture and the Inhumane."

60. Analyses were done using t-tests: case 1: $t(211) = 2.1$, $p = .039$; case 2: $t(208) = 2.2$, $p = .03$; case 3: $t(206)= .06$, $p = .95$; and case 4: $t(200) = 2.3$, $p = .022$.

61. See, e.g., Kohlberg, "Moral Stages and Moralization." See also Kohlberg, *The Psychology of Moral Development*.

62. See Walker, "Sex Differences in the Development of Moral Reasoning." See also Walker, "A Longitudinal Study of Moral Reasoning."

63. Gilligan, *In a Different Voice*. For a philosophical analysis of Gilligan's work, see also Calhoun, "Justice, Care, Gender Bias." For more on the differences between Kohlberg and Gilligan, see Flanagan and Jackson, "Justice, Care, and Gender."

64. Kolby and Kohlberg, *The Measurement of Moral Judgment*, referenced in Walker, "A Longitudinal Study of Moral Reasoning," 158. Congruencies between consequentialism and care-based ethics have also been argued for in Driver, "Consequentialism and Feminist Ethics."

65. See, e.g., Pratt, Golding, and Hunter, "Does Morality Have a Gender?" See also Walker, "Sex Differences in the Development of Moral Reasoning," and "Experimental and Cognitive Sources of Moral Development." Finally, see Friedman et al., "Sex Differences in Moral Judgments?"

    Results in experimental philosophy have been varied concerning the relationship between gender and utilitarian thinking; e.g., Greene et al. reported gender effects in some trolley case variants and not in others. See Greene et al., "Pushing Moral Buttons," esp. §§2.2, 4.2. See also Zamzow and Nichols, "Variations in Ethical Intuitions," esp. §2.

CHAPTER SIX

1. This strategy was originally developed in Allhoff, "A Defense of Torture." Treatments of utilitarianism and rights-based deontology previously appeared in Allhoff, "Terrorism and Torture."

2. For present purposes, the precise details of various utilitarian views are largely irrelevant and, regardless, would take us too far afield. My own view is closer to Bentham's than to Mill's—that is, without a distinction between higher and lower pleasures—but that does not matter for the following discussion.

3. See, e.g., Arrigo, "A Utilitarian Argument against Torture." See also Wynia, "Consequentialism and Harsh Interrogations."

4. Bufacchi and Arrigo, "Torture, Terrorism and the State," 360, 361–62.

5. Davis, "The Moral Justifiability of Torture."

6. Wolfendale, "Training Torturers."

7. For a good overview, see Brecher, *Torture and the Ticking Bomb*, esp. chaps. 2–3.

8. For example: "We argue that empirical evidence clearly suggests that institutionalizing torture interrogation of terrorists has detrimental consequences on civil, military, and legal institutions, making the costs higher than the benefits." Bufacchi and Arrigo, "Torture, Terrorism and the State," 362.

9. Wisnewski, "Hearing a Still-Ticking Bomb Argument." While it is irrelevant for present purposes, I think that Bufachi and Arrigo's empirical assumptions are misguided regardless. For more discussion, see chapter 7.

10. For more discussion, see Kershnar, "For Interrogational Torture."

11. In other words, it is probably the case that (most) rights are not forfeited absolutely. Consider killing in self-defense, and assume that this should be understood as a forfeiture of right to life by the aggressor. This forfeiture is qualified insofar as things like proportionality and necessity still matter for exonerating the attacked person. If the threat could be disarmed through nonlethal means, or if the threat was merely to a limb (rather than life), then the right of self-defense might not justify killing (i.e., the attacker's right to life has not been unqualifiedly forfeited). Or, to take another example, the negligent parent might not unqualifiedly forfeit his right to custodianship of his child since such a right could be reasserted if certain conditions were met (e.g., some corrective measures were taken). And the right of custodianship might not be unqualifiedly forfeited regardless, but rather only under the claim made by some legitimate authority, such as the state. In short, there are probably myriad qualifications on rights forfeitures.

12. This is especially true given the position that I will ultimately defend, namely, that torture can be justified even if the terrorist can successfully assert a right against torture. See the discussion below.

13. In the way of terminology, we can talk about rights being absolute, inalienable, nonderogable, and so on. More could be said about what these mean, differences among them, and so on, but I will not pursue that here. As *absolute* is the least technically laden, it will suffice for my purposes.

14. For more discussion, see chapter 3, n. 38.

15. There are more things to say here, though they are not central to the ensuing argumentation. For example, we might think that capital punishment threatens the right to life, but the right to life could be variously understood: it might n include, not a right not to be killed, but rather a right not to be killed unjustly. If capital punishment is justified, then it would, therefore, not violate the right to life understood as a right not to be killed unjustly. See Thomson, "A Defense of Abortion."

16. Dworkin, *Taking Rights Seriously*, ix.

17. Nozick, *Anarchy, State, and Utopia*, 28–33.

18. Dworkin, *Taking Rights Seriously*, 191.

19. We should observe that this approach will yield different results than utilitarianism. For example, consider the "spare parts surgeon" case, which is supposed to inveigh against utilitarianism: imagine that we can kill one innocent person to provide lifesaving organ transplants to five people who will otherwise die. We could make enough further stipulations to commit the utilitarian to the harvesting, though the aggregative deontologist need not have this commitment. The reason is that the harvesting violates one right (namely, that of the harvested) but not harvesting violates no rights (since the dying patients do not have a right to the organs of the healthy person). Since the harvesting does not minimize overall rights violations, it is, therefore, impermissible; this is the conclusion that many deontologists want.

20. See, e.g., Sen, "Rights and Agency," 187–223.

21. Nozick, *Anarchy, State, and Utopia*, 33.

22. Ibid., 30.
23. Allhoff, "A Defense of Torture." For nonphilosophers, the basic structure of this argument was that most major moral theories led to the same conclusion, but for some other set of moral theories. If this other set of moral theories can be rejected, then the conclusion is secured without having to adjudicate among that first set of moral theories, so long as the complete set of moral theories was exhaustive (i.e., none was left out). Formally, consider that the right moral theory is A, B, or C. Further suppose that C can be ruled out on some grounds. If φ is permissible on both A and B, then it is permissible full stop since one or the other of them had to be true once C was excluded. The advantage of this style of argument is that nothing has to be said about the relative merits of A vs. B; if those stood for utilitarianism and rights-based deontology, such an adjudication might be unlikely given the intractability of the debate.
24. Plato develops his account of virtue ethics through various dialogues, but the most straightforward is *The Republic*, esp. bks. 2–4. See also Plato, "Euthyphro," 2a1–16a5, and "Laches," 178a1–201c5. For Aristotle's account, see *Nichomachean Ethics*, esp. bks. 1.13–5.
25. See, e.g., Hursthouse, *On Virtue Ethics*. See also Foot, *Natural Goodness*. Foot's *Virtues and Vices and Other Essays in Moral Philosophy* was also important, though broader than just virtue ethics.
26. See, e.g., Doris, "Persons, Situations, and Virtue Ethics." See also Doris, *Lack of Character*.
27. See, e.g., Plato, "Laches," 441c3–445e2.
28. Aristotle, *Nichomachean Ethics*, 1119b20–1128b36.
29. Hutcheson, "Treatise II."
30. Hume, *A Treatise of Human Nature*, 3.2.1.
31. Hursthouse, *On Virtue Ethics*, 63–87.
32. Darwall, *Contractarianism/Contractualism*, 1.
33. Ibid., 1. This notion of *moral equality* is a tricky one, though I will return to it briefly in §6.4. While Darwall does not provide an account in *Contractarianism/Contractualism*, see his *Second-Person Standpoint*. See also Anderson, "What Is the Point of Equality?"
34. Hobbes, *Leviathan*, 74.
35. He writes: "To this war of every man against every man, this also is consequent; that nothing can be unjust. The notions of right and wrong, justice and injustice, have there no place. Where there is no common power, there is no law; where no law, no injustice." Ibid., 78. For more discussion, see Allhoff, "Evolution of the Moral Sentiments."
36. For example, John Harsanyi's "impartial observer argument" holds that we should make social decisions as if we had an equal chance of being anyone in the society. Since our case stipulates that there are a lot more non-terrorists who may lose their lives than terrorists who may suffer torture, the rational choice—on his view at least, Rawls's maximin principle would yield the contrary result—would be to support the legislation of torture. This support would, on average (even to near unity if the number of potential victims were high enough), be in the self-interest of the legislator. See Harsanyi, "Cardinal Utility in Welfare Economics," and "Cardinal Welfare,

Individualistic Ethics, and Interpersonal Comparisons in Utility." For the alternative view, see Rawls, *A Theory of Justice*, 132–36.

37. Rawls, *A Theory of Justice*, 132–33.
38. Ibid., 53.
39. Ibid., §28.
40. In "A Defense of Torture," I offer some treatment of moral pluralism and moral particularism as nonabsolutist theories. Given the space constraints and the following comments, it would not be useful to repeat those treatments here, but I direct the interested reader to §3.5 of that paper.
41. For example, I take "antiutilitarianism" to be a coherent—if unmotivated— moral theory: let this be the theory that always reaches conclusions opposite to those reached by utilitarianism. Allow that utilitarianism endorses torture in ticking-time-bomb cases, and, therefore, antiutilitarianism does not. Still, antiutilitarianism would provide for the moral permissibility of torture in *some* cases, namely, those in which utilitarianism does not. This theory rules out a consensus regarding the permissibility of torture in ticking-time-bomb cases but, nevertheless, still allows for the permissibility of torture in other cases.
42. In point of fact, I suspect that many who defend a-practice do so for methodological reasons and, in fact, would also defend the stronger a-principle. A-practice is simply much more plausible than a-principle, and to argue against torture in the real world—the goal of most opponents of torture— this weaker thesis is sufficient.
43. See, e.g., Mayerfeld, "In Defense of the Absolute Prohibition on Torture." See also Tindale, "Tragic Choices."
44. Scheppele, "Hypothetical Torture in the 'War on Terrorism,'" 287, quoted in McMahan, "Torture in Principle and Practice," 127 n. 2. As McMahan says, Scheppele ultimately goes on to defend something that looks more like a-practice, despite her clear statement of a-principle. A-principle and a-practice are often conflated, which is one reason why I emphasize the distinction.
45. Juratowitch, "Torture Is Always Wrong," 81.
46. McMahan, "Torture in Principle and Practice," 111.
47. At a workshop on this manuscript, Jeremy Wisnewski argued that such a claim was too quick; consider rape, slavery, or genocide, all of which we (presumably?) reject absolutely. However, our absolute rejection of these practices does not show that we endorse a-principle with regard to them as we might otherwise be endorsing a-practice. And, in fact, I suspect that we are since, unlike with torture or killing, there are no obvious circumstances in which rape, slavery, or genocide would preclude worse harms. In other words, we can reasonably deny that any of these ever *would* (cf. *could*) be justified, and that is (roughly) sufficient to accommodate our moral sensibilities. To be sure, we can invent cases to the contrary: imagine that a tyrant will kill an innocent population unless a second party rapes, enslaves, or effects genocide against some other, smaller population. These cases, however, have even less surface plausibility than ticking-time-bomb cases, so it is not surprising that the former fail to figure into our moral discourse. If they did, a-principle positions would surely appear, and my forthcoming arguments

would apply to those positions as well. Professor Wisnewski took this to be a disadvantage thereof, but I nevertheless remain committed to the position that lesser harms are always preferable to greater ones and maintain that a-principle is unable to accommodate this basic moral truism (i.e., by proscribing certain actions even when we can imagine that those actions minimize harms). To put it another way, if we want to absolutely reject some act, I propose that we solicit a-practice instead of a-principle.

48. McMahan, "Torture in Principle and Practice."

49. In the following paragraphs, it will be useful to draw distinctions between a-principle$_{torture}$ and a-principle$_{killing}$—i.e., absolutism with one but not necessarily the other act type—so the associated subscripts will be employed. When left unqualified, *a-principle* usually refers to absolutism in principle with regard to torture, so long as context does not clearly indicate the more generalized intent.

50. The converse, however, does hold: if φ is morally permissible and ψ is less bad (or more good) than φ, then ψ is morally permissible.

51. While it is irrelevant to the present discussion, I also find it implausible that all instances of torture are less wrong than the least-worst death. Some deaths—such as those provided for through euthanasia—are not wrong at all, and there are certainly cases of torture that are very wrong. Sometimes death is worse than torture, and sometimes torture is worse than death. For my attack on a-principle$_{torture}$, it is this first conjunct that matters, though I also endorse the second.

52. For simplicity of presentation, I will not continually repeat *maximally* in front of *promotes*. I take it to be possible that φ promotes (i.e., increases) V while, at the same time being inadvisable if some other act ψ promotes V to a greater extent. So maybe φ increases happiness in the world but does so less than ψ; if happiness is our sole moral value, then we should ψ rather than φ. I encourage the reader to substitute *maximally promotes* for *promotes* as he or she likes.

53. For our purposes, the ways in which dignity can be compromised are not important; the reader may supply these details given his account of dignity. Let the bomb blind, maim, paralyze, or scar. Let it have neurological impacts, leave its victims prone to self-mutilation, self-defecation, or whatever. So long as torture is supposed to compromise dignity, there surely must be other ways to do so.

54. McMahan, "Torture in Principle and Practice," 111. It bears notice that some with broadly Kantian sympathies nevertheless deny a-principle with regard to torture. David Sussman, e.g., does "not . . . contend that torture is categorically wrong, but only that it bears an especially high burden of justification." See Sussman, "What's Wrong with Torture?" 4. For more discussion of Sussman's account, see §4.3 above. For a more traditional Kantian approach, see Wisnewski and Emerick, *The Ethics of Torture*, chap. 3.

55. Statman, "The Prohibition against Torture," 161, quoted in Gross, *Moral Dilemmas of Modern War*, 146.

56. Shue, "Torture in Dreamland," 238 (emphasis added). In earlier work, after presentation of a ticking-time-bomb case, he writes: "I can see no way to deny the permissibility of torture in a case *just like this*." Shue, "Torture,"

141. He goes on to issue various disclaimers about whether these cases would actually attain, but he does not rule out the possibility. The more recent paper is unequivocal in its practical prohibition on torture.

57. See, e.g., Arrigo, "A Utilitarian Argument against Torture." See also Wynia, "Consequentialism and Harsh Interrogations."

58. Rejali, *Torture and Democracy*.

CHAPTER SEVEN

1. Rejali, *Torture and Democracy*, 446–47.
2. For more discussion, see Melzack and Wall, *The Challenge of Pain*. See also Deeley, *Beyond Breaking Point*.
3. Rejali, *Torture and Democracy*, 449.
4. Ibid., 455–56.
5. Ibid.
6. Ibid., 464. For more discussion, see Vrij, *Detecting Lies and Deceit*. See also Mann, Vrij, and Bull, "Detecting True Lies."
7. It is worth recognizing that this point is made by supposing a (false) dichotomy between torturing and doing nothing; the structure of the dialectic is set up only to show the limited force of the misinformation objection. More will be in §7.4 about alternatives to torture.
8. Rejali, *Torture and Democracy*, 458.
9. Ibid., 474.
10. Arrigo, "A Utilitarian Argument against Torture," 564 (emphasis added), quoted in Shue, "Torture in Dreamland," 236.
11. Bufacchi and Arrigo, "Torture, Terrorism, and the State," 362–66.
12. See Allhoff, "Physician Involvement in Hostile Interrogations." See also Allhoff, ed., *Physicians at War*.
13. See, e.g., Rejali, *Torture and Democracy*, 245–47.
14. Bufacchi and Arrigo, "Torture, Terrorism, and the State," 364.
15. Arrigo, "A Utilitarian Argument against Torture," 236.
16. Wolfendale, "Training Torturers," 270.
17. Shue, "Torture in Dreamland," 236.
18. Ibid., Wolfendale, "Training Torturers," 273, 274.
19. A related issue is whether we should think of torture in individual *cases* or else whether we should think about our social *policies*, which will either support or abhor torture. This idea is somewhat redolent of rule utilitarianism, but I would just say that our social policies should be to torture only in justified cases, and the associated moral rule should be to torture when doing so maximizes the moral benefits. It is a red herring to say that we need to pick between "always torture" and "never torture" as surely we do not. Policies just represent agglomerated treatments of individual cases, and there is nothing misleading about focusing on cases or else on proposing that our policies should be nuanced rather than blunt. The arguments regarding the institutionalization of torture in §7.3 are also relevant in terms of thinking about the policy issues, though I will return to these in the next chapter as well.

20. Fiala, "A Critique of Exceptions."

21. Shue, "Torture," 139.

22. Millgram, "Behavioral Study of Obedience." See also Milgram, *Obedience to Authority*. A short and accessible excerpt from the book is available as Milgram, "The Perils of Obedience."

23. Haney, Banks, and Zimbardo, "Interpersonal Dynamics in a Simulated Prison." See also Haney, Banks, and Zimbardo, "Study of Prisoners and Guards in a Simulated Prison."

24. See, e.g., Wolfendale, "Training Torturers."

25. Logically, there are two other possibilities as well. The first is that the alternatives are less effective and more morally costly, which obviously makes those alternatives ill advised. The second is that the alternatives are more effective and more costly, though I do not think that anyone holds this: the principal argument against torture is its moral cost, and it is hard to envision other intelligence practices that would carry an even higher burden. The alternatives that are proposed in the literature certainly do not bear out this possibility, so I take it that the two options mentioned in text are the ones that should be considered.

26. Alexander and Bruning, *How to Break a Terrorist*.

27. As a secondary theme to the book, Alexander paints a clash of cultures among the interrogators, contending that there is a deep divide between those advocating hostile and those advocating nonhostile means of interrogation.

28. Department of the Army, *Human Intelligence Collector Operations*, 8-6–8-20.

29. Ibid., 5-26, quoted in Alexander and Bruning, *How to Break a Terrorist*, 69. Alexander and Bruning actually have the wrong reference, citing to the *Army Manual* [sic] *Field Manual*, 34-52, i.e., Department of the Army, *Intelligence Interrogation*. *Human Intelligence Collector Operations* superseded *Intelligence Interrogation* in 2006. Given the publication date of Alexander's book, this oversight is curious.

30. Mathematically, let P_{Sx} stand for the probability that some technique will succeed in eliciting the necessary information, MC_x stand for the moral costs of that technique—whether successful or not—and MB stand for the technique's moral benefits (if successful). The question then is whether $P_{S\varphi} \times MB - MC_{\varphi} > P_{S\psi} \times MB - MC_{\psi}$. If so, we should φ; otherwise, we should ψ.

In other words, assume that torture has the same costs whether it is successful or not, which is at least a reasonable approximation. It might be false insofar as failed torture could raise more umbrage, distrust, and so on, but set that aside for simplicity. What we then care about is the probability that torture will work, times the moral benefits that would accrue if it does, minus its moral costs. That quantity then gets compared to the (lesser) costs of the alternative to torture, as subtracted from the expected moral benefit of that alternative. The unweighted moral benefits are the same on each side of the inequality since both torture and its alternatives aim at the same end. This is not to say that they have the same consequences, but I find it more intuitive to think that those different consequences play out under moral costs rather than under moral benefits (i.e., the alternatives to torture avoid certain moral costs rather than probabilistically aspiring toward different moral benefits).

31. Alexander and Bruning, *How to Break a Terrorist*, 31, 111, 158, 165.
32. United Nations Treaty Collection, IV.9.
33. Alexander and Bruning, *How to Break a Terrorist*, 103.
34. Ibid., 157–58, 160–63.
35. Bufacchi and Arrigo, "Torture, Terrorism and the State," 367.
36. Ibid., 368.
37. Rejali, *Torture and Democracy*, 111, quoting Mellor, *La torture*, 218.
38. Alexander and Bruning, *How to Break a Terrorist*, 236. The reference is to a colleague who is attempting to leverage hope in exchange for intelligence.
39. Ibid., 5, 277–79.
40. See also n. 19 above.
41. See table in chapter 2, n. 40.
42. At least if the disjuncts are distinct, and neither is necessarily false.
43. Sammon, "Cheney." There is no shortage of these sorts of quotes from Cheney. President George W. Bush has been somewhat more circumspect but has, ultimately, said similar things. See, e.g., Hamby, "Bush Defends Interrogation Program."
44. "September 11 Mastermind." There is at least some dispute as to how to count instances of waterboarding. See, e.g., Abrams, "Despite Reports."
45. Another al-Qaeda suspect, Abu Zubaydah, was allegedly waterboarded eighty-three times, yet a former CIA officer has maintained that this waterboarding did not engender any more information than Zubaydah was willing to give from the outset. "September 11 Mastermind." See also Rejali, *Torture and Democracy*, 504–7.
46. Thiessen, "The CIA's Questioning Worked."
47. Noah, "Water-Bored."
48. Dershowitz, *Why Terrorism Works*, 137. The more comprehensive account is found in Brzezinski, "Bust and Boom." See also Maass, "If a Terror Suspect Won't Talk."
49. Dershowitz, *Why Terrorism Works*, 137. Murad was caught somewhere around midnight on January 7, and the pope was scheduled to appear at the World Youth Day celebrations on January 15. We know that Murad was tortured for sixty-seven days, and Maass seems to allege that the assassination attempt against the pope was acknowledged only after the fact: if Murad did not confess until the end of the torture, then the confession would have been too late to have mattered for protecting the pope. See Maass, "If a Terror Suspect Won't Talk." Dershowitz does not discuss these details, and I have not seen an unequivocal discussion about when Murad confessed to the papal assassination attempt. Nevertheless, his ambitions in regard to the planes are not in dispute, particularly given the flight details recovered from his laptop.
50. Rejali, *Torture and Democracy*, 507–8. See also Brzezinski, "Bust and Boom."
51. Rejali, *Torture and Democracy*, 507.
52. Winik, "Security Comes Before Liberty," quoted in Rejali, *Torture and Democracy*, 508.

53. Brzezinski, "Bust and Boom," W09. Curiously, Rejali calls out Dershowitz on ignoring certain features of the Brzezinkski article but then fails to recognize that the Filipinos did reach out to the Americans. Rejali, *Torture and Democracy*, 762 n. 304.

54. Brzezinski, "Bust and Boom."

55. This is a rough approximation that will be revisited in subsequent chapters. For more discussion, see esp. chapter 9, n. 1.

56. Rubin, "3 Suspects Talk After Iraqi Soldiers Do Dirty Work." As the title indicates, the point of Rubin's article was, not to rejoice in this intelligence finding, but rather to lament the asymmetrical relationship between the American and the Iraqi forces: the Iraqis are characterized as overzealously trying to impress the Americans and, in so doing, cavalierly assaulting a detainee. By contrast, the American military leadership is characterized as being oblivious to the harms perpetuated by the Iraqis while, at the same time, tacitly supporting whatever methods generate positive intelligence results. Since I think that the beating was justified, I do not have these worries, at least in this particular case. That does not deny that there are ethical risks in the alliance between the Iraqis and the Americans, only that I do not see them herein manifest.

57. Miller, "Is Torture Ever Morally Justified?" 182–83. Miller attributes the case to John Blackler, a former New South Wales police officer. I thank Daniel Star for help in deciphering the Australian colloquialisms.

58. For several discussions of nefarious police beatings, see Rejali, *Torture and Democracy*. Obviously, I think that there should be some sort of safeguards to prevent wanton abuse. For example, it is certain that the detainee in the case in question is guilty, which relieves various epistemic worries.

59. See, e.g., Davis, "The Moral Justifiability of Torture."

60. See, e.g., Dershowitz, *Why Terrorism Works*, 150; Rejali, *Torture and Democracy*, chap. 22.

CHAPTER EIGHT

1. For details on CAT's legislative history, see §4.1, above.

2. See, e.g., Luban, "The Torture Lawyers of Washington." See also Strauss, "Torture," esp. §2.

3. The full quote was actually: "Great cases, like hard cases, make bad law. For great cases are called great, not by reason of their importance in shaping the law of the future, but because of some accident of immediate overwhelming interest which appeals to the feelings and distorts the judgment." *Northern Securities Co. v. United States*, 193 U.S. 197, 400 (1904) (Holmes, O. W., dissenting).

4. Recall from §4.1 that §2.2 of CAT states: "No exceptional circumstances whatsoever, whether a state of war or a threat of war, internal political in stability or any other public emergency, may be invoked as a justification of torture." More will be said about this issue in §8.3.

5. See, e.g., Miller, "Is Torture Ever Morally Justified?" See also Gross, "The Prohibition on Torture."

6. See, e.g., Luban, "Liberalism, Torture, and the Ticking Bomb." See also Miller, "Is Torture Ever Morally Justified?"

7. For a general discussion of judicial integrity, see Bloom, "Judicial Integrity." For a discussion of judicial integrity in regard to torture, see Sung, "Torturing the Ticking-Bomb Terrorist." See also Garg, "Unwarranted and Unnecessary." Judicial integrity will be discussed more in subsequent sections, but let me just register from the outset a dim view of how such integrity could be undermined by participating in, ex hypothesi, *justified* torture; it seems to me that such integrity *requires* that participation. Regardless, more on this to come.

8. Miller, "Is Torture Ever Morally Justified?" 188, 190.

9. Nozick, *Anarchy, State, and Utopia*, 28–33.

10. Miller, "Is Torture Ever Morally Justified?" 190.

11. Plato, "Crito," 43a–54e.

12. Langbein, *Torture and the Law of Proof*, 81–128.

13. Dershowitz, *Why Terrorism Works*, 158–59. See, more broadly, ibid., 158–60. See also Dershowitz, "Tortured Reasoning," and "The Torture Warrant."

14. For more extended discussion than I will provide here, see Wisnewski, "Unwarranted Torture Warrants."

15. This famous example—as well as a common failure to reason through it properly—comes from Tversky and Kahneman, "Extensional versus Intuitive Reasoning."

16. This list is roughly adapted from Wisnewski, "Unwarranted Torture Warrants," 308.

17. Kleinig, "Ticking Bombs and Torture Warrants." See also Steinoff, "Torture"; and Fiala, "A Critique of Exceptions."

18. For example, consider time constraints, judges' differing evidential standards, and so on. I thank Jeremy Wisnewski for discussion in this regard.

19. Sung, "Torturing the Ticking-Bomb Terrorist." See also Garg, "Unwarranted and Unnecessary."

20. Luban, "Liberalism, Torture, and the Ticking Bomb." See also Bufacchi and Arrigo, "Torture, Terrorism, and the State."

21. Sung, "Torturing the Ticking-Bomb Terrorist," 207. See also Bloom, "Judicial Integrity," 466.

22. Garg, "Unwarranted and Unnecessary," 5. See also *Olmstead v. United States*, 277 U.S. 438 (1928) (Brandeis, L. D., dissenting).

23. Sung, "Torturing the Ticking-Bomb Terrorist," 207, quoting *Casey v. United States*, 276 U.S. 413 (1928) (Brandeis, L. D., dissenting) (other internal references elided).

24. Dressler, *Understanding Criminal Law*, 558, quoted in Husak, "On the Supposed Priority of Justification," 558 (emphasis added).

25. Moore, *Placing Blame*, 674, quoted in Husak, "On the Supposed Priority of Justification," 559.

26. American Law Institute, *Model Penal Code*, §3.04. The *Model Penal Code* is not the code of any particular jurisdiction, though many jurisdictions have codified its precepts. We should, presumably, amend the *Model Penal Code* statement with a qualification that no other reasonable alternative be available to the agent.

27. Yoo, "Memorandum for William J. Hynes II," 79.

28. Moore, "Torture and the Balance of Evils," 323, quoted in Yoo, "Memorandum for William J. Hynes II," 79.

29. See, e.g., Luban, "The Torture Lawyers of Washington," 179: "Looked at dispassionately, necessity offers the strongest defense of torture on normative grounds. The necessity defense justifies otherwise criminal conduct undertaken to prevent a greater evil, and in extreme cases it is at least thinkable that torture might be the lesser evil." Luban nevertheless strongly opposes torture.

Note also that, since a 1999 High Court of Justice ruling, the necessity defense has formed the basis of Israel's torture policy; unfortunately, extended discussion in this regard would take us too far afield. For the court's ruling, see *Public Committee against Torture in Israel et al. v. Government of Israel et al.*, HCJ 5100/94 (1999). One point worth making is that torture has almost assuredly been underprosecuted in Israel. For example, the Public Committee against Torture in Israel (PCATI) alleges: "Since 2001, over 600 complaints of torture have been submitted to the law enforcement agencies in Israel by victims of torture. Not a single one of these complaints has developed into a criminal investigation—the first step in the process of indictment, conviction, and the meting out of justice." The Public Committee against Torture in Israel, "Accountability Denied," 15.

To be clear, I do not think that torture should be underprosecuted; Israel could, presumably, do better in this regard. (Some skepticism is due PCATI's predictably negative finding, particularly given the group's obvious political design. For example, no mention is made as to how many of the complaints were frivolous, which could well be a significant percentage.) There is no reason to think that Israel's failure to prosecute would transfer to other law enforcement or judicial jurisdictions or else that there is anything inherent to situations of necessity that would limit prosecution. In other words, however Israel has implemented the necessity defense vis-à-vis torture is neither here nor there with regard to how the defense could or should be implemented elsewhere. This does not deny that we can learn from Israel's experience or that correctives thereof could be part of our own.

30. American Law Institute, *Model Penal Code*, §3.02. For more discussion than I will provide here, see Christie, "The Defense of Necessity." For cases, see LaFave, *Modern Criminal Law*. See also n. 35 below. Different jurisdictions have implemented the *Model Penal Code* language in different ways. See, e.g., *United States v. Schoon*, 971 F2d 193, 195–97 (9th Cir. 2002), *United States v. Patton*, 451 F3d 615, 638 (10th Cir. 2006), and *People v. Bordowitz*, 115 Misc. 2d 128, 132–33 (N.Y. Crim. Ct. 1991). Cases referenced in Schwartz, "Is There a Common Law Necessity Defense in Federal Criminal Law?" n. 3.

31. This claim was defended in chapter 6, and I will not rehearse those arguments here. Refer to that earlier chapter for discussion.

32. For the sake of argument, I will assume that killing the gangster is always at least prima facie wrong (i.e., whether he is preparing to execute innocents or not). If the reader has a different intuition, then substitute some more complicated example, such as Bernard Williams's Jim and the Indi-

ans case. In this case, Jim is offered the opportunity to kill one innocent such that the other nineteen are let go; if Jim declines, all twenty will be killed. Should Jim accept this ill-fated bargain, he could presumably avail himself of the necessity defense since he chose the lesser of two evils. See Williams, "A Critique of Utilitarianism," 99.

Other paradigmatic cases include the destruction of property to save a life. For example, Joel Feinberg imagines a case wherein a backpacker is stranded by a blizzard; he stays alive by forcing his way into a cabin, consuming food he finds there, and burning furniture for warmth. Feinberg, "Voluntary Euthanasia," 102. Similarly, Jules Coleman proposes a diabetic who loses his insulin in an accident and must break into the house of another diabetic to obtain lifesaving insulin. Coleman, *Risks and Wrongs*, 282. Both cases are referenced in Christie, "The Defense of Necessity," 977.

To take an actual case, consider *Montana v. Leprowse*, 2009 MT 387 (2009), in which Lisa Marie Leprowse successfully defended herself against charges of drunk driving by establishing a physical threat from which she fled. The necessity defense worked in this case because the evil posed by her intoxicated flight was judged to be less than the evil she risked by not fleeing.

33. American Law Institute, *Model Penal Code* §3.02, comment 3 (Tentative Draft No. 8, 1958). See also ibid., §3.02, comment 3: "It would be particularly unfortunate to exclude homicidal conduct from the scope of the defense." Referenced in Christie, "The Defense of Necessity," n. 286.

34. *Ky. Rev. Stat. Ann.*, §503.030, states that "no justification can exist under this section for an intentional homicide." *Mo. Ann. Stat.*, §563.026, allows necessity in circumstances "other than a class A felony or murder." *Wis. Stat. Ann.*, §939.47, provides that necessity can reduce a charge of first-degree homicide to second-degree homicide. Referenced in Christie, "The Defense of Necessity," 279–81. See also Cohan, "Homicide by Necessity."

35. Interestingly, many of these cases pertain to survival cannibalism among castaways. For the landmark, see *R v. Dudley and Stephens*, 14 QBD 273 DC (1884). See also *United States v. Holmes* F. Cas. 360 (E.D. Pa. 1842); note that Holmes was able to receive some consideration vis-à-vis necessity insofar as he was convicted of manslaughter rather than first-degree murder. The ill-recorded "Saint Christopher case"—dating to the early seventeenth century—recognized necessity but, nevertheless, did not have a significant impact on *R v. Dudley and Stephens*. See Simpson, *Cannibalism and the Common Law*, 122–23.

36. Unlike homicide, note that torture is a federal crime; individual states cannot block or limit the necessity defense in regard to torture since the unqualified federal statute supersedes state law.

37. I first came across this issue in Luban, "The Torture Lawyers of Washington," n. 60, and I thank Professor Luban for subsequent discussion thereof. As he pointed out, note that the situation is different in Israel, where there is a statute creating the necessity defense; this defense can be used against charges of torture. For discussion of the Israeli approach, see Raviv, "Torture and Justification," 157–59.

38. For more discussion, see "The Necessity Defense to Prison Escape After *United States v. Bailey*," 367–71.

39. *United States v. Bailey*, 444 U.S. 394, 427 (1980).

40. For example, consider *Dixon v. United States* (2006). This case considered duress, which is not sharply distinguished from necessity in some rulings. The court ruled that the possession of a firearm by a felon was not "incompatible" with a duress offense, even if such possession violated federal law. *Dixon v. United States*, 548 U.S. 1, 13–14 and n. 6 (2006). See also Schwartz, "Is There a Common Law Necessity Defense in Federal Criminal Law?" 1268.

41. Schwartz, "Is There a Common Law Necessity Defense in Federal Criminal Law?" 1266.

42. For discussion of *Dixon*, see n. 40 above.

43. *United States v. Bailey*, 444 U.S. 394, 410, 411, (1980) quoted in Paust, "The Complicity of Dick Cheney."

44. Gaeta, "May Necessity Be Available," 785. See also Hunsinger, "Torture *Is* the Ticking Time-Bomb."

45. See, e.g., Schwartz, "Is There a Common Law Necessity Defense in Federal Criminal Law?" 1268–73.

46. Paust, "The Complicity of Dick Cheney."

47. Ibid.

48. See also Raviv, "Torture and Justification."

CHAPTER NINE

1. Imagine that either φ or ψ would prevent some bad outcome A; therefore, neither is necessary for its prevention. Suppose that φ is bad but that ψ is worse. So, even though φ is bad and not necessary to prevent A, it is our best course of action. Alternatively, imagine that φ had some probability of success, P_1, and that ψ had some other probability of success, P_2, where $P_1 > P_2$. Given our epistemic situation, we cannot say that φ is necessary to prevent A since ψ might work. Even if φ were morally worse than ψ, φ could still be justified given the associated probabilities. (That is, if φ were twice as bad as ψ but four times more likely to avert the moral harms of A, then our moral calculus would support it.) In other words, φ needs to be neither necessary to prevent A nor the least harmful action in order to be justified; the implications for torture more generally and the above wording in particular are transparent.

2. As I write, President Obama just today—March 29, 2010—signed into law a sweeping health care reform bill that does far too little to rectify this shortcoming; the principal focus of that bill is to increase access to care for the (previously) uninsured rather than to propose thoroughgoing reform as to how to prevent people from needing curative care in the first place.

3. This might sound like a strange claim, but remember that the point of terrorism is to use extreme fear in order to effectuate some sort of ideological change. In other words, there is nothing intrinsically motivating about the

fear itself; that fear is meant to be used instrumentally. Therefore, there is no reason that terrorists should want to perpetuate terrorism if they can achieve their ideological goals by alternative means; this is especially true given the costs and risks of terrorism. If all someone cared about were causing terror—i.e., rather than the ideological goals—then we would call him, not a *terrorist*, but rather a *sadist* or a *psychopath*. To be sure, there might be incompatible ideologies that different terrorists wanted to promote, thus, from their perspective at least, making terrorism a practical necessity. But, from either of their perspectives, there would be no reason to prefer more terrorism to less. For more discussion on the conceptual foundations of terrorism, see chapter 1.

4. Claims like this do not presuppose a thoroughgoing science of torture—such as that objected to by Darius Rejali (see §7.1 above)—but rather are just meant to be self-evident.

5. In other words, having a good reason to torture does not mean that there are not better, countervailing reasons not to torture. The existence of such reasons does not always presuppose that ignorance thereof is culpable, which is to say that a torturer might torture unjustifiably while, at the same time, not being blameworthy.

6. This case is loosely inspired by discussion in Alexander and Bruning, *How to Break a Terrorist*.

Bibliography

Abrams, Joseph. "Despite Reports, Khalid Sheikh Mohammed Was Not Waterboarded 183 Times." Foxnews.com, April 28, 2009. http://www .foxnews.com/politics/2009/04/28/despite-reports-khalid-sheikh-mohammed-waterboarded-times/ (accessed October 8, 2009).

Abruzzese, Sarah. "Maryland Parents Told to Have Children Immunized." *New York Times*, November 18, 2007.

Ackerman, Bruce. *Before the Next Attack: Preserving Civil Liberties in an Age of Terrorism*. New Haven, CT: Yale University Press, 2004.

———. "The Emergency Constitution." *Yale Law Journal* 113 (2004): 1029–91.

Alexander, Matthew, and John R. Bruning. *How to Break a Terrorist*. New York: Free Press, 2008.

Allhoff, Fritz. "Terrorism and Torture." *International Journal of Applied Philosophy* 17, no. 1 (2003): 105–18.

———. "A Defense of Torture: Separation of Cases, Moral Methodology, and Ticking Time-Bombs." *International Journal of Applied Philosophy* 19, no. 2 (2005): 243–64.

———. "Physician Involvement in Hostile Interrogations." *Cambridge Quarterly of Healthcare Ethics* 15 (2006): 392–402.

———, ed. *Physicians at War: The Dual-Loyalties Challenge*. Dordrecht: Springer, 2008.

———. "The Evolution of the Moral Sentiments and the Metaphysics of Morals." *Ethical Theory and Moral Practice* 12, no. 1 (2009): 97–114.

———. "The War on Terror and the Ethics of Exceptionalism." *Journal of Military Ethics* 8, no. 4 (2009): 265–88.

Altman, Andrew, and Christopher Wellman. "From Humanitarian Intervention to Assassination: Human Rights and Political Violence." *Ethics* 118 (2008): 228–57.

American Law and Legal Information. "Justification and Excuse: Similarities and Differences." Crime and Justice, vol. 2 (n.d.). http://law.jrank .org/pages/1114/Excuse-Theory-Justification-excuse-similarities-differences .html (accessed June 4, 2009).

American Law Institute. *Model Penal Code*. Philadelphia, 1962.

Anderson, Elizabeth. "What Is the Point of Equality?" *Ethics* 109, no. 2 (1999): 287–337.

Antiterrorism and Effective Death Penalty Act of 1996. Pub. L. No. 104-132, 110 Stat. 1214 (1996).

Aquinas, Thomas. *Summa theologica*. Translated by Fathers of the English Dominican Province. New York: Benziger, 1948.

Aristotle. *Nichomachean Ethics*. Translated by Terence Irwin. 2nd ed. Indianapolis: Hackett, 1999.

Arrigo, Jean Maria. "A Utilitarian Argument against Torture Interrogation of Terrorists." *Science and Engineering Ethics* 10, no. 3 (2004): 1–30.

Associated Press. "Poll Finds Broad Approval of Terrorist Torture." 2005. http://www.msnbc.msn.com/id/10345320 (accessed May 30, 2008).

Baender v. Barnett. 255 U.S. 224 (1921).

Bagaric, Mikro, and Julie Clarke. *Torture: When the Unthinkable Is Morally Permissible*. Albany: State University of New York Press, 2007.

Baker, Robert. "A Theory of International Bioethics: Multiculturalism, Postmodernism, and the Bankruptcy of Fundamentalism." *Kennedy Institute of Ethics Journal* 8, no. 3 (1998): 201–31.

Baldor, Lolita. "More Than Half of Guantánamo Detainees Not Accused of Hostile Acts." *Associated Press*, February 9, 2006.

Baron, Marcia. "Justifications and Excuses." *Ohio State Journal of Criminal Law* 2 (2005): 387–500.

Baur, Michael. "What Is Distinctive about Terrorism, and What Are the Philosophical Implications." In *Philosophy 9/11: Thinking about the War on Terror*, ed. Timothy Shanahan, 3–12. Peru, IL: Open Court, 2005.

Beccaria, Cesare. *Of Crimes and Punishments*. 1764. Translated by J. Grigson. London, 1964.

Bedau, Hugo Adam. *The Death Penalty in America: Current Controversies*. New York: Oxford University Press, 1998.

Belasco, Amy. *The Cost of Iraq, Afghanistan, and Other Global War on Terror Operations since 9/11*. Congressional Research Service Report for Congress. Washington, DC: Library of Congress, 2008.

Bentham, Jeremy. *An Introduction to the Principles of Morals and Legislation*. 1780. Mineola, NY: Dover, 2007.

———. "Of Torture." ca. 1776–80. Box 46, Bentham MSS, University College London Library.

———. "Of Torture." ca. 1778–79. Box 99, Bentham MSS, University College London Library.

———. "Of Torture." 1804. Box 74.b, Bentham MSS, University College London Library.

———. *The Works of Jeremy Bentham*. Edited by John Bowring. 11 vols. Edinburgh: William Tait, 1838–43.

Bentley, Amy. *Eating for Victory: Food Rationing and the Politics of Domesticity*. Urbana: University of Illinois Press, 1998.

Berryman, Phillip E., trans. *Report of the Chilean Commission on Truth and Reconciliation*. Notre Dame, IN: Notre Dame University Press, 1993.

Blimes, Linda J., and Joseph E. Stiglitz. "The Iraq War Will Cost Us $3 Trillion, and Much More." *Washington Post*, March 9, 2008, B01.

Bloche, M. Gregg, and Jonathan H. Marks. "When Doctors Go to War." *New England Journal of Medicine* 352, no. 3 (2005): 3–6.

Blomberg, S. Brock. "Perspective Paper 9.1." In *Global Crises, Global Solutions* (2nd ed.), ed. Bjørn Lomberg, 563–76. Cambridge: Cambridge University Press, 2009.

Bloom, Robert. "Judicial Integrity: A Call for Its Re-Emergence in the Adjudication of Criminal Cases." *Journal of Criminal Law and Criminology* 84 (1993): 462–501.

Boumediene v. Bush. 553 U.S. 723 (2008).

Brecher, Bob. *Torture and the Ticking Bomb*. Maiden, MA: Blackwell, 2007.

Brough, Michael. "Legitimate Combatancy, POW Status, and Terrorism." In *Philosophy 9/11: Thinking about the War on Terror*, ed. Timothy Shanahan, 205–22. Peru, IL: Open Court, 2005.

Brown, Gary D. "Proportionality and Just War." *Journal of Military Ethics* 2, no. 3 (2003): 171–85.

Bruff, Harold H., and Ernest Gellhorn. "Congressional Control of Administrative Regulation: A Study." *Harvard Law Review* 90, no. 7 (1977): 1369–1440.

Brzezinski, Matthew. "Bust and Boom." *Washington Post Magazine*, December 30, 2001, W09.

Bufacchi, Vittorio, and Jean Maria Arrigo. "Torture, Terrorism and the State: A Refutation of the Ticking-Bomb Argument." *Journal of Applied Philosophy* 23, no. 3 (2006): 355–73.

Bybee, Jay S. "Memorandum for Alberto R. Gonzales Counsel to the President, Re: Standards of Conduct for Interrogation under 18 U.S.C. §§2340–2340A." Washington, DC: U.S. Department of Justice, August 1, 2002.

Byrd, B. Sharon. "Wrongdoing and Attribution: Implications beyond the Justification-Excuse Distinction." *Wayne Law Review* 33, no. 4 (1987): 1289–1342.

Calhoun, Chesire. "Justice, Care, Gender Bias." *Journal of Philosophy* 85, no. 9 (1988): 451–63.

Carter, Jimmy. "Executive Order 12036: United States Foreign Intelligence Activities." January 24, 1978. http://www.fas.org/irp/offdocs/eo/eo-12036 .htm (accessed June 3, 2008).

Casey v. United States. 276 U.S. 413 (1928) (Brandeis, L. D., dissenting).

Cassel, Elain. *The War on Civil Liberties: How Bush and Ashcroft Have Dismantled the Bill of Rights.* Chicago: Lawrence Hill, 2004.

Chaddock, Russell G. "One Maryland County Takes Tough Tack on Vaccinations." *Christian Science Monitor*, November 19, 2007.

Christie, George C. "The Defense of Necessity Considered from the Legal and Moral Points of View." *Duke Law Journal* 48, no. 5 (1999): 975–1042.

Coady, C. A. J. "The Morality of Terrorism." *Philosophy* 60 (1985): 47–69.

———. "Defining Terrorism." In *Terrorism: The Philosophical Issues*, ed. Igor Primoratz, 3–14. New York: Palgrave Macmillan, 2004.

———. "Terrorism, Morality, and Supreme Emergency." *Ethics* 114 (2004): 772–89.

Cohan, John Alan. "Homicide by Necessity." *Chapman Law Review* 10 (2006): 119–86.

Cohen, David. "The Development of the Modern Law of Necessity: A Comparative Critique." *Journal for History of Law* 4 (1985): 215–34.

Coleman, Jules. *Risks and Wrongs.* Oxford: Oxford University Press, 1992.

Conroy, John. *Unspeakable Acts, Ordinary People: The Dynamics of Torture.* New York: Knopf, 2000.

Convention against Torture and Other Cruel, Inhuman, or Degrading Treatment or Punishment. United Nations, 1984. http://www2.ohchr .org/english/law/cat.htm (accessed May 26, 2011).

Cooper, Melinda. "Pre-Empting Emergence: The Biological Turn in the War on Terror." *Theory, Culture, and Society* 23, no. 4 (2006): 113–35.

Crawford, Neta. "Just War Theory and the US Counterterror War." *Perspectives on Politics* 1, no. 1 (2003): 5–25.

Dancy, Jonathan. "The Role of Imaginary Cases in Ethics." *Pacific Philosophical Quarterly* 66 (1985): 141–53.

———. "Defending Particularism." *Metaphilosophy* 30, nos. 1–2 (1999): 25–32.

———. *Ethics without Principles.* Oxford: Clarendon, 2004.

———. "Moral Particularism." *Stanford Encyclopedia of Philosophy.* 2001. rev. ed., 2009. http://plato.stanford.edu/entries/moral-particularism (accessed May 26, 2011).

Darwall, Stephen. *Contractarianism/Contractualism.* Malden, MA: Blackwell, 2003.

———. *Second-Person Standpoint: Morality and Accountability*. Cambridge, MA: Harvard University Press, 2006.

David, Steven R. "Israel's Policy of Targeted Killing." *Ethics and International Affairs* 17, no. 1 (2003): 111–26.

Davis, Lewis Anthony. "Review Procedures and Public Accountability in Sunset Legislation: An Analysis and Proposal for Reform." *Administrative Law Review* 33 (1981): 393–402.

Davis, Michael. "The Moral Justifiability of Torture and Other Cruel, Inhuman, or Degrading Treatment." *International Journal of Applied Philosophy* 19, no. 2 (2005): 161–78.

———. "Torture and the Inhumane." *Criminal Justice Ethics* 26 (2007): 29–43.

Dayan, Colin. *The Story of Cruel and Unusual*. Cambridge: MA: MIT Press, 2007.

Declaration of Tokyo. World Medical Association, October 1975. http://www.cirp.org/library/ethics/tokyo (accessed May 5, 2008).

Deeley, Peter. *Beyond Breaking Point*. London: Arthur Baker, 1971.

Department of Homeland Security. *Strategic Plan: One Team, One Mission, Securing Our Homeland*. Washington, DC, 2008.

Department of the Army. *Intelligence Interrogation*. FM 34-52. Washington, DC: Department of the Army, 1992. http://www.fas.org/irp/doddir/army/fm34-52.pdf (accessed September 21, 2009).

———. *Human Intelligence Collector Operations*. FM 2-22.3 (FM 34-52). Washington, DC: Department of the Army, 2006. http://fas.org/irp/doddir/army/fm2-22-3.pdf (accessed September 21, 2009).

Dershowitz, Alan M. *Why Terrorism Works: Understanding the Threat, Responding to the Challenge*. New Haven, CT: Yale University Press, 2002.

———. "The Torture Warrant: A Response to Professor Strauss." *New York Law School Law Review* 48, nos. 1–2 (2003/2004): 275–94.

———. "Tortured Reasoning." In *Torture: A Collection*, ed. Sanford Levinson, 258–80. New York: Oxford University Press, 2004.

Dixon v. United States. 548 U.S. 1 (2006).

Doris, John M. "Persons, Situations, and Virtue Ethics." *Noûs* 32, no. 4 (1998): 504–530.

———. *Lack of Character: Personality and Moral Behavior*. Cambridge: Cambridge University Press, 2002.

Doyle, Charles. "Patriot Act: Sunset Provisions That Expire on December 31, 2005." Washington, DC: Congressional Research Service, 2004. http://www.fas.org/irp/crs/RL32186.pdf (accessed May 9, 2008).

———. "USA PATRIOT Act Reauthorization in Brief." Washington, DC: Congressional Research Service, 2006. http://fpc.state.gov/documents/organization/51133.pdf (accessed May 9, 2008).

Dressler, Joshua. *Understanding Criminal Law*. 3rd ed. New York: Lexis, 2001.

Driver, Julia. "Consequentialism and Feminist Ethics." *Hypatia* 20, no. 4 (2005): 183–99.

Duncan, Craig, and Tibor Machan. *Libertarianism: For and Against*. Lanham, MD: Rowman & Littlefield, 2005.

Dworkin, Ronald. *Taking Rights Seriously*. Cambridge, MA: Harvard University Press, 1977.

Enders, Walter, and Todd Sandler. *The Political Economy of Terrorism*. Cambridge: Cambridge University Press, 2005.

European Commission on Human Rights. "*Ireland v. United Kingdom*." In *Council of Europe Yearbook of the European Convention on Human Rights: 1976*, 512–949. The Hague: Martinus Nijhoff, 1977.

Ex Parte Merryman. 17 F. Cas. 144 (1861).

Ex Parte Quirin. 317 U.S. 1 (1942).

FDIC v. Meyer. 510 U.S. 471 (1994).

Feinberg, Joel. "Voluntary Euthanasia and the Inalienable Right to Life." *Philosophy and Public Affairs* 7, no. 2 (1978): 93–123.

Feitlowitz, Marguerite. *A Lexicon of Terror: Argentina and the Legacies of Torture*. Oxford: Oxford University Press, 1999.

Fiala, Andrew. "A Critique of Exceptions: Torture, Terrorism, and the Lesser Evil." *International Journal of Applied Philosophy* 20, no. 1 (2006): 127–42.

Fife, Graeme. *The Terror: The Shadow of the Guillotine: France, 1792–1794*. New York: St. Martin's, 2006.

Flanagan, Owen, and Kathryn Jackson. "Justice, Care, and Gender: The Kohlberg-Gilligan Debate Revisited." *Ethics* 97, no. 3 (1987): 622–37.

Fleck, Dieter, ed. *Handbook of Humanitarian Law in Armed Conflicts*. New York: Oxford University Press, 2000.

Foot, Philippa. "The Problem of Abortion and the Doctrine of Double Effect" (1967). In *Virtues and Vices and Other Essays in Moral Philosophy*, 19–32. Oxford: Blackwell, 1978.

———. *Virtues and Vices and Other Essays in Moral Philosophy*. Oxford: Oxford University Press, 1978.

———. *Natural Goodness*. Oxford: Oxford University Press, 2003.

Ford, Franklin L. *Political Murder: From Tyrannicide to Terrorism*. Cambridge, MA: Harvard University Press, 1985.

Ford, Gerald R. "Executive Order 11905: United States Foreign Intelligence Activities." February 18, 1976. http://www.fordlibrarymuseum.gov/library/speeches/760110e.htm (accessed May 26, 2011).

Fotion, Nick. "The Burdens of Terrorism." In *Terrorism: The Philosophical Issues*, ed. Igor Primoratz, 44–54. New York: Palgrave Macmillan, 2004.

Friedman, William J., et al. "Sex Differences in Moral Judgments? A Test of Gilligan's Theory." *Psychology of Women Quarterly* 11 (1987): 37–46.

Gaeta, Paola. "May Necessity Be Available as a Defence for Torture in the Interrogation of Suspected Terrorists?" *Journal of International Criminal Justice* 2 (2004): 785–94.

Garg, Vishal. "Unwarranted and Unnecessary: An Argument against Judicially Sanctioned Torture." Unpublished manuscript, 2009.

Garrett, Stephen A. "Terror Bombings of German Cities in World War II." In *Terrorism: The Philosophical Issues*, ed. Igor Primoratz, 141–60. New York: Palgrave Macmillan, 2004.

Gill, Terry, and Elies van Sliedregt. "Guantánamo Bay: A Reflection on the Legal Status and Rights of 'Unlawful Enemy Combatants.'" *Utrecht Law Review* 1, no. 1 (2005): 28–54.

Gilligan, Carol. *In a Different Voice: Psychological Theory and Women's Development*. Cambridge, MA: Harvard University Press, 1982.

Gitmo: The New Rules of War. Directed by Erik Gandini and Tarik Saleh. Atma Media Network, 2005.

Global Fund to Fight AIDS, Tuberculosis and Malaria. "Current Grant Commitments and Disbursements." http://www.theglobalfund.org/en/commitmentsdisbursements (accessed April 14, 2009).

Goldman, Alan H. *Practical Rules: When We Need Them and When We Don't*. Cambridge: Cambridge University Press, 2001.

Gonzales, Alberto R. "Memorandum for the President." January 25, 2002. In *The Torture Papers: The Road to Abu Ghraib*, ed. Karen J. Greenberg and Joshua L. Dratel, 118–21. Cambridge: Cambridge University Press, 2005.

Graves, Robert. *Goodbye to All That*. Rev. ed. New York: Anchor, 1957.

Greene, Joshua D., et al. "Pushing Moral Buttons: The Interaction between Personal Force and Intention in Moral Judgment." *Cognition* 111, no. 3 (2009): 364–71.

Gross, Michael. "Assassination and Targeted Killing: Law Enforcement, Execution, or Self-Defence?" *Journal of Applied Philosophy* 23, no. 3 (2006): 323–35.

———. *Moral Dilemmas of Modern War: Torture, Assassination, and Blackmail in an Age of Asymmetric Conflict*. Cambridge: Cambridge University Press, 2009.

Gross, Oren. "The Prohibition on Torture and the Limits of the Law." In *Torture: A Collection*, ed. Sanford Levinson, 229–53. New York: Oxford University Press, 2004.

Haidt, Jonathan. "The Emotional Dog and Its Rational Tail: A Social Intuitionist Approach to Moral Judgment." *Psychological Review* 108 (2001): 814–34.

Hamby, Peter. "Bush Defends Interrogation Program in Michigan Speech." CNN.com, May 29, 2009. http://www.cnn.com/2009/POLITICS/05/29/george.bush.speech/index.html (accessed October 8, 2009).

Hamdan v. Rumsfeld. 548 U.S. 557 (2006).

Hamdi et al. v. Rumsfeld. 542 U.S. 507 (2004).

Haney, Craig, W. Curtis Banks, and Phillip G. Zimbardo. "Interpersonal Dynamics in a Simulated Prison." *International Journal of Criminology and Penology* 1 (1971): 69–97.

———. "Study of Prisoners and Guards in a Simulated Prison." *Naval Research Reviews* 9 (1973): 1–17.

Harsanyi, John. "Cardinal Utility in Welfare Economics and the Theory of Risk Taking." *Journal of Political Economy* 61 (1953): 434–35.

———. "Cardinal Welfare, Individualistic Ethics, and Interpersonal Comparisons in Utility." *Journal of Political Economy* 63 (1955): 309–21.

Haydar, Bashshar. "The Ethics of Fighting Terror and the Priority of Citizens." *Journal of Military Ethics* 4, no. 1 (2005): 52–59.

Henderson, Nathan. "The Patriot Act's Impact on the Government's Ability to Conduct Electronic Surveillance of Ongoing Domestic Communications." *Duke Law Journal* 52, no. 1 (2002): 179–209.

Hobbes, Thomas. *Leviathan.* 1668. Edited by Edwin Curley. Indianapolis: Hackett, 1994.

Hobijn, Bart, and Erick Sager. "What Has Homeland Security Cost? An Assessment: 2001–2005." *Current Issues in Economics and Finance* 13, no. 2 (2007): 1–7.

Hooker, Brad, and Margaret Little, eds. *Moral Particularism.* Oxford: Oxford University Press, 2000.

Hume, David. *A Treatise of Human Nature.* Edited by Paul H. Nidditch. 2nd ed. Oxford: Oxford University Press, 1978.

Hunsinger, George. "Torture *Is* the Ticking Time-Bomb: Why the Necessity Defense Fails." *Dialog: A Journal of Theology* 47, no. 3 (2008): 228–39.

Hursthouse, Rosalind. *On Virtue Ethics.* Oxford: Oxford University Press, 1999.

Husak, Douglas. "On the Supposed Priority of Justification to Excuse." *Law and Philosophy* 24 (2005): 557–94.

Hutcheson, Francis. "Treatise II." In *An Inquiry into the Original of Our Ideas of Beauty and Virtue*, 83–197. Indianapolis: Liberty Fund, 2004.

Informe de la Comisión Nacional Sobre Política y Tortura. Santiago: Presedencia de la República, 2004.

Ingierd, Helene, and Henrik Syse. "Responsibility and Culpability in War." *Journal of Military Ethics* 4, no. 2 (2005): 85–99.

In re Neagle. 135 U.S. 1 (1890).

Ireland v. United Kingdom. Eur. Ct. H.R. (ser. A, no. 25) (1978).

Jackson, Richard. *Writing the War on Terror: Language, Politics, and Counter-Terrorism.* Manchester: Manchester University Press, 2005.

Johnson v. Eisentrager. 339 U.S. 763 (1950).

Johnson, Alexander. "Habeas Corpus." In *Cyclopaedia of Political Science*, ed. Josh Joseph Lalor. New York: Maynard, Merrill, 1899. http://www.econlib.org/library/YPDBooks/Lalor/llCy521.html#LF-BK0216-02pt04ch001 (accessed May 22, 2008).

Juratowitch, Ben. "Torture Is Always Wrong." *Public Affairs Quarterly* 22, no. 2 (2008): 81–90.

Kagan, Shelly. *The Limits of Morality.* Oxford: Oxford University Press, 1991.

Kamm, Frances M. "The Doctrine of Triple Effect and Why a Rational Agent Need Not Intend the Means to His End." *Proceedings of the Aristotelian Society, Supplementary Volumes* 74, no. 1 (2000): 21–39.

———. "Failures of Just War Theory: Terror, Harm, and Justice." *Ethics* 114 (2004): 650–92.

———. "Terror and Collateral Damage: Are They Permissible?" *Journal of Ethics* 9, nos. 3–4 (2005): 381–401.

Kasher, Asa, and Amos Yadlin. "Military Ethics of Fighting Terror: An Israeli Perspective." *Journal of Military Ethics* 4, no. 1 (2005): 3–32.

Katya, Neal. "Sunsetting Judicial Opinions." *Notre Dame Law Review* 79, no. 4 (2003): 1237–46.

Kautsky, Karl. *Terrorism and Communism: A Contribution to the Natural History of Revolution.* Berlin: National Labour Press, 1919. http://marxists.org/archive/kautsky/1919/terrcomm/index.htm (accessed March 1, 2009).

Kershnar, Stephen. "Assassination and the Immunity Theory." *Philosophia* 33, nos. 1–4 (2005): 129–47.

———. "For Interrogational Torture." *International Journal of Applied Philosophy* 19, no. 2 (2005): 223–41.

Kleinig, John. "Ticking Bombs and Torture Warrants." *Deakin Law Review* 10, no. 2 (2006): 614–27.

Kohlberg, Lawrence. "Moral Stages and Moralization: The Cognitive-Development Approach." In *Moral Development and Behavior: Theory, Research, and Social Issues*, ed. Thomas Lickona, 31–53. New York: Holt, Rinehart & Winston, 1976.

———. *The Psychology of Moral Development.* Vol. 2 of *Essays on Moral Development.* San Francisco: Harper & Row, 1984.

Kolby, Anne, and Lawrence Kohlberg. *The Measurement of Moral Judgment.* 2 vols. New York: Cambridge University Press, 1987.

Kunreuther, Howard, Erwann Michel-Kerjan, and Beverly Porter. "Assessing, Managing, and Financing Extreme Events: Dealing with Terrorism." Working Paper no. 10179. Cambridge, MA: National Bureau of Economic Research, 2003. http://opim.wharton.upenn.edu/risk/downloads/archive/arch92.pdf (accessed March 23, 2009).

LaFave, Wayne R. *Modern Criminal Law: Cases, Comments, and Questions.* 4th ed. St. Paul, MN: Thomson/West, 2006.

Langbein, John. *Torture and the Law of Proof: Europe and England in the Ancien Régime.* 1976. Chicago: University of Chicago Press, 2006.

Lartéguy, Jean. *Les centurions.* 1960. Translated by Xan Fielding. New York: Avon, 1961.

Leggett, George. *The Cheka: Lenin's Political Police.* Oxford: Oxford University Press, 1981.

Leib, E. "Responsibility and Social/Political Choices about Choice; or, One Way to Be a True-Non-Voluntarist." *Law and Philosophy: An International Journal for Jurisprudence and Legal Philosophy* 25, no. 4 (2006): 453–88.

Levin, Michael. "The Case for Torture." *Newsweek,* February 7, 1982, 7.

Levinson, Sanford, ed. *Torture: A Collection.* Oxford: Oxford University Press, 2004.

Lewis, Paul H. *Guerillas and Generals: The "Dirty War" in Argentina.* London: Praeger, 2002.

Likert, Rensis. "A Technique for the Measurement of Attitudes." *Archives of Psychology* 140 (1932): 1–55.

Looney, Robert. "Economic Costs to the United States Stemming from the 9/11 Attacks." *Strategic Insights* 1, no. 6 (2002). http://www.hsdl.org/?view&doc=4347&coll=limited (accessed May 26, 2011).

Luban, David. "Liberalism, Torture, and the Ticking Bomb." *Virginia Law Review* 91, no. 6 (2005): 1425–61.

———. "The Torture Lawyers of Washington." In *Legal Ethics and Human Dignity,* ed. David Luban, 162–205. Cambridge: Cambridge University Press, 2007.

Maass, Peter. "If a Terror Suspect Won't Talk, Should He Be Made To?" *New York Times,* March 9, 2003.

Machiavelli, Niccolò. *The Prince.* ca. 1505. Translated by W. K. Marriott. 1908. http://www.constitution.org/mac/prince00.htm (accessed May 30, 2008).

Maestro, Marcello. *Voltaire and Beccaria as Reformers of Criminal Law.* New York: Columbia University Press, 1942.

Mann, Samantha, Aldert Vrij, and Ray Bull. "Detecting True Lies." *Journal of Applied Psychology* 89, no. 1 (2004): 137–49.

Marks, Jonathan H. "When Doctors Go to War." *New England Journal of Medicine* 352, no. 3 (2005): 3–6.

———. "9/11 + 3/11 + 7/7 = ?: What Counts in Counterterrorism." *Columbia Human Rights Law Review* 37, no. 3 (2006): 101–61.

Massey, Drew. "Shipping across State Lines: Wine and the Law." In *Wine and Philosophy*, ed. Fritz Allhoff, 275–87. Oxford: Blackwell, 2008.

Matravers, Matt. *Responsibility and Justice*. Malden, MA: Blackwell, 2007.

Mayerfeld, Jamie. "In Defense of the Absolute Prohibition on Torture." *Public Affairs Quarterly* 22, no. 2 (2008): 109–28.

McMahan, Jeff. "The Ethics of Killing in War." *Ethics* 114 (2004): 693–733.

———. "Torture in Principle and Practice." *Public Affairs Quarterly* 22, no. 2 (2008): 111–28.

McPherson, Lionel K. "Is Terrorism Distinctively Wrong?" *Ethics* 117 (2007): 524–46.

Meisels, Tamar. "Targeting Terror." *Social Theory and Practice* 30, no. 3 (2004): 297–326.

———. "Combatants—Lawful and Unlawful." *Law and Philosophy* 26, no. 1 (2007): 31–65.

Melgunov, Sergey Petrovich. *The Red Terror in Russia*. 1925. Westport, CT: Hyperion, 1975.

Mellor, Alec. *La torture*. Paris: Horizons Littéraires, 1949.

Melzack, Ronald, and Patrick Wall. *The Challenge of Pain*. Harmondsworth: Penguin, 1982.

Meyer, Jane. "The Predator War: What Are the Risks of the C.I.A.'s Covert Drone Program?" *New Yorker*, October 26, 2009.

Milgram, Stanley. "Behavioral Study of Obedience." *Journal of Abnormal and Social Psychology* 67 (1963): 371–78.

———. "The Perils of Obedience." *Harper's Magazine*, December 1973, 62–77.

———. *Obedience to Authority: An Experimental View*. New York: Harper & Row, 1974.

Milhizer, Eugene R. "Justification and Excuse: What They Were, What They Are, and What They Ought to Be." *St. John's Law Review* 78, no. 4 (2004): 725–895.

Mill, John Stuart. *Utilitarianism: Second Edition*. 1861. Edited by George Sher. Indianapolis: Hackett, 2001.

Miller, Seumas. "Is Torture Ever Morally Justified?" *International Journal of Applied Philosophy* 19, no. 2 (2005): 179–92.

Mills, Geoffrey, and Hugh Rockoff. "Compliance with Price Controls in the

United States and the United Kingdom during World War II." *Journal of Economic History* 47, no. 1 (1987): 197–213.

Montana v. Leprowse. 2009 MT 387 (2009).

Moore, Michael. "Torture and the Balance of Evils." *Israel Law Review* 23 (1989): 280–344.

———. *Placing Blame*. Oxford: Clarendon, 1997.

More, Thomas. *Utopia*. New York: Appleton-Century-Crofts, 1949.

Murphy, Sean, ed. "Ability of Detainees in Cuba to Obtain Federal Habeas Corpus Review." *American Journal of International Law* 98, no. 1 (2004): 188–90.

Nagel, Thomas. "War and Massacre." In *International Ethics*, ed. Charles R. Beitz, Marshall Cohen, Thomas Scanlon, and A. John Simmons, 53–74. Princeton, NJ: Princeton University Press, 1985.

"The Necessity Defense to Prison Escape After *United States v. Bailey*." *Virginia Law Review* 65, no. 2 (1979): 359–76.

Noah, Timothy. "Water-Bored: Al-Qaida's Plot to Bomb the Library Tower Was Not Worth Torturing Anyone Over." *Slate*, April 21, 2009. http://www.slate.com/id/2216601 (accessed October 8, 2009).

Northern Securities Co. v. United States. 193 U.S. 197 (1904) (Holmes, O. W., dissenting).

Nozick, Robert. *Anarchy, State, and Utopia*. New York: Basic, 1974.

Olmstead v. United States. 277 U.S. 438 (1928) (Brandeis, L. D., dissenting).

O'Neill, Onora. "Ethical Reasoning and Ideological Pluralism." *Ethics* 98 (1988): 705–22.

Orend, Brian. "War." In *Stanford Encyclopedia of Philosophy*. 2005. http://plato.stanford.edu/entries/war (accessed June 2, 2008).

Oxford English Dictionary. 2nd ed. Oxford: Oxford University Press, 1989.

Palmer, R. R. *Twelve Who Ruled: The Year of Terror in the French Revolution*. Princeton, NJ: Princeton University Press, 2005.

Paust, Jordan. "The Complicity of Dick Cheney: No 'Necessity' Defense." *Jurist*, May 18, 2009. http://jurist.law.pitt.edu/forumy/2009/05/complicity-of-dick-cheney-no-necessity.php (accessed February 3, 2010).

Payne, Leigh A. *Unsettling Accounts: Neither Truth nor Reconciliation in Confessions of State Violence*. Durham, NC: Duke University Press, 2008.

People v. Bordowitz. 115 Misc. 2d 128, 132–33 (N.Y. Crim. Ct. 1991).

Petit, Philip. "Responsibility Incorporated." *Ethics* 117 (2007): 171–201.

Plato. "Crito." In *Five Dialogues*, trans. G. M. A. Grube. Indianapolis: Hackett, 1981.

———. "Euthyphro." In *Five Dialogues*, trans. G. M. A. Grube. Indianapolis: Hackett, 1981.

———. "Laches." In *Laches and Charmides*, trans. Rosamond Kent Sprague. Indianapolis: Hackett, 1992.

———. *The Republic*. Translated by C. D. C. Reeve. 3rd ed. Indianapolis: Hackett, 2004.

Pogge, Thomas. "Making War on Terrorists: Reflections on Harming the Innocent." *Journal of Political Philosophy* 16, no. 1 (2008): 1–25.

Pratt, Michael W., Gail Golding, and William J. Hunter. "Does Morality Have a Gender? Sex, Sex Role, and Moral Judgment across the Adult Lifespan." *Merrill-Palmer Quarterly* 30 (1984): 321–40.

Priebe, Stefan, and Michael Bauer. "Inclusion of Psychological Torture in PTSD Criterion A." *American Journal of Psychiatry* 152 (1995): 1691–92.

Priest, Dana. "CIA Avoids Scrutiny of Detainee Treatment: Afghan's Death Took Two Years to Come to Light; Agency Says Abuse Claims Are Probed Fully." *Washington Post*, March 3, 2005, A1.

Primoratz, Igor. "State Terrorism." In *Terrorism and Justice: Moral Argument in a Threatened World*, ed. C. A. J. Coady and Michael O'Keefe, 31–42. Melbourne: Melbourne University Publishing, 2004.

———, ed. *Terrorism: The Philosophical Issues*. New York: Palgrave Macmillan, 2004.

———. "What Is Terrorism?" In *Terrorism: The Philosophical Issues*, ed. Igor Primoratz, 15–27. New York: Palgrave Macmillan, 2004.

Public Committee against Torture in Israel. "Accountability Denied: The Absence of Investigation and Punishment of Torture in Israel." 2009.

Public Committee against Torture in Israel et al. v. Government of Israel et al. HCJ 5100/94 (1999).

Quillen, Chris. "A Historical Analysis of Mass Casualty Bombers." *Studies in Conflict and Terrorism* 25, no. 5 (2002): 279–92.

———. "Mass Casualty Bombings Chronology." *Studies in Conflict and Terrorism* 25, no. 5 (2002): 293–302.

Quinn, Warren. "Actions, Intentions, and Consequences: The Doctrine of Double Effect." *Philosophy and Public Affairs* 18, no. 4 (1989): 334–51.

Quinton, Anthony. "Views." *Listener*, December 2, 1971, 757–58.

R v. Dudley and Stephens. 14 QBD 273 DC (1884).

Rachels, James. "Political Assassination." In *Assassination*, ed. Harold Zellner, 9–21. Cambridge, MA: Schenkman, 1974.

Raviv, Adam. "Torture and Justification: Defending the Indefensible." *George Mason Law Review* 13, no. 1 (2004): 135–81.

Rawls, John. "Fifty Years After Hiroshima." In *Collected Papers*, ed. Samuel Freeman, 565–72. Cambridge, MA: Harvard University Press, 1999.

———. *A Theory of Justice*. Rev. ed. Cambridge, MA: Belknap, 1999.

Reagan, Ronald. "Executive Order 12333: United States Intelligence Activities." 1981. http://www.fas.org/irp/offdocs/eo12333.htm (accessed June 3, 2008).

———. "Message to the Senate Transmitting a Protocol to the 1949 Geneva Conventions." January 29, 1987. Available at http://www.reagan.utexas.edu/archives/speeches/1987/012987b.htm (accessed May 23, 2008).

Rejali, Darius. *Torture and Democracy*. Princeton, NJ: Princeton University Press, 2007.

Rescher, Nicholas. "The Allocation of Exotic Medical Lifesaving Therapy." *Ethics* 79, no. 3 (1969): 173–86.

Rodin, David. "Terrorism without Intention." *Ethics* 114 (2004): 752–71.

———. "The Ethics of War: State of the Art." *Journal of Applied Philosophy* 23, no. 3 (2006): 241–46.

Rodley, Nigel S. *The Treatment of Prisoners under International Law*. 2nd ed. Oxford: Oxford University Press, 2000.

Rubin, Alissa J. "3 Suspects Talk After Iraqi Soldiers Do Dirty Work." *New York Times*, April 22, 2007, A1, A12.

Sammon, Bill. "Cheney: Enhanced Interrogations 'Essential' in Saving American Lives." Foxnews.com, August 30, 2009. http://www.foxnews.com/politics/2009/08/30/cheney-enhanced-interrogations-essential-saving-american-lives (accessed October 8, 2009).

Sandler, Todd, Daniel G. Arce, and Walter Enders. "Transnational Terrorism." In *Global Crises, Global Solutions* (2nd ed.), ed. Bjørn Lomberg, 516–62. Cambridge: Cambridge University Press, 2009.

Saving Private Ryan. Directed by Steven Spielberg. Amblin Entertainment and Mutual Film Co., 1998.

Scheppele, Kim Lane. "Hypothetical Torture in the 'War on Terrorism.'" *Journal of National Security Law and Policy* 1 (2005): 285–340.

Schwartz, Stephen. "Is There a Common Law Necessity Defense in Federal Criminal Law?" *University of Chicago Law Review* 75, no. 3 (2008): 1259–93.

Selgelid, Michael. "Ethics and Infectious Disease." *Bioethics* 19, no. 3 (2005): 272–89.

Sen, Amartya. "Rights and Agency." In *Consequentialism and Its Critics*, ed. Samuel Scheffler, 187–223. Oxford: Oxford University Press, 1988.

"September 11 Mastermind Khalid Sheikh Mohammed 'Waterboarded 183 Times.'" *The Times Online*, April 20, 2009. http://www.timesonline.co.uk/tol/news/world/us_and_americas/article6130165.ece (accessed October 8, 2009).

Shanahan, Timothy, ed. *Philosophy 9/11: Thinking about the War on Terror*. Peru, IL: Open Court, 2005.

Sher, George. *In Praise of Blame*. New York: Oxford University Press, 2006.

Shue, Henry. "Torture." *Philosophy and Public Affairs* 7, no. 2 (1978): 124–43.

———. "Torture in Dreamland: Disposing of the Ticking Bomb." *Case Western Reserve Journal of International Law* 37, nos. 2–3 (2006): 231–39.

Simpson, A. W. Brian. *Cannibalism and the Common Law: The Story of the Tragic Last Voyage of the Mignonette and the Strange Legal Proceedings to Which It Gave Rise.* Chicago: University of Chicago Press, 1984.

Singer, Peter. "Famine, Affluence, and Morality." *Philosophy and Public Affairs* 1, no. 3 (1972): 229–43.

Sorenson, Roy. *Thought Experiments.* New York: Oxford University Press, 1998.

Statman, Daniel. "The Absoluteness of the Prohibition against Torture." *Mishpat Unimshal* (Law and government in Israel) 4 (1997): 161–98.

———. "Targeted Killing." *Theoretical Inquiries in Law* 5, no. 1 (2004): 179–98.

———. "Supreme Emergencies Revisited." *Ethics* 117 (2006): 58–79.

Steinoff, Uwe. "Torture—the Case for Dirty Hands and against Alan Dershowitz." *Journal of Applied Philosophy* 23, no. 3 (2006): 337–53.

Strauss, David A. "Common Law, Common Ground, and Jefferson's Principle." *Yale Law Journal* 112, no. 7 (2003): 1717–55.

Strauss, Marcy. "Torture." *New York Law School Review* 48, nos. 1–2 (2003/2004): 201–74.

Sung, Chanterelle. "Torturing the Ticking-Bomb Terrorist: An Analysis of Judicially Sanctioned Torture in the Context of Terrorism." *Boston College Third World Law Journal* 23 (2003): 193–212.

Sussman, David. "What's Wrong with Torture?" *Philosophy and Public Affairs* 33, no. 1 (2005): 1–33.

Swisher, Carl. "Civil Liberties in War Time." *Political Science Quarterly* 55, no. 3 (1940): 321–447.

Taurek, John. "Should the Numbers Count?" *Philosophy and Public Affairs* 6 (1977): 293–316.

Taylor, Frederick. "How Many Died in the Bombing of Dresden?" *Spiegel Online*, October 2, 2008. Available at http://www.spiegel.de/international/germany/0,1518,581992,00.html (accessed March 1, 2009).

Teichman, Jenny. *Pacifism and the Just War.* Oxford: Blackwell, 1986.

———. "How to Define Terrorism." *Philosophy* 64 (1989): 505–17.

Thiessen, Marc A. "The CIA's Questioning Worked." *Washington Post*, April 21, 2009.

Third Geneva Convention. 1949. http://www.icrc.org/ihl.nsf/7c4d08d9b287a42141256739003e636b/6fef854a3517b75ac125641e004a9e68 (accessed May 5, 2008).

Thomson, Judith Jarvis. "A Defense of Abortion." *Philosophy and Public Affairs* 1, no. 1 (1971): 47–66.

———. "Killing, Letting Die, and the Trolley Problem." *Monist* 59 (1976): 204–17.

———. "The Trolley Problem." *Yale Law Journal* 94, no. 6 (1985): 1395–1415.

———. "Self-Defense." *Philosophy and Public Affairs* 20 (1991): 283–311.

Tindale, Christopher W. "Tragic Choices: Reaffirming Absolutes in the Torture Debate." *International Journal of Applied Philosophy* 19, no. 2 (2005): 209–22.

Trotsky, Leon. *Terrorism and Communism: A Reply to Karl Kautsky*. 1920. Edited by Slavoj Žižek. Ann Arbor: University of Michigan Press, 1961.

———. "A Defense of the 'Red Terror'" (1920). In *Terrorism: The Philosophical Issues*, ed. Igor Primoratz, 31–43. New York: Palgrave Macmillan, 2004.

Tversky, Amos, and Daniel Kahneman. "Extensional versus Intuitive Reasoning: The Conjunction Fallacy in Probability Judgment." *Psychological Review* 90, no. 4 (1983): 293–315.

Twining, W. L., and P. E. Twining. "Bentham on Torture." *Northern Ireland Legal Quarterly* 24 (1973): 307–56.

Tzu, Sun. *The Art of War*. Translated by Lionel Giles. 1910. http://www.gutenberg.org/etext/132 (accessed May 30, 2008).

United Nations Treaty Collection, IV.9. http://www2.ohchr.org/english (accessed May 16, 2009).

United States v. Bailey. 444 U.S. 394 (1980).

United States v. Holmes. F. Cas. 360 (E.D. Pa. 1842).

United States v. Oakland Cannabis Buyers' Cooperative, 532 U.S. 483 (2001).

United States v. Patton. 451 F3d 615, 638 (10th Cir. 2006).

United States v. Schoon. 971 F2d 193, 195–97 (9th Cir. 2002).

U.S. Congress. Alien and Sedition Acts. 1798. http://www.loc.gov/rr/program/bib/ourdocs/Alien.html (accessed May 27, 2008).

Universal Declaration of Human Rights. http://www.un.org/en/documents/udhr/index.shtml (accessed May 26, 2011).

USA PATRIOT Act. Pub. L. No. 107-56, 115 Stat. 272 (2001). http://gpo.gov/fdsys/pkg/PLAW-107publ56/html/PLAW-107publ56.htm (accessed May 26, 2011).

USA PATRIOT Improvement and Reauthorization Act of 2005. H.R. Rep. No. 109-333 (2005). http://thomas.loc.gov/cgi-bin/cpquery/R?cp109:FLD010:@1(hr333) (accessed May 9, 2008).

USA PATRIOT Act Additional Reauthorizing Amendments Act. Pub. L. No. 109-178, S.2271 (2006). http://intelligence.senate.gov/laws/pl109-178.pdf (accessed May 26, 2011).

Voltaire. "Commentaire sur le livre des Délits et des peines" (1766). In *Oeuvres complètes de Voltaire* (52 vols.), ed. Louis Moland, 25:539–77. Paris: Garnier, 1877–85.

———. "Prix de la justice et de l'humanité" (1777). In *Oeuvres complètes de Voltaire* (52 vols.), ed. Louis Moland, 30:533–86. Paris: Garnier, 1877–85.

Vrij, Aldert. *Detecting Lies and Deceit*. Chichester, NY: John Wiley, 2000.

Waldron, Jeremy. "Terrorism and the Uses of Torture." *Journal of Ethics* 8 (2004): 5–35.

———. "Torture and Positive Law: Jurisprudence for the White House." *Columbia Law Review* 105, no. 6 (2005): 1681–1750.

Walker, Lawrence J. "Sex Differences in the Development of Moral Reasoning: A Critical Review." *Child Development* 55, no. 3 (1984): 677–91.

———. "Experimental and Cognitive Sources of Moral Development in Adulthood." *Human Development* 29 (1986): 113–24.

———. "A Longitudinal Study of Moral Reasoning." *Child Development* 60 (1989): 157–66.

Wallace, R. Jay. *Responsibility and the Moral Sentiments*. Cambridge, MA: Harvard University Press, 1994.

Walzer, Michael. "Political Action: The Problem of Dirty Hands." *Philosophy and Public Affairs* 2 (1973): 160–80.

———. *Just and Unjust Wars*. 1977. 4th ed. New York: Basic, 2006.

———. "Terrorism: A Critique of Excuses." In *Problems of International Justice*, ed. Steven Luper-Foy, 237–47. Boulder, CO: Westview, 1988.

Ward, Thomas. "The New Age of Assassination." *SAIS Review* 25, no. 1 (2005): 27–39.

Weber, Max. "Politics as Vocation." In *From Max Weber: Essays in Sociology*, ed. H. H. Gerth and C. Wright Mills, 117–28. London: Routledge & Kegan Paul, 1948.

Wellman, Carl. "On Terrorism Itself." *Journal of Value Inquiry* 13 (1979): 250–58.

Williams, Bernard. "A Critique of Utilitarianism." In *Utilitarianism: For and Against*, ed. J. J. C. Smart and Bernard Williams, 75–150. Cambridge: Cambridge University Press, 1973.

Wine Institute. "State Shipping Laws." http://wineinstitute.org/initiatives/stateshippinglaws (accessed May 6, 2008).

Winik, Jay. "Security Comes Before Liberty." *Wall Street Journal*, October 23, 2001, A26.

Wisnewski, Jeremy J. "Unwarranted Torture Warrants: A Critique of the Dershowitz Proposal." *Journal of Social Philosophy* 39, no. 2 (2008): 308–21.

———. "Hearing a Still-Ticking Bomb Argument: A Reply to Bufacchi and Arrigo." *Journal of Applied Philosophy* 26, no. 2 (2009): 205–9.

Wisnewski, J. Jeremy, and R. D. Emerick. *The Ethics of Torture*. London: Continuum, 2009.

Wolfendale, Jessica. "Training Torturers: A Critique of the 'Ticking Bomb' Argument." *Social Theory and Practice* 32, no. 2 (2006): 269–87.

———. "Terrorism, Security, and the Threat of Counterterrorism." *Studies in Conflict and Terrorism* 30 (2007): 75–92.

———. "The Myth of 'Torture Lite.'" *Ethics and International Affairs* 23, no. 1 (2009): 47–61.

Woodward, Bob. "CIA Told to Do 'Whatever Necessary' to Kill Bin Laden." *Washington Post*, October 21, 2001, A01.

Wynia, Matthew. "Consequentialism and Harsh Interrogations." *American Journal of Bioethics* 5, no. 1 (2005): 4–6.

———. "Ethics and Public Health Emergencies: Restrictions on Liberty." *American Journal of Bioethics* 7, no. 2 (2007): 1–5.

Yoo, John. "Memorandum for William J. Hynes II, General Counsel of the Department of Defense, Re: Military Interrogation of Alien Unlawful Combatants Held Outside the United States." Washington, DC: U.S. Department of Justice, March 14, 2003.

Zamzow, Jennifer, and Shaun Nichols. "Variations in Ethical Intuitions." *Philosophical Issues* 19, no. 1 (2009): 368–88.

Zellner, Harold, ed. *Assassination.* Cambridge, MA: Schenkman, 1974.

Zweiniger-Bargielowska, Ina. *Austerity in Britain: Rationing, Controls, and Consumption, 1939–1955.* Oxford: Oxford University Press, 2000.

Index

103–10, 106f, 226nn50–51; torture of, 200–202

In re Neagle, 187

institutionalization of torture, 147–54, 170

intelligence gathering: detention v. torture, 53; gaining relevant intelligence through torture, 144–46

intensity considerations, 91

intentional use of force. *See* force, intentional

interrogational torture: characteristics, 76–77; justification of, ix; moral aspects, 76–77; rapport used in, 158–62; self-betrayal harm, 78–79, 80–81, 85

intrinsic harms of torture, 77–85

intuition: arguments against, 94–101; as excuse, 99–100; and experience, 95–98; as justification, 94; and moral considerations in torture, 92–101; and ticking-time-bomb cases, 95–101, 102–3

Iraq War, costs of, 29

Ireland, torture in, 65

Jassam, Mustafa Subhi, 169–70

judicial torture, 68–73

judiciaries, and torture warrants, 181–85, 237n7

Juratowitch, Ben, 128

jus ad bellum, 19–20

jus in bello, 19–20

justice, virtue, and torture, 122–23

justification: and absolutism, 128–35; compared to excuse, 99–100, 185; and intuition, 94

justification for torture: arguments against, 128–35; case examples, 165–73; as civil disobedience, 177–80; intuition, 94; national defense, 186–88; need for, 82; self-defense, 185–88; terroristic torture, 74–75; ticking-time-bomb cases, 3, 88–93, 204. *See also* moral theories and justification for torture; necessity defense

just war theory: definition, 19–20, 208n2; and noncombatant immunity, 9, 10, 19–22; self-defense and, 202; torture violations of, 79

Kamm, Frances, 8

Kantian moral theory on torture, 80, 82, 128, 132

Kautsky, Karl, 22

kidnapping, 3, 57, 171–72

killing and absolutism in principle, 129–30

Kohlberg, Lawrence, 109, 110

Kolby, Anne, 109, 110

Langbein, John, 69, 70

Lartéguy, Jean, 89

laws and statements on torture, 37, 58–64, 175, 213n6

Leahy, Patrick, 17

legislation and temporal exceptionalism, 42–44

lesser evil argument. *See* harms in torture

Levin, Michael, 88, 93

locations for torture centers, 150

Locke, John, 124

Looney, Robert, 28–29

Luban, David, 94

Machiavelli, Niccolò, 24, 37

Marks, Jonathan, 42, 43, 45, 216n29

Masuy, Christian, 161

McMahan, Jeff, 129, 132

McPherson, Lionel, 5–6, 15

medical treatment: costs in torture, 148; withholding of, 160, 161

military personnel: needed for efficient torture, 149–50, 151; as noncombatants, 9–10

Mill, John Stuart, 67

Miller, Geoffrey, viii, 39

Miller, Seumas, 178, 179

Model Penal Code, 188–89, 192

Mohammed, Khalid Shiekh, 164, 199

Moore, Michael, 99, 185, 187

moral theories and justification for torture: absolutism, 113, 128, 132–35, 177–78; aggregative approach, 120–21; contractarianism, 124–25; contractualism, 125–26; Kantian, 80, 82, 128, 132; nonabsolutism, 113, 121–22, 127; rights-based utilitarianism, 120–21; social contract theory, 124–27; virtue theory, 122–24. *See also* utilitarianism

More, Thomas, 37–38

Murad, Abdul Hakim, 165–67, 168, 235n49

Nagel, Thomas, 25

national defense as justification for torture, 186–88

Neagle, David, 187

necessity defense: arguments against, 191–92; basis for, 188–89; cost-benefit analysis, 193; defined, 100; federal courts' position, necessary defense (*cont.*)

    189–91; as justification for torture, 89,
179, 181–82, 185, 188–93, 238n29; legal
foundations for, 192–93; and reasonable
belief, 192; ticking-time-bomb cases, 167–
68, 188–93; and torture warrants, 193–94

9/11 terrorist attacks. *See* September 11
    terrorist attacks, 2001

noise exposure, use of, 65

nonabsolutism moral theories: defined, 113;
    and justification for torture, 121–22, 127

noncombatants: exceptions that override
protection of, 23, 26, 28; immunity of, 9,
19–22; justifiable infringement of rights,
20–21; status changed due to terrorism,
35–36; in terrorism definition, 9–11; terrorist violation of immunity, 19–20; torture victims as, 79; and utilitarian views
on torture, 115

nondiscrimination as terrorism characteristic, 4

nonhostile torture techniques, 158–62

nonviolent terrorism as form of terrorism, 7

normalization of torture, 154–57

norms, societal: assassination exceptions, 48;
balanced exceptions to, 23; changes due
to War on Terror, 35–40; dirty hands
theory allowing overriding of, 24; and exceptionalism, 40–42, 45–46, 50; exceptions
from, 23–25; torture in violation of, 46–48

Nozick, Robert, 120–21, 178

*Oakland Cannabis Buyers' Cooperative, United
States v.*, 189–90, 191

Obama, Barack, vii, viii

O'Neill, Onora, 101

pain and suffering: in defining torture, 58,
144; intrinsic harm of torture, 78; mental
forms, 63–64; U.S. definition, 60–64

Patriot Act as temporal exception, 42–44,
217n33

Paust, Jordan, 191–92

permissibility and intuition, 92–101

Plato, 122–23

police needed for effective torture, 149–50

political terrorism, 15, 207n37

Powell, Colin, 31

POWs, treatment of, 37, 38

preventative torture, 202–4

Primoratz, Igor, 5–6, 10, 11, 16, 17, 22

prisoners of war, treatment of, 37, 38

prolonged mental pain or suffering, 63–64

property destruction in terrorism, 11

propinquity considerations, 91

psychological torture, 158–62

psychologists needed for torture efficiency, 148

punitive torture, 71–73

purity considerations, 91

Quinton, Anthony, 88, 93

rapport as interrogational technique, 158–62

Rawls, John, 20, 124, 126–27

Reagan, Ronald, 38, 58

reasonable belief and necessity defense, 192

recidivism, effect of torture on, 72–73

recruitment of informants to combat terror-
    ism, 145–46

Rejali, Darius, 135, 142–46, 160–61, 166, 173

religious commitments of terrorists, impact
on interrogation, 160, 161

religious terrorism, 15–16, 207n38

revolutionary terrorism, 21–22

rights, individual: absolute, 118; aggregative
approach, 120–21; in conflict with terrorist rights, ix, 121–22; due process, 118;
restitution, 118–19; and torture, 117–22

rights-based utilitarianism, 120–21, 178–79

right to due process, 118

Rodin, David, 5–6, 8–9, 12, 15

Rousseau, Jean-Jacques, 124

Rumsfeld, Donald, viii

Russia, torture in, 21–22

sadistic torture, 67–68, 77

Scanlon, T. M., 124

Scharff, Hans, 160, 161

Scheppele, Kim Lane, 128

science applications in torture, 142–44, 149

Scottish Enlightenment, 122–23

self-betrayal harm in torture, 78–79, 80–81, 85

self-defense as justification for torture, 185–88

September 11 terrorist attacks, 2001: costs of,
28–29; effect on Bush presidency, vii–viii;
effects of counterterrorism after, 33–34

seriousness as justification for supreme
emergencies, 21, 22–23

severe punishment in torture, 61–66

Shue, Henry, 80, 88, 93, 99, 101–2, 129,
150–51, 154

Singer, Peter, 97

situationism, 123

sleep deprivation, use of, 65

social contract moral theory, and torture,
124–27

societal norms. *See* norms, societal

spatial scope in exceptionalism: ethical considerations, 49–50; example, 41; norms
not applied in, 45–46; torture not violation of, 47; and War on Terror, 45–46
specific intent in inflicting harm, 61, 64, 66,
220n8
standard of care and use of force, 8–9
statements and laws on torture, 37, 58–64,
175, 213n6
states and statehood: promoting terrorism, 17;
revolutionary terrorism against, 21–22;
and supreme emergencies, 22–23
Statman, Daniel, 128–29
Sung, Chanterelle, 184
sunset provisions and temporal exceptionalism, 42–44
Sun Tzu, 37
supreme emergencies: definition, 20; as justification for actions, 20–21; as justification
for terrorism, 22–28; not limited to state,
25; values' role in, 25–28
Sussman, David, 78–79, 80–84
symbolic costs of terrorism, 32–33

Tasers, and torture, 149
technology applications in torture, 142–44,
149
Teichman, Jenny, 11
temporal scope in exceptionalism: ethical
considerations, 49; example, 41; torture
not in violation of, 47; and War on Terror,
42–44
terror, definition of, 12
terror bombing. See World War II
terrorism and terrorists: attack records, 33,
211n40; author's definition, 5–6; Bush
administration impact, vii–ix; characteristics of, 4–6; combatant/noncombatant
status, 9–11, 19–20, 36; costs of, 28–29,
32, 210n26; differing views on, 4–6; dual
targets in, 16–17; and fear, 4, 11, 12–15, 16;
forms of, 15–16, 21–22; historical context,
4; ideological aims, 15–17, 36; and intentional use of force, 6–9; justification for,
20–28; nondiscrimination in, 4; and property, 11, 14–15; recruiting informants,
145–46; rights of, ix, 117–22; against the
state, 21–22; state-sponsored, 17, 73–75;
and supreme emergencies, 22–28; symbolic
costs, 32–33; thought experiments, 103–10,
226nn50–51; threat of, 6–7, 146, 206n14;
torture not solution to, 195–98; word
origin, 4

Third Geneva Convention on torture, 37, 38,
39, 175
Thomas Aquinas, Saint, 8
Thomson, Judith Jarvis, 8, 96–97
threats of violence, 6–7, 206n14
ticking-time-bomb cases: abstraction in, 101–2;
assumption failures, 140; case examples,
165–73; cases v. arguments about, 93;
critics of, 101–3, 116–17, 162–65; definition, 87; features of, 101–3; idealization
in, 101–3; imminence in, 167–68; intuition in, 102–3; justification for torture, 3,
88–93, 204; lack of experience with, 95–
101; lesser harms in, 116–17; methodology
in thinking about, 92–101; necessity defense, 167–68, 188–93; origins of concept,
88–92; purpose of, 92–93; rights conflicts
in, 121–22; thought experiments about,
103–10, 226nn50–51
time constraints, and torture, 145–46, 161–62,
165–68
Torture and the Law of Proof (Langbein), 69
torture and torturers: accountability, 198–204;
agent-centered view, 82–84; alternatives,
157–62, 234n25; arguments against, 59,
114–15, 116–17, 128–35, 140–46; authorization approaches, 175–76; case examples,
165–73; cost-benefit analysis, 142–54, 153f,
156–57, 159–62, 172, 185, 234n30; criteria,
92–93, 115–16, 155; definitions, 58–64;
effectiveness of, 140–46, 147–54, 153f;
factors to consider, 91–92, 146; forms of,
67–75, 77, 202–4; illegal status, 175; of
innocents, 200–202; institutionalization
of, 147–54, 170; intuition in considering,
92–101; laws and statements on, 37, 58–
64, 175, 213n6; legal reconsideration of,
176, 177–80; as lesser harm, ix, 116–17,
193–94, 195, 204; limits, 198–204; moral
harms of, 77–85; moral progression in,
155–57; normalization of, 154–57; not
solution to terrorism, 195–98; obtaining
relevant information through, 144–46;
oversight needed, 155–57, 180–82; pain
and suffering in, 58, 60–64, 78, 144; power
relationships in, 79–80; psychological
states in, 158–62; publicity lacking, 163–
65; punishment for, 177–78, 199; rapport
effectiveness, 158–62; reliability of, 140–46;
and rights of victims, 37, 117–22; security
concerns, 163–65; self-betrayal harm, 78–
79, 80–81, 84; severity of techniques, 61–
66; specific intent, 61, 220n8; techniques,

torture and torturers (*cont.*)
    viii, 62–63, 65–67, 142–44, 149, 158, 163–
    65; thought experiments, 103–10,
    226nn50–51; time constraints' impacts on,
    145–46, 161–62, 165–68; training for tor-
    turers, 150–52; unjustified, 155–57, 181–
    83; victim-centered view, 82–84; warrants
    for, 175, 180–85, 193–94. *See also* interro-
    gational torture; justification for torture;
    moral theories and justification for tor-
    ture; necessity defense
Trotsky, Leon, 21

uncertainty considerations in torture, 103–10,
    107f, 226nn50–51
UN Convention against Torture and Other
    Cruel, Inhuman or Degrading Treatment
    or Punishment (CAT): definition of torture,
    58–61, 175; state requirements in, 58–59;
    U.S. ratification of, 59–64, 61
United States: authorization of covert action,
    38; banning assassinations, 38; citizens'
    views on torture, 37, 214n9; counter-
    terrorism expenditures, 30, 31, 210n38;
    and enemy combatants' treatment, 38–40;
    Iraq and Afghanistan conflicts, costs of,
    29; 9/11 terrorist attacks, costs of, 28–29;
    position on torture, viii, 59–64, 175; Yoo
    arguments for torture, 186–88
United States v. Bailey, 190, 191, 194
United States v. Oakland Cannabis Buyers'
    Cooperative, 189–90, 191
Universal Declaration of Human Rights, 175
unjustified torture: concerns about spread of,
    155–57; reduced with torture warrants,
    181–83
USA PATRIOT Act as temporal exception,
    42–44, 217n33
utilitarianism: criteria for use of torture,
    115–16; as form of consequentialism, 117;
    gender influences, 110; and justification

of torture, 114–17; noncombatants and,
    115; and opponents of torture, 114–15;
    on pain and suffering, 82; and punitive
    torture, 72–73; and sadistic torture, 67–68;
    thought experiments, 103–10, 226nn50–
    51; in ticking-time-bomb situations, 90–91

veil of ignorance, 126
victims of torture: compliance by, 79–80; self-
    betrayal harm, 78–79, 80–81; victim-
    centered view, 82–84
Videla, Jorge, 73
violence to promote fear, 4, 6–7
virtue moral theory position on torture, 122–24

wall standing, use of, 65
Walzer, Michael, 10, 19–21, 22–24, 25, 27
war: changes due to terrorism, 36; compart-
    mentalization in, 42; definition, 9, 19–20;
    role of assassinations in, 37–38; status in,
    9–10, 35–36, 39; traditional understanding
    of, 35–36
War on Terror: and exceptionalism, 36–39,
    42–49, 52–54; torture techniques, 65–66;
    use of phrase, 35
warrants, torture: arguments against, 182–85;
    arguments in favor, 180–82; cost-benefit
    analysis, 185; democratic values and, 183;
    and necessity defense, 193–94; practicality
    of, 183
waterboarding, use of, viii, 163–65
Weber, Max, 24
Wellman, Carl, 7
Winik, Jay, 166
Wolfendale, Jessica, 30–31, 33, 65–66, 150, 151
World War II: bombings, 17, 20, 21, 75;
    interrogation techniques, 160, 161

Yoo, John, 37, 61–63, 64, 186–88

Zarqawi, Abu Musab al, 158